HEROES
OF
MODERN
JEWISH
THOUGHT

by
DEBORAH KARP

KTAV PUBLISHING HOUSE INC.

Design and Art Supervision by EZEKIEL SCHLOSS

Library of Congress Catalog Card No. 66-28527

Manufactured in the United States of America

TABLE OF CONTENTS

ACKNOWLEDGEMENTS

If you want to learn more about the Hafetz Hayyim you may read about him in *Saint and Sage* by Rabbi Moses M. Yoshor, Bloch Publishing Company.

PHOTOGRAPH CREDITS

American Friends of the Hebrew University
Israel Office of Information
Hadassah
The Jewish Museum, New York
Jewish Theological Seminary
Scharfstein, Joel
Union of American Hebrew Congregations
Yeshiva University
Yivo Institute for Jewish Research
Yoshor, Rabbi Moses
Zionist Archives

To my mother
Stella Cohn Burstein
Many daughters have done valiantly;
but thou excellest them all.

ON THE STREET WHERE YOU LIVE

On the street where you live there are many families. All of them live very much the way your family does, and are interested in many of the same things. The parents, like yours, try to be good citizens. They take good care of their homes and families; they are concerned with what goes on in their community and in the world.

If they have children the same age as you, those children are your friends. All of you go to school, and many of you have lessons after school. You study and learn so that when you grow up you will know how to be good parents, good citizens, good workers at whatever job you choose.

All the families on your street are the same in many ways, but each one is different from every other. Each has its own name, its own particular love for its own members, its own special interests—perhaps in books, or in art, or in music, or in pets, or in sports, or in politics, or in charity. It may be possible to learn something from every one of these families, to see things that you don't see in your own home. But of course, you would not trade your own family for any of the others!

FREEDOM OF RELIGION

In a very important way, the families on your street are different one from the other. Each attends its own church or synagogue. Each family loves and keeps its own customs and holidays. Even among families that are Jewish you will find different ways of living. In some homes there is very little observance. In some the children find joy in many customs and celebrations, in services and songs that the whole family can share together. There are different ideas in different families about how to live as a Jew. Yet all are proud to be Jewish and glad that they can live according to their faith.

You know that only in a democracy can such freedom be enjoyed— freedom to live equally with others; freedom to be different from others. As a Jew, you can especially appreciate the blessings of democracy.

If you have read *Heroes of Jewish Thought,* or any other book about the Jewish people, your ancestors, you know that for many centuries they were not free anywhere in the world. They were not allowed to be full citizens of any country. They had to live only in certain places and to get special permission to go elsewhere. They could not buy land or work as they pleased. The children could not go to regular schools, and universities were out of the question. The Jews were considered to be strange and wicked people. They had no rights in the court, and they were subject to hatred, ridicule and false charges of crime. Violence broke out against them, now in one country, now in another.

Through it all they kept their faith, and lived good lives according to Jewish law. In the worst of times they trusted that help would come.

All this is very hard to believe now. It is hard to believe that even in America there were times and places where Jews could not vote or hold office.

THE RIGHTS OF CITIZENS

You now are enjoying all the benefits your ancestors hoped and prayed that you would have. You and your family live where you want to, and your father does the work he wants to do to support his family. You can attend a fine synagogue or temple. You are respected by all your neighbors for doing so.

You can enter the college that you qualify for, and can plan to take up any career you want. When you grow up, you may vote, join a political party, run for office. You may be elected, if you are good enough, to any position in our government, even the highest in the land.

When did this change take place? How did the Jews gain their freedom and their rights? What happened to the Jews in their own homes, in their own minds, when they no longer were kept separate from the people around them?

WHEN FREEDOM CAME

This book will tell you how the Jews entered the modern world. Freedom did not come all at once, and there were and are many setbacks. The Jews themselves reacted to freedom in different ways. Some thought they should become exactly like the Gentiles. Others knew that there were values in Jewish tradition that would be good for the whole world to know; they worked to teach their own people these values. Many felt the Jews must learn their faith and keep their laws more faithfully than before, in order not to become lost among the other groups. When the Gentile world did not always prove friendly, the Jews knew they would have to do all they could to help their own people themselves.

In this book you will read about the leaders and teachers who have worked for the Jewish people in modern times, who have taught them ideas and helped them know how to live among the nations of the world.

You will read of saints and scholars of Europe, of men who served their people in England and in America, of thinkers and planners who helped bring about the State of Israel. You will hear of men who helped you not only to be free, but to be free to think and live as a Jew.

Perhaps you will understand better how the ways and ideas of your own family came to be.

YOU AND YOUR HERITAGE

Each family on your street has something of its own that is worthwhile. Your family has its own heritage from which it can choose and by which it lives. In this heritage is much that can make life finer and happier for you; there is also much that, if known and followed, could make the whole world a better and a happier place.

You are the heir to this heritage. The more you know and keep of your inheritance, the richer you will be: not rich in money, but rich in ideas and ideals, in good and happy ways of life.

Everyone on your street wants to lead a good life, to be a good citizen, to help make your community a better place. The more you know of the teachings of the great men in this book, the more you will know how you, as a Jew, can lead the best possible life.

You will know better how to be a good neighbor on your street, a useful citizen of your country, an individual who lives by ideas and ideals that can help bring justice and peace to our troubled modern world.

UNIT ONE

THE HEART AND MIND
OF EASTERN EUROPE

For hundreds of years, well into the twentieth century, Eastern Europe was the center of Jewish life. In countries that were called Russia, Poland, Lithuania, Austria, Hungary, lived the largest number of Jews in the world. Your own family, grandparents or great-grandparents, probably came from that part of the world sometime during the last hundred years.

Besides being greatest in numbers, the Jews of Eastern Europe were a loyal and learned community. Great rabbis and teachers went forth from the *yeshivot* of Eastern Europe to communities in Western Europe and America. Most of the Jews of America, and the founders of the State of Israel came from that area, as well.

Why did so many Jews live in that part of the world? For one reason, they had been invited to come there. The early rulers of Poland in the thirteenth and fourteenth centuries wanted Jews and others from Western Europe to settle in their territory. These rulers knew that their people were not as modern or as well educated as those of the French and German provinces.

Poland was a country of farms and forests. There were noblemen who owned large estates, and there were poor and ignorant serfs who farmed the land for them. King Boleslav and King Casimir wanted to build up towns and cities, and to carry on trade with other countries. They were happy when Jews from German-speaking lands came to settle in Poland, bringing their education and their knowledge of trade. They made rules that the Jews should be allowed to live in peace and to take care of their own government.

The Travels of the Jews

Let us look back at the travels and adventures of the Jewish people.

We know that Jews had been living in many countries of the world since the time of their first exile to Babylonia (586 B.C.E.) from their own country, Palestine. Many had returned to rebuild the Temple in Jerusalem and to found the Second Commonwealth; but many had also remained outside the land.

By the time of the Roman Empire, Jews lived not only in Babylonia, but also in Egypt, especially in the great city of Alexandria; in the thriving cities of North Africa; in Rome itself. After the destruction of the Second Temple in the year 70 C.E., many Jews were exiled. As Roman rule became more and more harsh, more Jews left Palestine.

Jews outside the land still loved their homeland. They sent help and, if they could, came to study in the land of Israel. However, we recall that after the time of the great teacher Judah Ha-Nasi (200 C.E.), Babylonia gradually became the center of Jewish life. As many as a million Jews lived there at one time. It was there that the Mishnah was studied and the Talmud developed, telling Jews how to live proper lives. Scholars in other countries sent questions to the *Geonim*, the heads of the schools of Babylonia.

After a thousand years of leadership, the community in Babylonia became less important. By this time Jews lived in every country of Europe, North Africa, and the Near East. They were under the rule of Christians in French, German, and Italian provinces; and of Moslems in Spain, North Africa, and Persia-Babylonia.

The Jews of Spain flourished under Moslem rule and enjoyed a golden age. With such teachers as Judah Ha-Levi and the great Moses Maimonides, the Spanish community was the leader of world Jewry for several centuries.

At the same time there were important

settlements in North Africa, places we now know as Algeria and Morocco; in Turkey and its neighboring lands; in France, where Rashi wrote his commentaries; in Germany, and in Italy.

Religious Persecution

The communities of Europe suffered a great deal at the hands of the Christian majority. In most places, the Jews were considered outsiders. They were not allowed to own land, so they could not be farmers. They were not allowed to join the various guilds of craftsmen. More and more they had to become storekeepers and traders. In one way, they were well fitted for trade and commerce. Because of their wanderings, Jews knew other languages; they had relatives and friends in other countries, and they were able to carry on business with faraway cities.

The worst hardship, we remember, was religious persecution. The Church wanted the Jews to leave their religion. In Germany the Jews had to wear special clothes and pointed hats, so that the common people would look on them as strange and evil. In many places, at different times, Jews were forced to become Christians or be killed. Noblemen and kings always had the right to drive the Jews out of their lands and take all their property.

We know of the terrible persecutions that came at the time of the Crusades (12th and 13th centuries). These were religious wars waged by the Christians of Europe who wanted to free the Holy Land from the Moslems. Many soldiers of the Crusades killed and robbed during their long journey to the Near East. Most particularly they felt free to kill Jews, since these, too, were "infidels," outside the Church. In the German towns along the Rhine River, complete Jewish communities were wiped out.

Flight to the East

Living under such oppression, it is no wonder that many Jews of the German provinces wanted to find a new and a safer home. Many traveled eastward to the open countries of Poland and Lithuania.

A medieval artist's idea of a discussion between Christians and Jews.

A group of Khazars, members of the Jewish nation in Southern Asia, as they are thought to have looked in the Middle Ages.

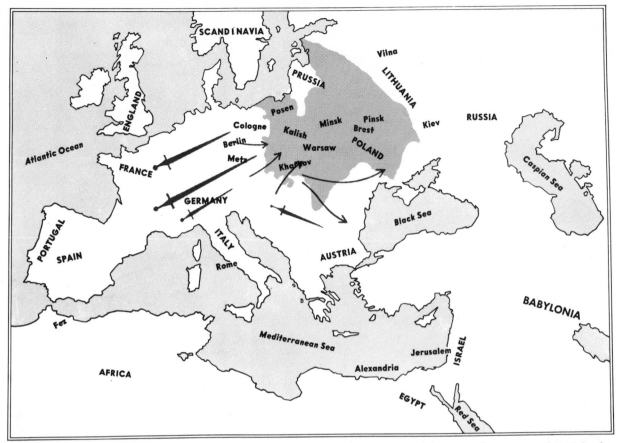

Persecutions and expulsions from German states 1350 to 1648. The many expulsions sent Jews eastward to Poland, where they were welcomed, and where they helped build up industry and trade.

Just a few years after King Casimir invited the Jews to live in his land (1344) new persecutions broke out in Germany. The dreadful plague called the Black Death spread across all of Europe. No one knew at that time about germs; doctors were helpless. In this time of fear many ignorant people, wanting to find some cause they could understand for this evil, decided the Jews were to blame. They turned against their Jewish neighbors. There were massacres in hundreds of towns, and Jews were expelled from places where they had lived for generations.

Thousands of Jews moved eastward from the German provinces and nearby areas. They were joined by others from the more southern countries, which had been part of the Eastern Roman Empire, and from Crimea

near the Black Sea. Some of these may have been descendants of the Khazars, the kingdom that converted to Judaism about the year 600.

A historian's picture of a riot against the Jews at Frankfurt, Germany, in 1614. The leader, Vincent Fettmilch, was later executed; and the Jews of the city celebrated a second Purim.

7

Self-Government

The new communities were allowed to govern themselves under the system called the *Kahal*. The Jewish residents of each town had their own president, their own charities, their own schools, and even their own civil courts. They collected taxes and passed them on to the Polish government. The Jews were

Polish coins with Hebrew inscriptions.

able to follow the laws of the Talmud in their daily lives and in their business. They often wrote contracts or bills of sale in Hebrew or Aramaic. There were even times when Jewish business men struck their own coins, using Hebrew lettering.

In the sixteenth century a council of Four Lands, representing the districts known as Major Poland, Minor Poland, Red Russia and Lithuania, was set up to look after Jewish interests. A Jewish ambassador was sent to the Polish court.

In the midst of a rather backward society, the Jews of Poland could be said to have had their own civilization. While most of the people were illiterate, every Jewish child learned to read and write. Far beyond that, studying was considered the most important task of every man throughout his life.

Larger towns had their *yeshivot*, their schools of higher learning. Those students

Page from the pinkas (minute-book) of the Council of Four Lands, with signatures of delegates.

who had the best minds might spend their whole lives studying the Talmud and commentaries, and advising the people. Every Jew, however, spent some of his time studying *Tehilim*, (the Psalms), or the Mishnah.

Jewish housewives and mothers, who had little time for learning, knew the many Talmudic laws for daily living and followed them

Young boys in Heder, children's school in Eastern Europe.

faithfully. And from the time they could talk even the children knew Talmudic words and ideas.

A Jewish Language

Up to this period, besides the Hebrew they all learned at school, Jews had always spoken the language of the country they lived in. Rashi spoke French; Saadia and Maimonides spoke and wrote Arabic. The Jews coming from German-speaking areas in the thirteenth, fourteenth and fifteenth centuries spoke German.

Separated for the most part from the Polish peasants among whom they lived, they kept their German language among themselves.

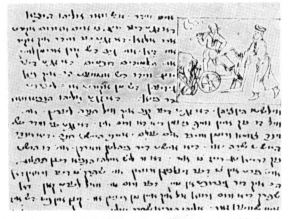

Page from a sixteenth century collection of Yiddish tales.

In Germany itself, the language of the Middle Ages changed into Modern German, which is somewhat different, mainly in pronunciation. The German of the Middle Ages which the Jewish wanderers brought with them to Eastern Europe became Yiddish.

The Yiddish language is more, however, than Middle High German with certain changes in pronunciation. It includes Hebrew and Aramaic, particularly Talmudic words and expressions. All the names for Jewish holidays and observances are, of course, from the Hebrew; and much else besides.

Ladino edition of Bahya ibn Pakuda's "Duties of the Heart," printed in Venice in the seventeenth century.

For instance, in everyday speech, a learned man would be called a *talmid hohem,* from the Hebrew words for "wise student"; a bride was always called *kallah;* to speak the truth was to speak *emes*—all Hebrew words, in their *Ashkenazi* or Germanic pronunciation.

Some Polish words or whatever other language was spoken in the neighborhood would also creep in. The Yiddish language was always written, and later printed, in Hebrew letters, for these were the letters that every Jew knew.

Interestingly, among the Spanish or *Sephardi* Jews who lived in the southern countries of Europe, another Jewish language

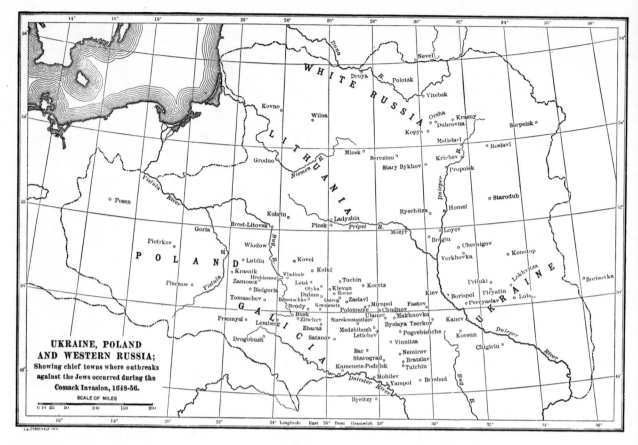

Map of the area where the Cossack invaders under Chmelnitzki destroyed many Jewish communities, in the years 1648 to 1656.

grew up. Called *Ladino,* it too was written in Hebrew letters. Over two hundred thousand Jews left Spain during the horrors of the Inquisition, the majority being expelled in the year 1492. These refugees, settling in Portugal, Italy, Turkey, North Africa, and later in Holland, England, and the Americas, carried with them their own culture, including the Ladino language.

Evil Times in the East

Conditions seemed good for the Jews of Eastern Europe who had escaped from violence in the lands of their birth. They soon found, however, that the Catholic Church of Poland was their enemy, and that the peasants among whom they lived could be easily

Bogdan Chmelnitzki, rebel leader responsible for the death of hundreds of thousands of Jews.

aroused against them. Life in the towns was often difficult. On some large estates, land-owners protected a small number of well-educated Jews, who could help them in their business and in collecting taxes.

The association of Jews and landowners led to disaster. In the sixteenth century, Polish nobles came to rule over the Russian territory called the Ukraine. They were hated by the peasants, who had to pay heavy taxes to the landlords—taxes sometimes collected by a Jewish overseer.

In the year 1648, a Ukrainian officer named Bogdan Chmelnitzki, joined by wild Cossack horsemen and the Tatars of the East, rebelled and invaded Poland. Thousands of Poles were killed, but in every town the Jews were the first victims. In the years of war and confusion which followed, hundreds of thousands of Jews were killed. At the end of that time, the Poles, suffering and disunited as they were, still turned their hatred against the Jews.

At the same time, Western Europe was

The synagogue of the ARI, in Safed, Israel.

suffering the results of the Thirty Years War. Strife and destruction seemed to be the condition of man.

Hope for a Miracle

This period was one of the lowest points in Jewish history. For one thing, after the Chmelnitzki massacres, the Jewish population all over the world was less than one million. At the time of the destruction of the Temple by Rome, nearly 1,600 years before, there had been at least five million Jews in the world. The slaughter during the rebellions against Rome, exile and flight and selling into slavery, forced conversions, religiously inspired massacres like those of the Crusades, and deaths through poverty and hardship had nearly destroyed the Jewish people.

When times are desperate, people hope for a miracle to save them. The Jews had long looked for the Messiah who would lead them back to the land of Israel and would bring

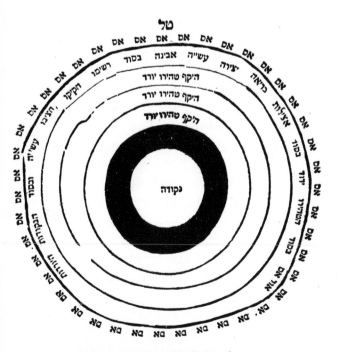

A drawing of the Kabbalistic spheres.

peace and justice to the world. In the dark centuries that were the Middle Ages, many Jews found hope in studying the mystical writings of the *Kabbalah*. Particularly in the school of Safed in Israel during the sixteenth and seventeenth centuries, devoted students searched through writings that told how to come nearer to the knowledge of God.

The most important work of the Kabbalah, which means "tradition," was the book called the *Zohar*. In its pages seemed to be the promise that the Messiah was soon to come.

Jacob Frank, false Messiah.

False Messiahs

In the gloom of the year 1648, a false Messiah by the name of Sabbetai Zvi arose in Smyrna, a city of Turkey. He traveled to Cairo and Jerusalem, gaining followers. Out of the depths of their despair, Jews all over the world began to believe that this was truly God's messenger who would save mankind. Many sold their possessions and came to Constantinople in the year 1666, when Sabbetai Zvi was supposed to be proclaimed king.

Instead of being acknowledged by the rulers of the world, as he had promised, Sabbetai Zvi was arrested by the Sultan. Afraid of further punishment, he gave up all his claims, and converted to Islam.

The disappointment all over the Jewish world was tremendous. Many could not give up their hopes. They claimed the Messiah had just gone into hiding. Others arose who claimed they were the true redeemers. One hundred years later another pretender, Jacob Frank, gained many followers by saying he was Sabbetai brought back to life. Eventually he and some of his followers left Judaism and became Catholics.

It is easy to see why people living under persecution should want to believe that some one might come to save them. Learned men and serious leaders warned the people against such vain superstition. They reminded the Jews to study Torah, to live righteously, and to keep faith in God. In the world to come, or at the end of days, they would gain their reward. Still the Jews looked for miraculous help in the darkness of their hour.

The Baal Shem Tov

Two great leaders, whom we remember from *Heroes of Jewish Thought*, arose in the eighteenth century in Eastern Europe. One spoke to the heart of the people. This was Israel Baal Shem Tov, who brought warmth and joy into their sad lives.

The Baal Shem taught that God is everywhere, close to the poor and ignorant as well as to the wealthy and learned. He taught that God wants all of His children to be happy; that He loves them all, even the least of them, and wants them only to return His love through joyful devotion and sincere prayer. The Baal Shem said that the truly righteous leader, the *tzaddik,* is the guide for the people in their journey towards God.

Tzaddikim

The followers of the Baal Shem were called *hasidim*, meaning "pious ones." Hasidism spread rapidly through a large part of Eastern Europe. After the death of the Baal Shem, other leaders arose. One was Rabbi Dov Ber of Mezritch, called the *Maggid*, or "preacher." The Maggid of Mezritch, with his gift for speaking and influencing others, was the tzaddik who did most to spread the teachings of the Baal Shem.

The descendants of the Baal Shem and the pupils of the Maggid became *tzaddikim* who led groups of hasidim in different towns. In the house of the tzaddik, or *rebbe*, the hasidim would eat, pray, sing and dance; they would bring gifts to the rebbe and ask his advice and blessing. Often, when a tzaddik died, his son would become the leader.

Rabbi Isaac Elhanan Spector of Kovno, leading rabbi of Lithuania.

Many of the tzaddikim were extraordinary men. Such were Shneur Zalman of Ladi, a pupil of the Maggid, who had a fine Talmudic background and emphasized learning as the basis for the service of God; Levi Isaac of Berditchev, a saint whose heart overflowed with love and pity for his people; and Rabbi Nahman of Bratslav, who told parables which show the miracle of God's love and care for the world.

Followers of tzaddikim still live in small groups throughout the world. The message of Hasidism—its faith in God and love for fellow man, its wondrous stories, its soul-stirring songs and dances—has become known and beloved among all peoples.

Elijah Gaon of Vilna

Hasidism was most successful in Poland and Galicia, spreading to some extent in Lithuania and nearby northern areas, where Jews lived in larger and more learned communities. However, there was much opposition. The "Opponents," or *mitnagdim,* saw

The great scholar Elijah, Gaon of Vilna.

in Hasidism a rebellion against learning and authority. They said it was not proper for Jews to show reverence for any man, to claim that a tzaddik had special influence with God and could help others through this power. Only through learning could a man gain the right to advise others.

The greatest rabbinic teacher of the eighteenth century was Elijah Gaon of Vilna. He spoke to the mind rather than to the heart of the Jews of Eastern Europe. His delight in study was so great that he never stopped studying; he wished to raise every Jew to the highest possible level of learning. He saw no value in Hasidism and opposed it strongly.

The Gaon of Vilna studied and taught not

Jewish officers and soldiers in the Polish National Guard, during the uprising against Russia in 1831.

by the method of *pilpul*, which showed keenness of mind in discussion of points of law in the Talmud and its commentaries, but by the direct method. In order to find out the true meaning of the laws of the Talmud, Rabbi Elijah studied history, languages, mathematics—everything that might help him understand the thoughts and background of the rabbis of the Talmud.

Such reasoned study of the Talmud was carried on after the death of Elijah Gaon by other scholars. His greatest pupil, Hayyim of Volozhin, established a famous yeshivah in his city. Other scholars who continued the traditions of the Vilna Gaon were the saintly Rabbi Israel Salanter, Rabbi Isaac Elhanan Spector, leading rabbi of Lithuania, and Rabbi Israel Meir Kagen, called the "Hafetz Hayyim" after the name of his first book.

Caricature by the French cartoonist Daumier, showing the real motive of Czar Nicholas I in persecuting the Jews in the Russian empire.

Life Under the Czars

There were many problems the Jews of Eastern Europe had to face as the nineteenth century began. Poland had been divided and conquered and was now ruled by Russia. The peasants and nobles of the great half-civilized territory of Russia still followed the religion and ways of life of the Middle Ages. Jews had not been allowed to settle in Russia for centuries.

In 1794 the Czarina Catherine declared that the million Jews who now were under her rule must return to the towns where they used to live. They were confined to the "Pale of Settlement" which ended with the former boundary of Poland. Thus a vast number of Jews were placed in what was really a large ghetto.

It was a time of change in the world: the American Revolution and the French Revolution had just been fought. Napoleon, with his declared policy of Liberty, Equality, and Fraternity, was on the march, conquering most of Europe. There was hope abroad for freedom for all men.

The defeat of Napoleon brought a strong reaction. The rulers of Europe, at the Congress of Vienna in 1815, resolved to be more strict than before.

Persecution in Russia

In the court of Russia, though the rulers liked to think they were "enlightened" and modern, there was backwardness and tyranny. Czar Alexander, at first trying to be liberal, appointed a committee to study the Jewish question. He then issued a "Constitution of the Jews," which took away from them their rights of self-government, forbade them to live in small towns or on farms, and urged them to attend government schools where they might get a Christian education.

The many restrictions of Alexander seemed kind, compared with the harsh rules of the next Czar, Nicholas. His first and most terrible anti-Jewish decree was that Jewish boys were to be drafted into the Russian army at the age of twelve, for six special years of training before the regular army term of twenty-five years. Being drafted into the Russian army was a hard fate for anyone; for these young Jews it was a method meant either to kill them by cruelty or to force them to convert. Jews tried to hide their sons or to bribe government officials in order to save them.

In another attempt to do away with the Jewish people, Czar Nicholas tried to establish a school system for the Jews where they would learn Russian subjects and gradually give up their Jewish traditions. Few Jews attended these government schools.

Jews were told to leave one town after another; they were urged to become farmers in Siberia, but those who tried met freezing weather and failure. There was strong censorship, control of the use of the Yiddish language, and restrictions at every turn.

The Life of the People

Under all this oppression, the Jews of Eastern Europe continued to live good Jewish lives. Whether they were hasidim or mitnagdim, they sent their children to *heder*, supported learning in the yeshivot, took care of their poor, and faithfully and joyfully kept the laws of Jewish tradition. Holidays were times of thanksgiving; Sabbaths were a foretaste of the happiness of the world to come.

While war, revolution, change and the reaction to change disturbed the peace in many lands, the life of the largest Jewish community in the world went on very much as it had gone on since the Middle Ages. Modern science and industry had little impact on the Pale of Settlement. Jews had never enjoyed freedom and civil rights under Russian rule. Western culture was unknown to them.

However, as the historian Solomon Grayzel has said, "If the measure of a culture's success is the development of beautiful character, these poverty-stricken, socially degraded and politically rightless people shed a brilliant luster on their culture and religion. . . . As a matter of fact, it would be hard to find a period in the history of the Jews in Europe which produced more beautiful living, more pious souls, more happy homes, than the nineteenth century in Eastern Europe."

Levi Isaac of Berditchev

1740-1809

It was the Eve of Yom Kippur, the Day of Atonement, the holiest time of the year.

The good Jews of the town of Berditchev were gathered together in their synagogue. During the week which had passed since the celebration of Rosh Hashanah, they had searched their hearts. They had gone to all their friends and asked them to forgive any wrong they had done to them in the past year.

Now, dressed in white, they were prepared to fast and pray for the forgiveness of their sins. The most moving prayer of the year, Kol Nidre, was about to begin.

It did not begin. The cantor stood silent. The sun set, and the time for Kol Nidre passed. But the service could not begin. Their rabbi, the gentle and beloved Levi Isaac, was not there.

A messenger was sent to the rabbi's house, and brought back the report that Levi Isaac had left long before. In fear, some of the men left the synagogue to look through the streets for any sign of the rabbi.

From the half-open door of a poor hut on a side-street came the sound of soft humming. Two of the hasidim, the followers of Levi Isaac, looked in. There sat their rabbi in his white robe, holding on his lap a sleeping baby. He looked up at them and signalled them to be quiet.

Placing the child gently back in its crib,

Page from an illustrated siddur printed in 1803, during the time Levi Isaac was rabbi of Berditchev.

Rabbi Levi Isaac explained, "When I passed this house on my way to *schul,* I heard this child crying. His mother had left him alone while she went to services. Of course I had to stop to take care of the child."

This was the rabbi of Berditchev, a man of love and compassion. No one was too small or unimportant; no one was too foolish or even too sinful to merit the love of this true tzaddik, this truly righteous man.

Miedziboz, the town of the Baal Shem Tov, founder of Hasidism.

A True Tzaddik

Levi Isaac was one of the tzaddikim who took over leadership of groups of hasidim after the death of the Baal Shem Tov. The Baal Shem had been the founder of Hasidism. He had brought to the poor, hardworking Jews of Eastern Europe new faith and new joy in life. True feeling and devotion in prayer bring any Jew close to God, he taught. God is with man always and everywhere. "Can a child be told when he may speak to his father?" he asked.

The tzaddik, said the Baal Shem, is the one who through his example and teaching can help the people become holy.

When the Baal Shem died, the hasidim, or Pious Ones, as his followers called themselves, accepted Rabbi Dov Ber as their tzaddik. Called the Maggid, or Preacher, Dov Ber of Mezritch was able to teach the message of Hasidism well, and to gain thousands of new hasidim.

Soon there were groups of hasidim in many towns of Eastern Europe, all through Poland, each group following its own *rebbe*, its own tzaddik. The leaders of the hasidim spoke to the heart rather than to the mind of their people. They spoke of God's love for every individual, and of the love that each hasid ought to feel for God and for every fellow

A Hassidic Rabbi giving his blessing to a young follower, about 1815.

man.

Perhaps the most truly worthy of the name of tzaddik was Rabbi Levi Isaac. He never looked for honor because of his position. His honesty and humility, his love and compassion for his people were so great that even the mitnagdim, the opponents of Hasidism, could not criticize him.

Levi Isaac Becomes a Hasid

Levi Isaac was born in 1740 into a family which loved learning. His father, Meir, was himself a rabbi. Like all Jewish boys of Eastern Europe, he spent his childhood in study. The Jews had their own school in each town, the *heder*, where they learned Hebrew, Bible, prayers and Talmud. All who could continue their studies went on to *yeshivot*, schools of higher learning.

Because he was a brilliant student, any family would have been proud to win young Levi Isaac for a son-in-law. A wealthy merchant was happy not only to have Levi Isaac

A Polish student of the last century.

marry his daughter, but also, as was customary, to support him while he continued his studies.

The father-in-law was not happy, however, when the young man wanted to leave his home and family and go to study in another town. Levi Isaac had his way, and went first to study with a certain Rabbi Samuel, who had been a pupil of the Maggid. Soon Levi Isaac decided to go to study with the Maggid himself, in his "court" at Mezritch.

The house where the Maggid lived and taught was in many ways like a royal court. Rabbi Dov Ber sat in his own large throne-like chair at the head of the table. Hasidim came every day to eat with him, to ask his advice, and to receive his blessing. They listened with reverence to every word he said.

The Great Synagogue at Berditchev.

Levi Isaac felt himself lifted to new heights at the court of the Maggid. He listened to Dov Ber and learned from him. One day a disciple was angry to see a well-known sinner enter the house of the Maggid, and told him to leave. The Maggid, upon hearing of this, sent after the sinner, saying, "Learn from me to tolerate the wrongdoer. Ignore the wickedness in him; seek, and you will find some good."

Levi Isaac also learned from the Maggid that such love and understanding brings a burden of pain. "Do you think it is a comfortable thing to be a tzaddik and a leader of many?" asked Rabbi Dov Ber. "Know better,

then, that it is a thicket of thorns. For the heart of the true tzaddik bleeds for others, and is weighed down with the sorrows of the people."

Levi Isaac became a devoted hasid, a follower of Dov Ber, the Maggid of Mezritch. He could not, however, remain long in the court of the Maggid. He received letters that his father-in-law could no longer support his family, and his children were hungry. Levi Isaac looked about for a position as rabbi so that he might be able to feed his family.

To the Town of Berditchev

The fact that he had become a hasid did not help him. In two communities to which he went, there were mitnagdim who upheld the order of the Gaon of Vilna, saying that no Jew should follow Hasidism. The words of the Gaon were not law, since there was, of course, no central ruler over the Jewish people. However, there was such respect for the Gaon, greatest scholar of the century, that many Jews obeyed him.

Finally an end came to Levi Isaac's period of wandering. He was asked to become the rabbi of Berditchev, not a large town and not a small one, but a good community with a history of four hundred years of Jewish settlement. Berditchev became famous because of its rabbi.

Types of Jews in Warsaw in the eighteenth century.

At first there were some who opposed the new rabbi. All doubts were soon overcome. It was not that Rabbi Levi Isaac was a great preacher who fascinated his audience. It was not that he was so learned that he could out-argue his opponents. In fact, he never gave long sermons, nor did he ever seek out or try to win an argument. He won the love of his friends and his enemies only through the goodness of his heart.

The Compassion of Rabbi Levi Isaac

Reb Levi Isaac was everything a true tzaddik was supposed to be. He gave his whole life to service and help of others; he lived simply and without pride. He never was too busy to speak to the humblest Jewish village-dweller, unlearned as he might be. All the Jewish people were dear to him. Like an overly fond parent who cannot see anything wrong in his beloved child, Levi Isaac saw

Wearing tefilin at morning prayer. The box on the forehead, fulfilling the commandment "And they shall be for frontlets between thine eyes," contains passages from the Torah.

only good in every Jew. In his prayers, he even reminded God of their virtues.

Stories about Levi Isaac show his belief in the Jewish people. Of course, the rabbi was a pious man, who kept every word of the law. He believed all Jews were as good and as pious as he was himself. One morning he saw a wagon-driver, still wearing his *tefilin* wrapped around his forehead and arm, greasing the wheels of his wagon.

The tefilin are worn only during morning prayers, to remind the worshiper of the holiness of service to God. The driver, a hasty man, could not wait until he finished his prayers and took off his tefilin to start his heavy day's work.

Not only a rabbi, but any Jew should have been shocked at this doing of grimy work in the attire of holiness. But Levi Isaac lifted his eyes to heaven and exclaimed: "Lord, what holy people the Jews are! They remain holy, they keep on praying and thinking of You, even while they are doing the lowliest of labor!"

Another wagon-driver came to Levi Isaac, saying, "I have hardly any time to pray, and none to study. I drive a wagon and carry

A Jewish wagon-driver of Poland.

people and packages from one town to another."

"When a poor man needs a ride," asked Levi Isaac, "do you take him free of charge?"

"Yes," said the coachman.

"Then you in your way are serving God by doing good deeds, and are just as dear in His eyes as the man who prays and studies," said the rabbi.

Another time, on the Fast Day of the Ninth of Av, one of the followers of the rabbi came running to him to whisper that another Jew was breaking the fast. He was eating on the day of memory for the destruction of the Temple, when no food was supposed to pass his lips.

Rabbi Levi Isaac was grieved to hear this. He knew it was his duty to speak to the offender. He went to the home of the sinner and asked hopefully, "My son, have you forgotten that today is the Ninth of Av?"—for he knew that sinning by accident is not a real sin.

"No, I haven't forgotten," said the man.

"Then it must be that you aren't feeling

Girls learning Jewish law from a woman teacher.

well, and must eat for the sake of your health," pleaded the rabbi. "In that case, you are doing a good deed."

"That's not it at all," said the man, "My health is fine. I just don't feel like going hungry."

A smile came upon Levi Isaac's face. Instead of scolding the other, he praised him, saying, "What a truthful people the Jews are! This man might so easily have told a lie, excusing himself by saying that he had forgotten the date, or that he was ill. Instead, rather than commit the sin of telling a lie, he admits that he has done wrong of his own free will."

Levi Isaac Appeals to God

The rabbi himself kept every feast and fast of the Jewish year with devotion. The Ninth of Av was a day that afflicted him greatly. On this day he recalled with all other Jews the destruction of the First and Second Temples, the exile of the Jews from their land, and their wandering and suffering all

Jews assembled in the synagogue to hear a maggid, a traveling preacher.

over the world. Because of his tender heart, he felt the pain of his people more than anyone else.

His followers told how on one evening of the Ninth of Av, he watched at the window, hoping that the Messiah would come, feeling that God must surely send the Messiah on the same day that He had previously sent destruction. When night came and the Messiah had once more not arrived, the rabbi, although an old and dignified man, broke into tears like a child.

How could God keep His children in exile? How could He look on their suffering and not save them? Rabbi Levi Isaac wept for his people and pleaded for them before God.

The Kaddish of Reb Levi Isaac

The time of year when Levi Isaac really stood up as a defender of his people was the time when the Jews feel they are on trial,

The Rabbi's Blessing, by the famed artist M. Oppenheim.

the holy days of Rosh Hashanah and Yom Kippur. On Rosh Hashanah, the New Year, God is thought of as the Judge of the world, who reads the record of each soul and decides what will be its fate during the coming year. On Yom Kippur, the verdict is made final. It was on Yom Kippur that Rabbi Levi Isaac spoke most movingly to God.

So great was his feeling of closeness to the Almighty that he spoke, not in formal words of prayer, but as one might speak to some one standing in front of him. So great was Levi Isaac's love for his people Israel, that he dared to challenge God for their sake.

Thus spoke Rabbi Levi Isaac before he recited the Kaddish on Yom Kippur:

"Good morning to You, Master of the world.

"I, Levi Isaac, son of Sarah, of Berditchev, have come in behalf of my client Israel, to summon You to a trial.

"Tell me, I ask You, what have You against Your people Israel? Why do You allow Your people of Israel to suffer? What have they done that is so terrible?

"Always it is 'Speak to the children of Israel'; 'Command the children of Israel that they do this and that.'

"Father of mercy, there are so many other nations in the world—Persians, Babylonians, Greeks and Romans. Why do you not command them?

"The Russians, what do they say? 'Our czar is the highest king.'

"The Germans, what do they say? 'Our kaiser is the greatest ruler.'

"The English, what do they say? 'Our king is the mightiest.'

"And I, Levi Isaac, son of Sarah, of Berditchev, what do I and Your people Israel say?

"'Magnified and sanctified be His great name in the world which He created by His word; may His kingdom be established!'"

"Moreover I, Levi Isaac, son of Sarah, of Berditchev, will not move from my place, I will not leave this spot, until I know that You have forgiven Israel for their sins, and will put an end to their sufferings."

It would be hard to say whether love of God, or love of his people was the strongest feeling in Levi Isaac's heart. Perhaps it was all one. As Levi Isaac, Defender of Israel, said himself. "Whether a man really loves God can be seen only by the love he shows toward his fellow men."

The Day After Sukkot

When Levi Isaac was ill and in misery, he expressed his love for God and his acceptance of whatever God sent him, saying,

"Lord, it is not that I am unwilling to suffer. It is not that I wish to know the reason for my suffering. All I want to know is that it is for Your sake."

When, finally, on Yom Kippur in his seventieth year, the tzaddik knew he had not long to live, he prayed for one thing for himself. His greatest joy, besides the Sabbath, was in keeping the Festival of Sukkot. He prayed only to live through the week of Sukkot, to enter the *sukkah* and to say the blessings over *lulav* and *etrog* once more. This was granted him, and the day after Sukkot, he died.

From the time of Levi Isaac's death there was no rabbi in Berditchev. The congregation could find no one to fill his place.

"Kedushat Levi," a book containing teachings by and about Rabbi Levi Isaac, printed in 1919.

Shneur Zalman of Ladi

1747-1813

"Let me not waste time on sleep," said the young rabbi. "I must stay awake as long as I can, and study more and more." And he removed the chairs from his room, so he would not be tempted to rest while reading. Standing, he leaned over the volumes of the Talmud, devoting all his hours to learning the Law.

"It is too much," said his father-in-law. The merchant of Vitebsk had wanted his daughter to marry the young scholar. No one was more respected in the Jewish community than a student of Talmud. Shneur Zalman was an *ilui,* a young genius, who had been called a rabbi in the town records the same year he became a Bar Mitzvah. No wonder the wealthy man had been happy to gain him for a son-in-law.

Now, however, after some years, the father-in-law was getting impatient. He wished to see Shneur Zalman in the position of rabbi in the community. He wanted the young man to get out into the world and make a name for himself. But Shneur Zalman was not ready.

A painting of Rabbi Shneur Zalman.

Buildings in the town of Vitebsk.

Two Directions

As a youth, he had mastered the Talmud, that tremendous work, with all its commentaries. He also studied the Kabbalah, books of Jewish tradition which contained not discussions of law but descriptions of the way God worked and ideas on how men might understand His will.

Though he loved learning with all his heart, he was not yet satisfied with his studies. He felt that knowledge should bring him to a feeling of joy and nearness to holiness.

"I must leave this town and travel to study with a great master," decided Shneur Zalman. Two choices were before him. He could go to Vilna, the world center of Jewish learning, where Elijah, Gaon of Vilna, taught a few selected students. This would have been the life's ambition of any scholarly young man of Lithuania.

He could also go to Mezritch, to the court of the great Maggid or Preacher, Dov Ber, who carried on the joyous teachings of the Baal Shem Tov. There Shneur Zalman felt he might find the true feeling of holiness which he was seeking.

The mind of the young rabbi told him to go to Vilna. His heart, his feelings, told him to make the second choice.

He discussed the trip with his young wife.

ספרי – אוצר החסידים – ליובאוויטש

קובץ
שלשלת האור

שער
שלשה עשר

היכל
חמישי

קיצורים והערות

לספר
לקוטי אמרים

מ א ת

כבוד קדושת אדוננו מורנו ורבנו הגדול
הגאון האמתי האלקי חסידא קדישא
אור עולם נזר ישראל ותפארתו
קדוש ה'
מרנא ורבנא מנחם מענדל נבג"מ זי"ע
מליובאוויטש

יוצא לאור על ידי מערבת
"אוצר החסידים"
שנת חמשת אלפים שבע מאות ושמנה לבריאה
770 איסטערן פארקוויי   ברוקלין, נ. י.

Title-page of an explanatory work on the Tanya of Shneur
Zalman, written by Menahem Mendel of Lubavitch, heir to
his teachings.

It would mean leaving her for some time. Unlike her father, she felt that whatever her husband wanted to do was right. If he wanted to study, no matter where or how long, she felt it was her privilege to help him do so. She took some money which her father had told her to keep for herself, and gave it to her husband so that he could make the journey to Mezritch.

The Lithuanian Among the Hasidim

The hasidim of Mezritch were surprised to see the Lithuanian Talmud scholar. Most Lithuanians, or Litvaks, as they were called in Yiddish, were proud of their learning and looked down on the hasidim who were from Poland or Galicia. The hasidim did not devote their lives to study, but preferred to listen to the words of their rebbe. Yet, though they wondered at his being there, they welcomed Shneur Zalman into the court of their rabbi.

In the court of Rabbi Dov Ber, Shneur Zalman found the enthusiasm and the sense of holiness that he had longed for. Said the rabbi of Mezritch: "A man should think holy thoughts. If he must leave them to think of ordinary things, let him feel that he has left his true home for a while, but intends to return as soon as possible.

"Every man should keep some sense of holiness even when he is doing wrong. When a coal still has one spark, it may be rekindled into flame. There are sparks of holiness in everything, even in sin. What is the spark of holiness in sin? It is the possibility of repentance."

Shneur Zalman felt that the rabbi of Mezritch was a saint; that the spirit of God really could be heard in the words of the rebbe. For the first time, he said, he felt the true fear and love of God. He was filled with joy.

The Maggid himself knew that he had found an extraordinary pupil. He loved the newcomer from the beginning. He could say about this follower what he had said about others: "I found a house full of candles that were unlit. I kindled them and the house is full of light." Because Shneur Zalman was by far the most learned of all his disciples, he was asked to become the teacher of the Maggid's son.

A Teacher of the Hasidim

Shneur Zalman wanted to use his knowledge to instruct all the hasidim who were not as learned as he. For many years he studied the codes of Jewish law. In the sixteenth cen-

tury Joseph Caro had compiled the *Shulhan Arukh*, intending it to be the final simple statement of all laws for daily life. Changes and commentaries had now made it difficult to follow Caro's code. Shneur Zalman considered which customs were basic, where different observances had started, what was no longer necessary. Over a period of years he put out a clear new version of the *Shulhan Arukh* in five volumes.

Rabbi Menahem Mendel of Lubavitch, founder of the Lubavitcher Hasidim, who emphasized learning in the tradition of Shneur Zalman.

He also wrote *Tanya*, meaning "We have learned," which contained his philosophy of Hasidism. In it he taught that everything is holy, and depends completely on God. There is something holy in every man, the spark of the Divine in his soul. A devoted Jew can fan the spark, can make it flame so that he feels more and more the holiness that is in him. The doing of the good deed, or *mitzvah*—particularly *tzedakah*, kindness and charity—was the way to kindle the spark of holiness.

The New Leader

It was only for a few years that Shneur Zalman was able to listen to the wise words of the Maggid of Mezritch. Dov Ber was old and weary. It was at a time of conflict between the hasidim and their opponents that the Maggid, pupil and successor of the Baal Shem, died and left the leadership to his old pupil, Rabbi Menahem Mendel, and his new follower, Shneur Zalman.

Why should there be any quarrel between hasidim and mitnagdim, wondered the new tzaddik. In himself were contained the best elements of both. If the warmth, enthusiasm and loving kindness of Hasidism could be combined with the learning of the Lithuanian Jews, thought Shneur Zalman, then indeed would Judaism flourish.

With Menahem Mendel, Shneur Zalman journeyed to Vilna. He wanted to speak to Elijah, the great Gaon, to persuade him that there was good in Hasidism, that a hasid could also be learned and pious. The Gaon, who seldom appeared in public, would not enter into discussion with them. Shneur Zalman regretted this, but continued to respect the Gaon of Vilna. He told his followers that such a genius had never before arisen in Israel.

A medal commemorating the emancipation of the Jews by Alexander I.

Betrayed and Imprisoned

A man of peace, the new leader of the hasidim soon found that he had enemies. He was denounced with twenty-two other hasidim to the Russian government. All were arrested and accused of disloyalty to the Czar, the ruler of Russia. The police soon saw that their prisoners were harmless and let them go, all except their leader, Shneur Zalman. He was charged with being the founder of a harmful sect, spreading dangerous ideas, and collecting money to be sent to Palestine for some unknown reason. He was taken in chains to St. Petersburg, to be tried in the national court.

Weeks went by before he could be freed. While the learned rabbi defended himself in a long document, his followers collected a defense fund of sixty thousand rubles. Finally, Czar Paul ordered the release of the prisoner, but warned that all hasidim would be watched for signs of disloyalty.

The good rabbi returned home in triumph. He was now considered a martyr and a hero as well as a teacher. Stories grew up about how impressed the Czar had been with his wisdom.

Two years later Rabbi Shneur Zalman was again arrested. Further accusations had been made that he was arousing his followers to treason. It was reported that he told his hasidim to fear no one but God, which was true. The claim was made that this meant his followers were supposed to disobey the laws of the state, which was not true. This time, however, the rabbi was kept in prison for only three weeks.

Finally, under Czar Alexander, the government announced that the hasidim were a recognized religious group with the rights of any other group. There was rejoicing among the hasidim. They felt that their leader's suffering in prison had helped bring about this welcome declaration.

Now a great leader, known throughout the provinces of Russia, Shneur Zalman was no longer condemned by his wife's family. In fact, they would have been very proud to have him return and live with them as he had done when he was first married, in the town of Vitebsk. The rabbi, however, politely refused the invitation. He and his wife and children lived in Lozna, where he had been born. Later they moved to Ladi, which gained the honor of becoming the town by whose name he is known; for Shneur Zalman is called the rabbi of Ladi.

Learning Above All

The rabbi of Ladi knew that many hasidim put too much value on feelings of joy and closeness to God, and not enough on the study of the law of God. They emphasized the heart at the expense of the mind. He taught them: "The true delight of the soul comes only after understanding the mysteries of the Torah." While the hasidim considered prayer the most desirable activity, Shneur Zalman taught, "You should not interrupt the study of the Law for prayer. Every law is the wisdom and will of God."

"Let the mind always rule over the heart," said the rabbi of Ladi. Although he himself had a heart full of enthusiasm, and though he, like most hasidim, often expressed his feelings in song rather than in careful speech, he influenced his followers to love books and pursue knowledge.

The closest disciples of the rabbi of Ladi joined him in devotion to wisdom, reason and knowledge. The first letters of the three Hebrew words, *Hakhmah, Binah, Deah,* were made into the name HaBaD. The Habad Hasidim, now called Lubavitcher hasidim, became the ones who established fine schools and yeshivot, and spoke of learning as the pathway to the highest spiritual joy.

Napoleon Invades Russia

The last years of Shneur Zalman's life were not spent in peaceful study and teaching. The Jews under Russian rule had been cut off from much knowledge of what was going on in the rest of the world. World events suddenly became important to them.

The French Revolution, with its message of Liberty, Equality and Fraternity, had frightened the rulers of every country. Now the revolution was being spread by the great French general, Napoleon, who invaded and soon controlled every country of Western Europe. To spread the ideal of brotherhood and to gain the loyalty of the Jews, Napoleon promised equal rights for the Jews wherever he went. Many Jews of Europe saw him as their redeemer.

Napoleon now began his last campaign. He easily conquered the western territories of Russia. The Jews of Poland, however, with most of the other Jews under Russian rule, remained loyal to the czar.

Why did they not turn to Napoleon? In part, because of the influence of Shneur Zalman. He warned them that Napoleon could be defeated at Moscow. And that is exactly what happened.

Shneur Zalman also instructed his followers that the freedom Napoleon promised might give them some advantages, but that the purpose of this freedom was to make them forget and leave their Jewish religion. That, in truth, was Napoleon's aim, for he

A famous picture entitled "Golus," showing the bitterness of exile. Artist Samuel Hirszenberg shows Jews, young and old, forced to leave their homes in Russia by one of the many cruel decrees of the Czar.

was not religious himself and would have liked to end all differences among the people he ruled.

Because he had spoken against Napoleon, the rabbi of Ladi was forced to escape from the city with his family when the French army drew near. For some time he and his family were refugees, wandering from one town to another.

Eventually the aging rabbi fell ill. He was brought to the home of a Russian peasant in a backward village where there was not even a doctor. Dying, in a strange bed, the rabbi still felt the presence of God.

Defeat and Fulfilment

The rabbi of Ladi died in 1813, the year Napoleon was defeated at Moscow. He did not live to see much that his people suffered: how Czar Alexander, who had seemed friendly to the Jews, made life more and more difficult

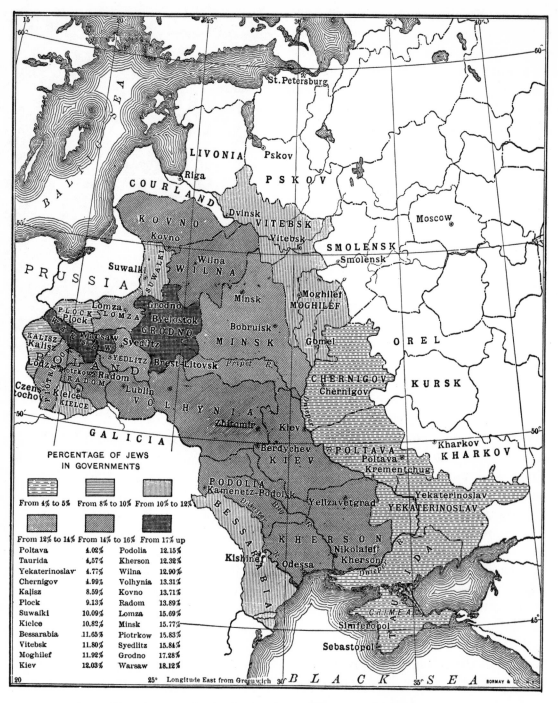

Map of western Russia showing the Jewish Pale of Settlement.

for them; how all over Europe, following the defeat of Napoleon, the rights which had been given to the Jews were cancelled. He did not see what would have broken his heart: how some Jews, wishing to gain the rights they had been promised, scorned and left their Jewish birthright.

What he did foresee was that Hasidism would continue. His trust was fulfilled. His descendants continued his work in the city of Lubavitch. The Lubavitcher Hasidim to this day live by the principles of Habad. They found schools and devote their lives to learning. Believing, as Shneur Zalman did, that there is a spark of holiness in every man, they show tolerance and love for all men.

To this day hasidim believe that God dwells in the world and in the hearts of His worshippers. There are hasidic groups following their *rebbes* all over the world — although most of them are in America and in Israel. Hasidim are known as the most observant of Jews. Wishing to follow every tradition of their founders, they often even dress as their ancestors did in the towns of Poland two centuries ago.

Hasidim are now few in number, but their influence has reached not only all Jews, but all the western world. Their music, their exuberant faith, their wonderful stories that teach lessons for life, have come to be loved by people of all groups.

Whenever a Jew feels his heart lifting in joy and love of God, he may be said to be feeling what the saintly Baal Shem wished every Jew to feel. When a Jew comes to spiritual joy through devoted study of Torah, he can be said to be living the tradition of Shneur Zalman, rabbi of Ladi.

Modern Jews celebrating the joy of the Torah in song and dance on Simhat Torah.

Israel Salanter

1810-1883

When dining with a great man, the guests are likely to be very careful about how they behave. They may wish to impress him with their own wisdom or goodness. The great man, however, will not be trying to impress the others; he has his own standards.

One cold winter day two rabbis sat at the table of an inn with the great Rabbi Israel Salanter. Rabbi Israel was known for his devotion to all the laws of the Torah; every minute of his life he followed the commandments.

When it came time for the washing of the hands before the meal, a positive commandment in Jewish law, the two rabbis allowed much water to be poured over their hands. They wanted to be sure Rabbi Israel saw they were fulfilling the mitzvah with all their might.

When it came the turn of Rabbi Israel to wash his hands, he used a few drops of water, as little as he could.

The others waited until all had said the blessings and eaten the piece of bread to open the meal. Then one of them dared

Implements used for scoring or raking matzot during baking, so that they will not rise.

to ask, "Rabbi Israel, why were you so sparing in the use of water?"

"From where I sit," answered Rabbi Israel, "I can see through the window. It is cold outside, as you know. I have seen the poor serving-girl go back and forth fetching water from the well in two heavy buckets. One should not gain credit for being exceptionally strict in obeying the law at the expense of someone else."

Keeper of the Commandments

Rabbi Israel was indeed known for his own exceptional strictness as a *shomer mitzvot*, a keeper of the commandments. He taught his followers, and lived by the rule, that every action of man's life should be in obedience to the law. He never spared or excused himself, and was never satisfied with his own righteousness.

Every Jew ate *matzah* on Passover, but Rabbi Israel was not content with his fulfilment of the mitzvah unless he had *matzah shemurah,* special supervised matzah made from wheat he himself ground. His students had great respect for the care with which Rabbi Israel watched the making of his own matzah from start to finish, making sure that there should not be the least suspicion of *hametz,* leaven, in his unleavened bread.

A Jew carrying matzot for delivery in an East European town.

Once the rabbi was ill a short time before Passover. He called two of his pupils. "I cannot go to the bakery to supervise the baking." he said. "You go and watch in my place."

"What shall we particularly guard against?" asked the pupils, expecting to be given detailed instructions about how the dough should be handled.

"You must take care," said the rabbi, "not to speak unkindly to the woman who kneads the dough. She is a poor widow, and her heart is sad. Be patient with her."

The law of God, the Torah the Jews must follow, was, above all, the law of goodness and kindness to fellow men. There was no merit,

One of the many institutions for giving help to the poor in an East European town. Here food and clothing were given out.

he emphasized, in keeping laws of prayer and holidays, ritual law, if one did not keep laws of justice and righteousness and mercy in dealing with others. The good Jew must do both.

Examples to Follow

In Eastern Europe at that time, in the early and middle nineteenth century, most Jews wanted to observe all of Jewish law. This was certainly true in Lithuania, where

Israel Lipkin was born in 1810, near the German city of Konigsberg. His father was a rabbi and a teacher of Talmud. The young student was famous by the time he was ten as an *ilui*, a child genius.

The boy Israel was able to amaze adults with his *pilpul*, his clever explanations of verses in the Talmud and their commentaries. Wanting his son to become more deeply learned in the real message of the Law, Rabbi Wolf Lipkin sent the boy to the town of Salant. There Israel studied the Talmud from beginning to end with Rabbi Hirsch Braude, who, though a poor man, would take no money for the privilege of working with such an unusual and beloved pupil.

Another rabbi of Salant had an even greater influence on the young scholar. This was Joseph Zundel, who did not hold a position as rabbi or even as teacher. He earned a living as a rather unsuccessful merchant, dressing and acting like any humble unlearned Jew, not wanting to gain any honor or reward for his learning.

Rabbi Zundel had studied for years at the famous Yeshivah of Volozhin under its founder, Rabbi Hayyim. Hayyim of Volozhin, greatest disciple of the Gaon of Vilna, carried on his master's tradition of disciplined, thorough study of the Talmud. Like the Gaon, he believed that all knowledge was

The Yeshivah of Volozhin.

34

good in that it led to better understanding of Jewish tradition. Like the Gaon, he tried not to devote his time to pilpulistic discussion, but to find the true basic meanings of the laws of the Talmud and to apply them to life.

Rabbi Zundel, although never a pupil of the Gaon of Vilna, absorbed his teachings through Rabbi Hayyim. He felt he was like a grandson of the Gaon. The influence of the great Elijah of Vilna went even further, for now Israel in turn came under the guidance of Rabbi Zundel.

This was not in a classroom, for Rabbi Zundel did not conduct classes. It was in observing the way of the man's life that Israel gained new direction for his own.

One of the Thirty-six

Though he would have been shocked to hear it, Rabbi Zundel was thought by some to be one of the *lamed-vav tzaddikim,* the "thirty-six righteous men." There is an old legend that in each generation there are that number of true saints in the world, who by their great goodness make the world worthy to survive. There is so much wickedness in the world, the legend states, that surely God ought to permit it to be destroyed; but the merit of these righteous ones keeps the world going.

The *lamed-vavnik* is supposed to be unrecognized by other men; and is himself unaware of his distinction. He is never a hero, a ruler, a powerful or well known person. He is a humble, lowly man whose actions are completely righteous, who does simple deeds of goodness, is helpful and kindly to others all the days of his life.

Some stories about Rabbi Zundel show how he "walked humbly with God." With his own hands he paved a muddy alley that led to the synagogue, so that his mother could walk there. When the door-knob of

Rabbi Hayyim Soloveichik (1853-1920), rabbi at Brest-Litovsk, formerly head of the Volozhin Yeshivah.

his house became rusted and hard to turn, he hastened to have it fixed, only so that beggars or those seeking his help might be able to enter his home with no trouble.

Once, when he went to Vilna, some one asked him to deliver a letter to Rabbi Gershon of that city. Rabbi Zundel, dressed in his usual poor though clean clothing, knocked on the door and offered the letter. Thinking that a wagon-driver or coachman stood before him, Rabbi Gershon asked him in and gave him a tip that such a man would appreciate. Rabbi Zundel, not to shame his host, accepted the tip and did not say who he was.

Rabbi Gershon, knowing the man was from Salant, began to ask questions about the saintly Rabbi Zundel. "How is the great man? How lucky you are to live in his city! What mitzvot has he been devoting himself to?" Rabbi Zundel could say nothing. Finally

A view of the city of Vilna.

Rabbi Gershon, seeing the unhappiness of his guest, realized that only Rabbi Zundel himself would not be answering and joining in the praises of himself.

"Israel, Learn Musar"

This simple, humble man inspired the young student Israel. The boy used to follow him about, even when the older man would walk in the fields or forest, as he often did, to think alone. Sometimes Israel would see the saintly man weeping or praying, for on these walks Rabbi Zundel was searching his soul, trying to teach himself to become a better man.

Once Rabbi Zundel turned around and saw the boy standing near him. He expressed no surprise. All he said was, "Israel, study *musar,* so that you may become a pious man."

This one sentence became the foundation for Rabbi Israel's life. From then on, he knew what his course of action should be. He was to raise himself, make himself as holy and as nearly perfect as a man might become, through obeying all Jewish laws and strengthening himself in humility and self-control. He was also to try to teach musar to others, so that all Jews might become more righteous.

What is musar? It can be called ethics or morals, the teaching of standards that one ought to follow. But it is more than that. The best translation might be "discipline." To live according to musar, one must be strong in conquering one's own evil tendencies. One must work hard to improve one's mind and character. It is a way of life based on the fear of God, on the overwhelming desire to obey God's word in every action of one's life.

"Know Thyself"

The student of musar must first examine his own soul, and then work to correct and improve himself. To learn what is the right way, he may read in all the works of Jewish tradition: Bible, Talmud, Kabbalah. There are also many works devoted completely to "duties of the heart." Rabbi Israel used many books, written in different centuries by scholars of many countries.

One book that is especially interesting to us is *Heshbon Ha-Nefesh* ("Examination of the Soul") written by a Polish Jew, Mendel Lefin. In it the author copied from the work of the American sage Benjamin Franklin, who was also much interested in self-improvement. Franklin had listed thirteen virtues that a man ought to test himself on, every day. He had made a chart with spaces for each day of the week, so that a man might check whether each day he had been temperate, frugal, industrious, and so forth.

The city of Kovno.

The Slobodka Yeshiva, located in a suburb of Kovno. It was one of the greatest institutions of learning.

In the Jewish work, the following virtues were listed on the chart: Tranquility of the Soul, Patience, Orderliness, Diligence, Cleanliness, Humility, Justice, Thrift, Industry, Silence, Gentleness, Truth, Self-Control.

Raising oneself in virtue was not possible, taught Rabbi Israel, if one lived apart from one's fellow man. "True salvation," he taught, "can come only to a person who gives service to the community."

The Need for His Teaching

Rabbi Israel taught musar as head of a yeshivah in Vilna. When he moved to Kovno, the other large Lithuanian center of learning, he opened a small study room where adults could come to "heal their souls" as they would come to a hospital to heal their bodies. He later traveled all over Europe, even to the westernized communities of Germany and France, founding small congregations and preaching to the people to return to true Jewish ethical living.

There was nothing new in what Rabbi Israel Salanter taught. All of it—the concern for fellow man, justice and honesty in all dealings—was part of Jewish law from the

time of Moses. The message of Jewish ethics, however, needed new emphasis at this time.

On the one hand, the Jews of Eastern Europe who lived according to the laws of the Talmud easily became mechanical in the fulfilment of these laws—they did not always carry out their duties with all their hearts. They were careful in ritual observances, but often, as Rabbi Israel warned, they forgot the lessons behind the observances; they would let slip an unkind word, or act in an unfeeling manner towards another. He reminded them that they must turn their hearts to all of the law, particularly that of behavior to one's fellowman.

On the other hand, there were some Jews who no longer lived by the law. Many of them were *maskilim,* believers in *Haskalah,* or Enlightenment (from the Hebrew word *sekhel,* meaning "intelligence"). They wished to make the Jews more like the educated non-Jews of Europe. They wrote books about modern science, as well as novels and poems, in the Hebrew language, and tried to break down the people's devotion to Talmud and the traditional way of life.

Rabbi Israel knew that, while science and new inventions might bring about changes in everyday life, there was no new way of ethical living that was better than the ancient Jewish way. People had certainly not learned any modern way of peace and justice and brotherhood that was better than the way

An 1860 copy of Ha-Melitz ("The Advocate"), the daily newspaper of the Hebrew Haskalah movement in Russia, which served as the proving ground for many a young writer and intellectual.

taught by the Talmud. He wanted to show his people the value of Jewish tradition, the beauty of Jewish ethical law; to prove to them that in their own culture they had a priceless treasure.

The Highest Duty of All

A remarkable incident, that became famous in song and story, showed Rabbi Israel's belief that the good of the community was the highest duty of all.

At noon on Yom Kippur, the most solemn day of the year, when every Jew fasts and asks for forgiveness, Rabbi Israel Salanter, the most pious leader of his generation, ate and drank in front of his congregation in the synagogue.

There was, of course, a reason. A terrible epidemic of cholera was raging through the country. Before Yom Kippur, the rabbis had informed the people that they ought to shorten their prayers and not exhaust themselves on the holy day; and that anyone who felt weak should eat a small amount of the cake that was to be kept in each synagogue. Doctors had warned that the strain of fasting might make many people fall victim to the disease.

Rabbi Israel looked around during morning service. He saw that not one of his congregation was allowing himself to break his fast. Many looked pale and weak, but they remained at the service without leaving their places, determined not to destroy the holiness of the most solemn day of the year. Yet, Rabbi Israel knew that the preserving of human life was more holy than any other law.

He appealed to the congregation. "Man owes a debt to his own body, to keep it a worthy dwelling place for the soul," he said. He reminded the congregation that upon giving the commandments, God had said, "You shall live by them"—not die because of them.

No one moved.

It was then that Rabbi Israel beckoned to the *Shammash,* who immediately brought out a tray bearing wine and cake. Standing on the *bimah,* the platform before the Holy Ark, and facing the worshippers, the rabbi took a sip of wine and a bite of cake. Then other Jews came forward and did the same.

In all his life Rabbi Israel had never consciously broken a single commandment that it was in his power to keep. Like many heroes he was aroused to the action by the need to save human life.

Interior of the old synagogue at Wilna.

Courage and Faith

Rabbi Israel showed heroism in many other quiet ways as well. He remained a poor man all his days, denying himself any more than his basic needs. The only property that he was able to leave for his children consisted of his *talit* and *tefilin*.

Yet he refused the offer of a position as director of a new Rabbinical Seminary, because he felt the Russian government, through this school, hoped to train rabbis who would lead the Jews away from their devotion to the law.

The ark and bimah of an old East European synagogue.

His faith in his people was also heroic. Rabbi Israel saw little result from all his efforts. He did not see the establishment of the yeshivot of Slobodka, Telz, and other towns, where his doctrine of musar was the core of study. After his visit to Paris, especially, he blamed himself for not being more successful with the free-thinking, unobservant Jews of that city. "If I were a better man, worthy of my task," he said, "I would have had more influence."

It took courage and faith to try to reform his people. The appeal of easier living, the possibility of making more money, the desire to be just like everyone else—all of these

Young yeshivah students.

made Jews forget their law. Israel Salanter never condemned; he always tried to improve. In a port city whose Jews were known to be Sabbath-breakers, he tried gently to lead the residents back to observance. He felt that any small observance was better than none; that doing a little bit might lead the doer back to more.

"I know you must unload the boats when they dock, even if it is Shabbat, in order to make a living," he said. "But you are not required to load every day. Can you not put off that job? And can you not avoid all extra work, such as writing records, so that you will remember the day of rest?"

While the Candle Burned

The story is told that Rabbi Israel learned a lesson of faith and perseverance from a cobbler. One night as he passed the cobbler's shop the rabbi noticed that the shoemaker was still working by the last flickering light of his candle.

"Your candle is almost out," Rabbi Israel said to his friend. "Isn't it time for you to stop working and go to sleep?"

"No, I'll keep working," said the cobbler. "As long as there is any light at all, I can still do some repairing."

Rabbi Israel Salanter often repeated this

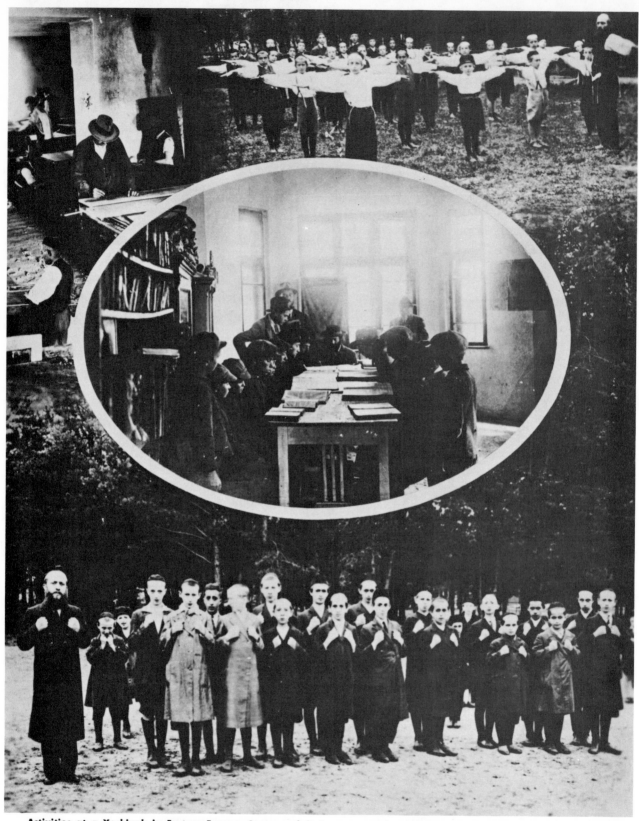

Activities at a Yeshivah in Eastern Europe. At upper left is a scene showing vocational training; at upper right, class calisthenics. The central study, that of Torah, is shown in the middle of the page.

story. In his life as devoted teacher and messenger to his people, as healer of their souls, he remembered this lesson.

As long as the least bit of light remained, as long as a Jewish heart still beat, as long as there was any hope at all, he knew he should keep working. His was the task to bring his people back to their heritage, to guide them towards the life of righteousness and brotherhood that God desired for all His children.

A Jewish shoemaker hard at work.

The Hafetz Hayyim

1838-1933

Rabbi Israel Meir Kagan, the Hafetz Hayyim.

Every Shabbat morning, Israel Meir sat next to his father in the small synagogue in the Polish town of Zhetel. Every week he was able to read better and faster; some day soon, he hoped, he would be able to keep up with the grown men as they raced through the early parts of the service. Try as he would, he never could read every word of the *Tehilim*, the Psalms, in the section called "Passages of Song." But there was one passage that he always read. It was dear to his heart, and had been his favorite as far back as he could remember. It seemed to be speaking directly to him.

From the thirty-fourth Psalm, it read:

"Come children, listen to me; I will teach you the fear of the Lord.

"Who is the man who desires life, and longs for many days of happiness?

"Keep your tongue from evil, and your lips from speaking falsehood;

"Depart from evil, and do good; seek peace, and pursue it."

The question and its answer fascinated the youngster. Who doesn't desire life? Even as a young child Israel Meir knew that everyone wants long life. Would being careful of what one says be sure to bring one length of days? The child thought of this often, and tried to follow the good advice. He never would say anything bad about anyone.

The Life to Be Desired

All too soon, however, the child saw that being good and kind does not always bring the reward of long life. His beloved father died when the boy was only ten. The mother made sure Israel Meir could continue his studies. They moved to Vilna, the center of learning. Sadly, Israel Meir came to realize that the question in the Psalm really meant: "Who desires worthwhile life, the right kind of life, however short or long, that is pleas-

Jewish street in Vilna.

43

ing to God, that leads to true goodness?"

Three times a day following the *Amidah* prayer, the boy continued to say the words taken from the Psalm: "O Lord, guard my tongue from speaking evil, and my lips from speaking falsehood." He resolved to devote himself to this ideal. Then his own life, whatever its length, would be a blessing.

Education for the Holy Life

After some difficult years, his devoted mother was remarried to a widower who also had children. They moved to the village of Radun but Israel Meir remained in Vilna to study. There his brilliance brought him early notice.

The Hebrew poet A. D. Lebensohn was a well-known Jewish citizen of Vilna. He was a founder of the *Haskalah*, the movement to bring modern culture to the helm of Jewish life, and to make the Jews resemble the other people of the countries in which they lived. His own talented son, Micah Joseph, also a Hebrew poet, had recently died at a young age. Perhaps the older man hoped that the young scholar Israel Meir could take the place of his son.

At any rate, Lebensohn became friendly

A. D. Lebensohn, Hebrew writer.

with Israel Meir and suggested that he leave his study of Talmud and Jewish law, and turn his attention to biblical Hebrew and modern studies. Then, said the *maskil*, Israel Meir could teach at a government school and be assured of a good future.

The young man was not attracted by the offer. To him the only study of value was the one that would teach Jews how to live righteous lives. He wished to devote himself to Torah, and to the education of his people in good deeds.

While still very young, Israel Meir married Frieda, the daughter of his stepfather. Not ambitious for honor or desirous of living in a big city, he settled in the village of Radun. His young bride knew she had the privilege of being married to a scholar, and was glad to live simply and to try to support the family by opening a small grocery shop.

Teacher and Writer

Israel Meir, however, was not meant to be a merchant. He could not bear to take sufficient profit from the customers for his family to live on. He made sure that no one left another merchant to come to him. Caring more for others than for himself, he could not be successful in business.

He was happy to turn to the teaching of Talmud. After some years, he was able to found a small yeshivah in his town, later to be known as Yeshivat Hafetz Hayyim. Most yeshivah students were penniless and could not pay for their stay. So Israel worked hard to support the yeshivah, collecting money from wealthier Jews who were interested in supporting learning. From the funds he collected, he spent almost nothing on himself or his family.

A teacher can become the teacher of thousands by writing books. Israel Meir published his first book, entitled *Hafetz Hayyim*, "He

Who Desires Life," without putting his own name on the title page. It was not necessary. The book became well known throughout the Jewish world, and the author became known by the name of his book. From the time of publication, Israel Meir Ha-Kohen of Radun became known as the "Hafetz Hayyim."

Guarding the Tongue

The subject of the book is easy to guess. The author reviewed for his readers the teachings of Jewish tradition concerning the wrongfulness of the "evil tongue." Telling tales about others, spreading gossip and slander, he pointed out, could lead to the destruction of life. He quoted such statements as "Slander kills three: the speaker, the slandered one, and the one who listens." "Gossip is a sin," he reminded his readers, "even if it is true."

The author recommended that everyone should think carefully before speaking, and to keep silent if in doubt as to the good effect of his words.

The scholar Rabbi Moses M. Yoshor recalls an incident he witnessed, showing the seriousness and yet the humor with which

A Hebrew letter written by the Hafetz Hayyim.

Rabbi Israel Meir believed in the virtue of silence:

Once a rabbi, a student of the Hafetz Hayyim, complained to him that he had preached a long sermon, two hours in length, and that it seemed to have had no effect on the congregation. The Hafetz Hayyim replied that the sermon surely did great good.

"Remember the Midrash," he said, "that states: 'For each and every second that a man keeps silent, with no evil talk, he will enjoy the rays of heavenly light in the Hereafter.'

"If such a treasure," the sage said with a smile, "is promised for only one second of silence, think of the reward you will have for keeping your whole congregation silent, without a word of evil talk, for two whole hours."

Further Books

The Hafetz Hayyim went about to sell his book himself, in different towns. He was too modest to tell people that he was the author, and did not want to influence them to buy the book on that basis.

Many other books followed. Rabbi Israel Meir looked about him and saw what were the needs of his people. He knew that with more freedom being given to the Jews, many of them were leaving their own traditions, "selling their birthright for a mess of pottage." Jews wanted to become exactly like the majority around them, like Russians in Russia, like Germans in Germany. Persecutions in Eastern Europe forced many Jews to leave and most of them went to America. In a new and strange land, driven by the need to make a bare living, Jews found it difficult to keep to their traditions.

The works of the Hafetz Hayyim were intended to help Jews to keep the commandments wherever they were. One book was written especially for the Jewish soldier in camp or in battle, explaining what laws he must still keep and what violations he might be allowed for the sake of preserving life.

For the Jews leaving their homes to go to distant America, he wrote a book of warning, sympathy and advice. He urged especially the priority of keeping the Sabbath. "It serves as a symbol of the Almighty's presence in the Jew's life and heart, inspiring and filling his soul with serenity and happiness."

The most important treatise of the Hafetz Hayyim is called the *Mishnah Berurah*, which explains the first section of the *Shulhan Arukh* by Joseph Caro. The six volumes of this great scholarly work are used by all who seek guidance in a code of Jewish law.

Maasim Tovim — Good Deeds

In his teachings and in his life, the Hafetz Hayyim always emphasized the doing of good deeds, *maasim tovim*. "The performance of

The Yeshivah Hafetz Hayyim of Radun.

good deeds," he said, "is the ultimate goal of Jewish ethics. Devotion may be important, but it has no merit when not accompanied by action. The Torah consists mainly of 'Thou shalt' and 'Thou shalt not.' Doing, action, is needed."

A stranger visiting the Hafetz Hayyim found out how strongly his host believed in the actual doing of the mitzvah. He protested when he saw the honored rabbi making up the bed for the guest with his own hands.

"You should not trouble yourself, Rabbi," pleaded the guest. "At least let me finish the job."

"No, no, dear sir, you must not help me," said the Hafetz Hayyim. "It is my mitzvah, not yours. When you saw me putting on tefilin this morning at the synagogue, did you then offer to do the job instead of me? Just as you cannot substitute for me in the mitzvah of putting on tefilin, so you cannot substitute for me in this mitzvah of hospitality."

The complete piety of the Hafetz Hayyim helped to persuade other Jews to remain observant. Once a mere half-serious reminder of his devotion to pure speech influenced a congregation to do the right thing.

The sage was making an appeal for charity, for the Passover fund, before a large but ungenerous congregation. "Friends," he finally

Title-page of the Mishnah Berurah, commentary on the Shulhan Arukh.

46

said, "I want your advice. I am growing old, as you see, and before long I expect to be called before the heavenly court. Suppose I should be asked, 'Israel Meir, you were in Smilowitz. Tell us something about your brethren there.' What should I then reply?

"To say that you are charitable would not be the truth; and in all my life I have never lied. To tell the truth, that you are not charitable, would, on the other hand, involve evil speech, which as you know, I also guard myself against. What should I do?" The people responded with large contributions.

Length of Days

Throughout his life, this great soul continued to make his home in the small town of Radun. He lived there through Czarist

The Hafetz Hayyim in the last year of his life.

persecutions, through times of change and violence. Though several times during war and revolution he had to flee his home, he always returned. From the town of Radun his influence was felt in the establishment of yeshivot and in his efforts to unify the support of Jewish students throughout the world.

A thank-you note written by the Hafetz Hayyim to General Sikorski, later prime-minister of Poland, for aiding him in his return to Radun from Russia after World War 1.

One of his great desires was to go at last to the land of Israel, but his people could not bear to see him go. At one point he argued, "I am too old to be of any use to you." One of the rabbis replied, "Just having the father at the table, though he may be old and broken by age, inspires the children with respect."

Not seeking a long life, but a good one, the Hafetz Hayyim attained both in good measure. He lived the noble life span of ninety-five years. His death in the year 1933 brought as much grief as though he had passed away in the midst of vigor and activity.

* * * *

The year 1933 was an ominous one. In that year Hitler came to power in Germany. It marked the beginning of the terrible destruction that put a tragic end to all the mighty Jewish community of Eastern Europe.

For more than four hundred years, that community had been devoted both to learning and to good deeds. The life of the people, grounded in the Talmud, was one of faith and of spiritual beauty, in the midst of poverty and persecution. The highest point in its tradition of learning was reached with the coming of the Gaon of Vilna. Untempted and untouched by the many influences of oppression, emancipation, reform, war and revolution, the Hafetz Hayyim had carried that tradition into the modern age.

The gravestone of the Hafetz Hayyim. At the bottom are listed some of his works and accomplishments.

The funeral of the Hafetz Hayyim.

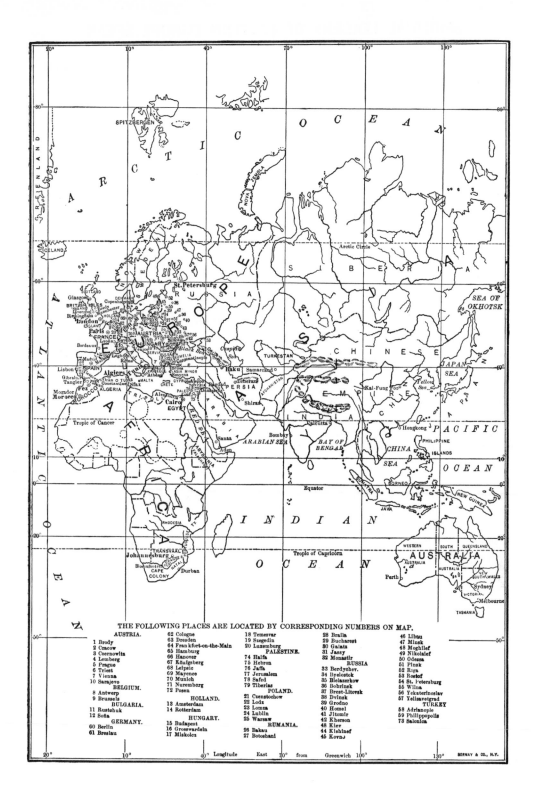

THE FOLLOWING PLACES ARE LOCATED BY CORRESPONDING NUMBERS ON MAP.

AUSTRIA.
1 Brody
2 Cracow
3 Czernowitz
4 Lemberg
5 Prague
6 Triest
7 Vienna
10 Sarajevo

BELGIUM.
8 Antwerp
9 Brussels

BULGARIA.
11 Rustchuk
12 Sofia

GERMANY.
60 Berlin
61 Breslau

62 Cologne
63 Dresden
64 Frankfort-on-the-Main
65 Hamburg
66 Hanover
67 Königsberg
68 Leipzic
69 Mayence
70 Munich
71 Nuremberg
72 Posen

HOLLAND.
13 Amsterdam
14 Rotterdam

HUNGARY.
15 Budapest
16 Grosswardein
17 Miskolcz

18 Temesvar
19 Szegedin
20 Luxemburg

PALESTINE.
74 Haifa
75 Hebron
76 Jaffa
77 Jerusalem
78 Safed
79 Tiberias

POLAND.
21 Czenstochow
22 Lodz
23 Lomza
24 Lublin
25 Warsaw

RUMANIA.
26 Bakau
27 Botoshani

28 Braila
29 Bucharest
30 Galatz
31 Jassy
32 Monastir

RUSSIA
33 Berdychev.
34 Byelostok
35 Bielozerkow
36 Bobrinsk
37 Brest-Litovsk
38 Dvinsk
39 Grodno
40 Homel
41 Jitomir
42 Kherson
43 Kiev
44 Kishinef
45 Kovno

46 Libau
47 Minsk
48 Moghilef
49 Nikolaief
50 Odessa
51 Pinsk
52 Riga
53 Rostof
54 St. Petersburg
55 Wilna
56 Yekaterinoslav
57 Yelisavetgrad

TURKEY
58 Adrianople
59 Philippopolis
73 Salonica

Map of the eastern hemisphere in the early 1900's showing chief centers of Jewish population.

49

SPIRITUAL LEADERS OF EASTERN EUROPE SPEAK

Whether a man really loves God can be determined by the love he bears toward his fellow men.

*   *   *   **

The mind is the Holy of Holies, and to admit evil thoughts is like setting up an idol in the Temple.

*   *   *   **

Why does each tract of the Talmud begin with page 2, and not with page 1? To remind us that no matter how much we study and learn, we have not yet come to the first page!

LEVI ISAAC OF BERDITCHEV

As lightning springs out of its concealment in dark clouds to flash through the world, so the divine light, imbedded in matter, emerges through charitable deeds. Thus through charity, a sort of divine revelation occurs in the soul.

*   *   *   **

Charity removes the stain of sin.

*   *   *   **

Charity is one of the remedies against alien thoughts.

*   *   *   **

Love for Israel must be a fire burning in the Jew's heart.

*   *   *   **

Don't attempt to drive folly out of your mind by force. Rather ignore evil thoughts, and concentrate on God.

*   *   *   **

The source of all virtue is wisdom, reason, knowledge.

SHNEUR ZALMAN OF LADI

Everyone can raise himself, but only by his own actions.

*   *   *   **

Be not slaves of gold. The more they own, the more anxious they are.

*   *   *   **

Be satisfied with little, and manage your household according to your means.

NAHMAN OF BRATSLAV

Even atheism can be uplifted through charity. If someone seeks your aid, act as if there were no God, as if you alone can help.

*   *   *

True love of man is to know his pain and bear his sorrow.

MOSHE LEIB OF SASOV

Man owes it to keep his body clean, as a worthy dwelling for the soul, God's portion from on high.

*   *   *

Promote yourself, but do not demote another.

*   *   *

It is not good, if it entails evil for others.

*   *   *

You may learn three things from a railroad: if you are late one minute, you miss it; the slightest deflection from the rails leads to catastrophe; a passenger without a ticket may expect punishment.

*   *   *

Before studying ethics, I blamed the whole world and justified myself; after I started the study, I blamed myself and also the world; but finally I blamed only myself.

*   *   *

Writing is one of the easiest things; erasing one of the hardest.

ISRAEL SALANTER LIPKIN

Despair not. It is darkest before dawn. . . . Before light was created, all was darkness upon the face of the deep.

*   *   *

On Judgment Day, God will not ask to what sect you belonged, but what manner of life you led.

*   *   *

The study of Torah is more essential than Eretz Israel, yea, even more than the building of the Temple.

ISRAEL MEIR KAGAN, THE HAFETZ HAYYIM

UNIT TWO

THE NEW LEARNING

No people on earth has valued learning more highly than the Jews. The great declaration of Jewish belief is *Shema Yisrael,* which we read in the book of *Dvarim,* or Deuteronomy, chapter VI, verse 4:

"Hear O Israel, the Lord our God, the Lord is One."

Immediately after this, the Jews are told to love the Lord, and to keep these words in their hearts, and to teach them to their children. "Thou shalt teach them diligently to thy children" is a basic law of the Torah. The mitzvah to educate one's children and to love learning has been followed by every generation of Jews from Bible times to the present day.

"An ignorant man cannot be pious," said Hillel two thousand years ago. The Talmud states that every town must have a school, and that every father is responsible for the education of his children. Through centuries of darkness, when only a privileged few among the general population knew how to read, every Jewish child learned his letters.

In the self-contained communities of Eastern Europe, and in the ghettos of Germany

A medal in honor of the emancipation of the Jews in the German province of Westphalia in 1808.

and Italy, the Jews remained true to their tradition. Children spent their time in learning and not in play. Bible and Talmud were familiar to them in their earliest years. The dearest wish of their fathers was to have more time in their hard-working lives for study.

The learned man was respected above all others. The parents of a girl wished only that she might marry a scholar, and would often support him so that he could continue studying. The mother sang to her baby:

"What is the best way of life? My little one shall study Torah."

Enlightenment in Europe

The majority of the people in the Middle Ages lived in poverty and ignorance, listening to what their rulers and the Church told them. They were content to remain as they were. By the fifteenth century, however, Europe had begun to change. This was the period of the Renaissance, the time of rebirth. Travel and trade broadened men's minds. Knowledge of the past was revived. Greek philosophy and art, which had been

הקצין הדר הירש גאלד שמיד
הקצין פו כהרר משה קליווא
הקצין פו כהרר אהרן כהן
האלוף התורני כהרר הירש כ״ן
האלוף הרר אנשיל עשווי
המעלה כהרר יואל פילא
היקר כה אלי קראטשין

First page of the book of minutes of the Berlin Jewish community, 1723.

known to the Moslems, now became an inspiration to the Christian world. Gradually, with the growth of cities, the expansion of trade, and the increase in number of workers and middle-class merchants in the towns, more people began to receive some form of education.

The eighteenth century in Europe has been called the Age of Enlightenment and the Age of Reason. The feudal system of the Middle Ages was disappearing. No longer did everyone believe in the "divine right" of kings, the idea that God had given power to rulers and that they must be obeyed without question. Rationalism, the reliance on man's mind to solve all problems, became the philosophy of the age.

All Men Are Equal

The new ideas spread particularly in France, England, and the colonies in America. French philosophers like Voltaire and Rousseau taught that all men were equal and that the right kind of education would produce good, free and happy people. This teaching helped inspire those who led the American Revolution and those who, in 1789, raised the banner of rebellion against king and aristocracy in France.

The French Revolution and the wars of Napoleon sowed the ideals of Liberty, Equality and Fraternity throughout Europe.

The governments of Europe felt the challenge of the demand for freedom for all their citizens. Kings trembled. Those that were near to France, thus feeling the full power of the French armies, were quick to agree to equality. Others, hoping to keep their subjects faithful to them, also grudgingly granted some rights. Wherever Napoleon's armies conquered, freedom for all became the official policy of the state.

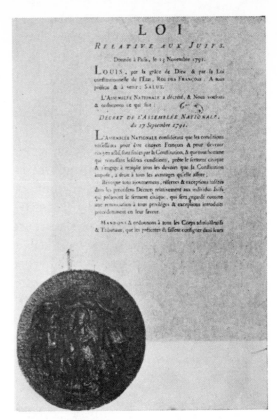

Decree of the French National Assembly, granting equal rights to Jews, September 27, 1791.

Civil Rights for Jews

The Jews of Europe were not, of course, the only group hoping for greater civil rights. Millions of persons of every land wished to become full and equal citizens of their countries. Members of the middle-class, the townspeople, demanded representative government, rather than rule by aristocrats.

It was the Jewish group, however, which found it hardest to break out of the shell of prejudice and restrictions which surrounded them. In each country where freedoms were offered to other groups, there was opposition to rights for the Jews.

In France itself, of course, the ideals of the revolution had to be carried out. Rights were granted first to the respected Sephardi community of southern France. Despite the opposition of delegates from Alsace-Lorraine, who scorned the Jews as money-lenders, the General Assembly in 1791 granted full citizenship to all Jews of France.

A leader of the Jews of Alsace-Lorraine, Lippman Cerf-Berr, wept with joy at the announcement, and wrote to his fellow-Jews: "God chose the noble French nation to restore us to our rights, just as he chose Antiochus of old to persecute us. This nation asks no thanks, except that we show ourselves worthy citizens."

In Holland, the Italian states, and all the Confederation of the Rhine, full rights were given to the Jews. The governments of Austria and Prussia continued to treat Jews as outsiders without legal rights; but even there, some terms had to be made, and some taxes were abolished.

Emperor Napoleon and His Sanhedrin

Napoleon proclaimed himself ruler of France in 1799. It was Emperor Napoleon, carrying out his plan of gaining the allegiance of all Europe, who demanded of the French Jews that they indeed prove themselves "worthy citizens."

In 1806, Napoleon called together an Assembly of Jewish Notables, a group of 112 leading rabbis and businessmen, to meet in Paris. To this group were presented such

Medal in honor of the Sanhedrin called by Napoleon, 1807.

questions as: Do Jews in France consider France their country? Are they willing to obey its laws and fight in its defense? Does Jewish law tell Jews to be money-lenders, and does it forbid them to enter the professions?

The delegates to the Assembly, knowing what was expected of them, did not answer that until that time Jews had been forbidden to be citizens, and had not been allowed to enter the professions. They answered eagerly that France was of course their country; that they would defend it until death; that they would be glad to enter all fields of labor; that Jewish law was to be followed only in strictly religious matters, and that the state was supreme in all others.

Pleased with the answers, Napoleon now came up with a master-stroke. He issued a call for a *Sanhedrin*, to put these decisions into the form of law.

The ancient Supreme Court of seventy-one members had not decided legal questions for the Jewish people as a governing body since the destruction of the Temple in the year 70 C.E. Though the Jewish community knew that there was no authority in such a gathering, the delegates gathered at Napoleon's invitation.

Anxious to win full rights for the Jews, the delegates to the Sanhedrin went as far as they could to give the answers that Napoleon desired. They condemned money-lending. They said they were first and foremost

The meeting of Napoleon's Sanhedrin.

Title-page of the prayers recited at the meeting of the Sanhedrin.

Frenchmen, and that the laws of France stood above their own. They disowned any hope for returning to Palestine or becoming a separate people once more. "We no longer are a nation within a nation," they said. "France is our country."

The declaration was thus made that Judaism was only a religion, a denomination like any other. Like the Catholic and Protestant faiths, Judaism became an "official" or permitted religion of France. Every Frenchman had to belong to the consistory of one of the religions. Religious leaders, now including rabbis, had to be appointed by the state, and had to preach what the state approved.

Though such requirements gave less rather than more freedom to the Jews in the practice of their religion, and though new laws were decreed that singled out the Jews, forbidding them to change residence and demanding of them an extra large quota for the draft, still Napoleon posed as the great liberator of the Jews.

Liberalism and Reaction

In 1812, the Emperor, who had reached too far, was defeated at Moscow when his armies could not survive the cold and hunger of a Russian winter. When they were sure Napoleon could not rise again, the rulers of Europe, including the kings of Prussia, Russia and Austria, gathered together at Vienna in 1815 to restore their countries to what they had been before.

A declaration of the Congress of Vienna read that "all rights granted by the states" were to be kept. Since, however, the rights had been granted by governments imposed by Napoleon, and since now the original monarchs were returned to power, it could be argued that the true governments, the states themselves, had never granted any rights. The freedoms gained under Napoleon's influence were no longer to be allowed.

Still, all progress could not be stopped. The millions who had heard about "the rights of man," and had perhaps for a short time really enjoyed them, were not forever to be denied their freedom.

Moses Mendelssohn, cultural leader in Berlin in the eighteenth century, who wished to educate his fellow Jews so that they might be accepted as German citizens.

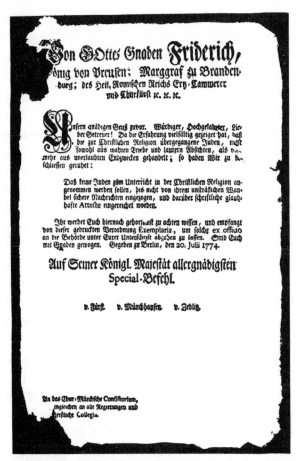

Edict of Frederick the Great, ruler of Prussia in the time of Mendelssohn. The decree regards the conversion of Jews to Christianity, demanding proof of true belief rather than self-seeking motives.

A good part of the history of the nineteenth century in Europe shows the conflict between liberal forces—those which wanted freedom—and the forces of reaction. In mid-century, revolutions broke out in German and Italian states. The revolutionaries were headed by intelligent young educated leaders, who combined a love for their countries with their democratic ideals. Though the rebellions were put down, the gains they strove for eventually came about.

The Influence of Mendelssohn

Many of the Jews of the German states were highly cultured, loyal to the idea of a strong Germany, and active in the liberal cause. The influence of Moses Mendelssohn had opened the world of Western culture and the promise of equality to them. In Berlin, especially, where Mendelssohn had been a cultural leader during the second half of the eighteenth century, the educated Jews wanted desperately to be accepted as good Germans, and as equal citizens.

Mendelssohn had risen, through his intelligence and fine character, to become a beloved philosopher and leading writer in Berlin. His example had proved to the non-Jewish world that a Jew could be a noble human being. He had also tried to show his fellow Jews that they must speak the German language and study German as well as Jewish culture. Although all his life he himself was not allowed to become a citizen, he had faith that if the Jews took part in German culture, it would help them to gain their rights.

The effect of Mendelssohn's example was far-reaching. Full rights were not granted to the Jews in the nineteenth century; prejudice against them remained. But many Jews of Germany decided that they should drop their Jewish ways and become exactly like the Gentiles around them. Fortunately Mendelssohn, who was an observant Jew, did not live to see his children and grandchildren become converts to Christianity.

Aaron Beer, first cantor in Berlin.

M. Oppenheim fec.   Verlag von Louis Lamm, Berlin C. 2.

Painting by M. Oppenheim of a Sabbath evening in a Jewish home.

Emancipation and Reform

In their longing for emancipation, many German Jews did the same. They felt that the only way they could become full citizens and find success in their careers was to leave Judaism completely.

Ignorance of Jewish tradition was one cause for their treason. They saw no value in Judaism, only strange customs that set them apart. Keeping Jewish laws about food and the Sabbath and holidays seemed only a hardship. Not knowing Hebrew, they could not take part in Hebrew prayer.

There were leaders who knew that in Jewish tradition are found the highest ethical standards, the noblest lessons for living that the world has ever known. They wanted to help other Jews to appreciate the ideals of Judaism, to respect their faith and to remain loyal to it.

Some leaders thought it necessary to reform Jewish practices in order to preserve the content of Jewish teaching. They felt that Jews had a mission to remain true to their ideals of one God and ethical living, and to teach these ideals to the world. The forms and rituals of Judaism, however, could be changed to fit the modern world. The synagogue service, they felt, could be carried on in the language of the land, and could be made more acceptable by use of organ and choir music, as was the custom in the services of most other religions.

During the years following Napoleon's rule, Reform congregations, called "Temples" instead of synagogues or "schuls," were set up in such large cities as Berlin, Hamburg, and Leipzig.

An important change in all these early Reform services was leaving out all mention of Zion, the Messiah, the return to Palestine and the rebuilding of the Temple in Jerusalem. Like the Sanhedrin called by Napoleon, these Jews wished it known that they were loyal to their native country, and had no ties to any other land.

Haham Isaac Bernays, Orthodox rabbi of Hamburg.

Orthodoxy and Reform

There was strong opposition to these early attempts at reform. The majority of Jews wished to observe their religion in all its details exactly as it had been handed down to them. These were named "Orthodox" by the Jews who believed in reform. In an effort to prevent the breaking down of Jewish tradition, rabbis like Isaac Bernays of Hamburg opposed even small changes in the prayer book. Isaac Bernays, however, and other "Orthodox" leaders saw the value in certain reforms: a sermon in the language of the country, so that young educated people might be willing to listen; a service that was orderly and dignified.

Two rabbis, both of whom studied Talmud in their youth, both of whom then went to the university, and both of whom believed in being good modern citizens of their country, show the different points of view.

Rabbi Samuel Holdheim, rabbi of the Reform congregation of Berlin from 1847 till his death in 1860, was in favor of extreme reform. He claimed that "Palestinian laws have no justification in the midst of a modern state." Seeing none of the rituals as binding, he said that circumcision was not necessary, and that there should be no Jewish form of marriage ceremony. He went so far as to observe the Sabbath on Sunday instead of Saturday in his congregation.

Rabbi Samson Raphael Hirsch, who became rabbi of the Orthodox community of Frankfurt-am-Main in 1851, insisted that the Torah was above time and change. Man had no right to alter the word of God. Jews who followed their religion faithfully, he taught, would be better citizens and better human beings than those who put aside the yoke of the Torah. People in every age must change themselves in order to follow the Law; not change the Law in order to suit themselves.

Medal struck in commemoration of the erection of the Frankfurt synagogue in 1852.

Jewish Science

The challenge of the modern world brought about a new way of learning for the Jewish people. Jews, through the ages, had devoted themselves to the books of their sacred tradition, and had studied them as though every word was holy. They had delved deep to find the lessons contained in the books, the instruction for righteous living. When and where a certain book was written, what influences had made a certain scholar think the way he did, were not important to them. Indeed, such investigation of the Bible and Talmud would have seemed sinful.

Now Jews were able to attend German

Jewish reading-room and library in Germany.

universities, to learn the thorough methods of German research. It was necessary to be scientific in approach, to prove one's points, to study past history and compare Jewish writings with other books of the same time. Proud of their tradition, young Jewish scholars wanted to bring Jewish learning up to the scientific level of other studies in the universities.

In 1819, a small group of students in Berlin founded a "Society for the Culture and Science of Judaism." They wanted to improve education among Jews and to show that, from a modern standpoint, Jewish tradition had value.

Although others did not, Leopold Zunz, the most important member of this group, remained faithful to Judaism and to the purposes of the Society. Among Zunz's many profound works of research were writings on the origin and history of books of the Bible, of the prayers in the *siddur,* and of the synagogue sermon. All his works contributed to the new "Science of Judaism."

Teachers of Others

Other scholars who studied Judaism from a scientific, historical point of view were Moritz Steinschneider, who catalogued all the Semitic manuscripts in the Bodleian Library at Oxford, England, as well as in other famous libraries; Abraham Geiger, a leader of German Reform; and Zechariah Frankel, teacher

Moritz Steinschneider, authority on books and manuscripts.

of the historical point of view.

Geiger wrote a "critical" history of the Bible. Like other Bible critics, he treated the books of the Bible not as a perfect divinely-inspired work but as a collection of writings by many different authors at many times. In his study he found wide variations in laws and in points of view, proving to him that Judaism had changed much even in its early history, and was still able to be changed by man. This idea of a developing and changing religion encouraged the growth of Reform Judaism.

Frankel also wrote that Judaism was a living and developing culture, but objected to making radical changes. Adjustments would come through the will of the people and its leaders if they were really needed and really appropriate to the spirit of Judaism, he said. His view came to be known as "Historical" Judaism.

Eastern and Western Europe

The language of the new scientific study of Judaism was German, and its ways and methods were patterned after the ways of the German universities, centers of careful research. A few Hebrew writings in the field of Jewish Science came from Eastern Europe, carrying on the revival of Hebrew that had been started by the *maskilim,* the novelists and essayists of Jewish "enlightenment."

The outstanding Hebrew "scientific" work was the "Guide to the Perplexed of Our Time," by Nahman Krochmal (1785-1840) of Galicia. Taking his title and theme from the great "Guide to the Perplexed" of Maimonides, he tried to justify the value of Jewish tradition in the eyes of its followers. He saw in Judaism (and the Jewish people) its own particular spiritual talent, always present and developing through the ages.

Another scholar of Eastern Europe was

Grave of Nahman Krochmal in Galicia. He wrote in Hebrew on Jewish history and philosophy.

Rabbi Solomon Judah Rapoport, who not only wrote biographies of Jewish sages in Hebrew, but translated French plays and poetry into that language. A brilliant scholar was Samuel David Luzzatto of Padua, Italy, who loved Hebrew literature and the Hebrew language. He believed Jews should remain a separate group with their own way of life. In Russia, the scientific historian Albert Harkavy was appointed librarian of the Hebrew department of the Public Library of St. Petersburg. Others in France and later in England and in America carried on the work of "Jewish Science."

Solomon Judah Rapoport, modern Jewish scholar of Eastern Europe, who wrote many works in Hebrew.

The most important of the nineteenth century historians was Heinrich Graetz, whose great work, *History of the Jews,* presents Jewish life from its beginnings to the year 1870. The six-volume English translation published by the Jewish Publication Society of America near the turn of the century is still read and enjoyed.

In Eastern Europe, despite the efforts of a few scholars to modernize Jewish education, the majority of the Jews followed their traditional way of life. Under the rising tide of persecution, there was little chance for university study. The revolutionary movement in all its aspects came later to Russia than to Western Europe.

In the German environment, where research and study were encouraged, Jewish Science grew and flourished. Together with it went the attempt to explain and justify Judaism, and, in various ways, to adapt it to the modern day.

The greatest effect of the new learning, and the greatest impact of Reform and Historical teachings, were eventually felt in the new community springing up in America. That, however, is a story for a later time.

Heinrich Graetz, professor and leading modern historian.

Leopold Zunz

1794-1886

The distinguished professor of history at the University of Berlin stood before his desk in the large lecture hall. Earnestly, the young men seated before him tried to note down his inspiring words.

"Every nation has its own spirit," said the professor. "The spirit of our beloved German nation, as we know, has been one of might and genius, of strength and of sentiment." The students listened eagerly.

"The study of history is the study of ideas and virtues. Nations lacking in virtue, which no longer have any reason for existence, have fallen. For example, the Jewish nation. It made its contribution when it gave the Bible to the world."

A Jewish student, Leopold Zunz, sitting near the back of the room, leaned forward.

"Since that time, Judaism has been a fossil. It has ceased to produce; it has ceased to exist as a living thing. Only a remnant has remained as witness to the fact that once there was a Jewish people.

"The German nation, on the other hand, is vital and alive. The highest expression of its genius, of which we have already had so much evidence, is yet to come."

The lecture over, the students trouped from the hall. "It makes you proud," said one, "to be a German at a time like this, when Berlin is the world center of culture and when our professors speak of our great past."

"And even greater future," said another. "The true German spirit of which he spoke is more alive than ever. We will be a united people soon, and the whole world will recognize our superiority."

One student walked out slowly, thoughtfully, alone. The Jewish listener had found no glory and inspiration in the morning's lecture. On the contrary, he was filled with dismay. How could the professor believe that the Jews had produced nothing since the

Title-page of an issue of the monthly magazine of Jewish History and Science, first published by Zechariah Frankel.

time of the Bible?

With all his heart he wished to learn wisdom from his professors. He had come to the university only with great difficulty. As a poor but brilliant orphan boy, he had managed to complete the course of studies at the *gymnasium,* or government high school, in his home town. Supporting himself by teaching and directing at the Samson School, the academy for Jewish children, he had not been able to enter the University till he was twenty-one. He lived poorly, eating little, earning small amounts by tutoring and translating. His whole soul was directed towards higher learning.

The Great Heritage

He had spent his childhood studying Bible and Talmud, Midrash and commentaries. He knew of the philosophy of Saadia and Maimonides, the poetry of the Golden Age in Spain, the ethical works and the pious odes written by Jews through the ages in every

Leopold Zunz.

land. He knew Jewish thought had flourished when Christian Europe was living through what his professors called the Dark Ages.

"We must raise Jewish learning to the level of all other learning," said Leopold Zunz, speaking to other young Jews like himself. There were among them Moses Moser, a business man of integrity; Eduard Gans, a law student so brilliant that even though a Jew he was allowed to tutor at the University; Heinrich Heine, an unsuccessful law student who wrote poetry and worked for liberal causes.

"Jewish literature has not been presented in a form that Christian scholars can understand or respect," said Eduard. "The Jews have not studied it systematically either. They read only to find out how to obey the laws."

"We must present Jewish history and literature in the careful, detailed, scientific way that general history and literature are presented," said Leopold Zunz. "Then it will become recognized as a study worthy to be included in all universities. Then Jews as well as Christians will know that their tradition is a worthy one."

"One good result," said Moses Moser, "will be that young educated Jews will not feel inferior to their neighbors. They will not be tempted to convert away from their faith."

"Only be sure," said Heinrich Heine, the poet, "that all your writings are done in ex-

cellent German."

The Work of the Society

To their group, Gans, Moser and Zunz gave the name of "Society for the Culture and Science of Judaism." With ambition and zeal, the young men vowed to devote themselves to their cause. They were going to teach the world to respect Judaism. They intended also to educate the Jews to take their part in German life, to enter agriculture and the professions, to appreciate art and music, to improve their manners. Then, thought the young students, the Jews would deserve and receive the freedom and rights they had been promised.

Zunz had already done some work towards the aims of the Society. He had written an essay on a rabbinic work; in part of the essay, he spoke of the ignorance of non-Jewish scholars about Judaism and the many writings of the rabbis of Palestine and Babylonia.

The Society proposed to sponsor lectures and to publish a scholarly magazine to spread the knowledge of Judaism. Gans gave lectures on laws concerning Jews in ancient Rome, and on European Jewish history. His lectures, as well as learned articles by Zunz, the editor, were printed in the "Journal for the Science of Judaism." The magazine was a good one, but for lack of support did not continue long. None of the young men was blessed with a good income.

Eduard Gans.

Defection from the Ranks

The hopes of young reformers are often defeated. It is often, unfortunately, the young zealots themselves who give up their hopes as soon as they seem difficult to attain.

Eduard Gans had started with high ideals. Finding that despite his talents he could never, as a Jew, rise above the lowest teaching position at the University of Berlin, he asked to be baptized. He was immediately appointed associate professor of law, and soon became full professor, lecturing to overflow classes at the University.

In the same year, 1825, the poet, Heine, was also baptized. He admitted that he made this move only for the hope of benefit, but benefit did not come. He was not asked to become a professor, nor even accepted as a lawyer. Never fitting in with any society, the self-exiled Jew became renowned as one of Germany's beloved poets and as a worker for liberal causes.

Leopold Zunz remained faithful: "Let individuals traffic with the Eternal for the sake of temporal goods; we shall cling all the more steadfastly to Judaism."

Serving by Study

In the beginning of the nineteenth century, Reform temples had been founded in several German cities. Among the first reforms introduced was the delivery of a sermon in the language of the country.

Not only traditional Jews but also the governments of the German states at first objected. The governments hoped to keep the people under their rule away from any ideas of change or revolution, whether in public or in private life. Prussian authorities said that the Jews could not introduce the sermon into their services.

With this as his spur, Zunz undertook to write a book on the history of sermons in

Heinrich Heine, poet and exile.

the Jewish past, showing that the tradition of preaching was as old as Judaism, that sermons to teach and inspire the people were quite in keeping with Jewish customs, and not an imitation of the customs of others.

More important than the facts in this book, "The Religious Discourses of the Jews," was the preface wherein the author took the German government to task for its prejudiced treatment of the Jews.

"It is high time," he wrote, "that the Jews be given, not rights and liberties, but right and liberty; not miserable, humiliating privileges, but complete, elevating citizenship." That these words disturbed the government can be shown by the fact that censors cut out the preface from most copies of the first edition.

More important also than the facts was the way the facts were presented. In reviewing Midrash, Talmud, and prayer-book, Zunz showed Judaism not as one finished and perfect system of law, but as a growing and developing culture. He showed how new forms and new ideas had entered into Jewish life

An old Hanukah Menorah from Frankfurt.

at different periods.

Further studies by Zunz showed the same "scientific" or "historical" approach to the study of Judaism. This was the attitude also of the early Reform leaders. They thought, as he did, that Judaism had grown and changed through the ages. They felt, further, that this meant they could change Jewish tradition in whatever way seemed best to them.

"Suicide Is Not a Reform"

When some of the reformers went to the extent of discarding the Hebrew language, and prayers, hopes and customs that had been considered sacred for thousands of years, Zunz said, "Suicide is not a reform." He was not Orthodox in his beliefs; he felt that ob-servances such as the dietary laws were "symbols"—but he wished to keep these symbols as signs of commitment to Judaism.

"We must reform ourselves and not our religion," wrote Zunz. "We should attack only evil practices that crept into our religious life from within or from without, but not the holy heritage."

A Lifetime of Study

His long life of ninety-one years was devoted to this "holy heritage." Zunz was never willing to serve as a rabbi, although he was often asked to do so. He preached occasional sermons, gave private lessons, did editorial work and directed small schools for many years in order to earn a living. Several times he refused or resigned from positions where he might have been secure. His devoted wife Adelheid was willing to live with him in lowly circumstances so that he might devote himself to study.

Often particular events called forth a special study by Zunz. At one point the government wanted to forbid Jews to call themselves by "Gentile" names. Zunz produced a study of Jewish names through the ages, showing that the names in question had long been used by Jewish families.

When Reform prayer books were published with almost all the traditional Hebrew prayers eliminated, and when many congregations were trying at least to shorten their services, Zunz felt it was important to write a history of the prayer book and its contents. His book on "Synagogue Poetry" showed where and when each of the many extra poems, or *piyyutim*, had been introduced. Although he did not defend keeping all the piyyutim in the service, he showed the value and meaning of these writings.

Self-Respect

In teaching the Jews self-respect, Zunz gained great respect for himself. He was admired by his Gentile neighbors, who chose him to represent them in elections. He spoke often to his countrymen about the need for progress and democracy.

On his seventieth birthday and again on his ninetieth, scholarly works by others were published in his honor. The Zunz "Jubilee Book" contained a wealth of articles, showing that many Jewish scholars were following in his path.

The Birthright

When, in the search for emancipation and success, young Jews like Gans and Heine left their faith, Zunz lamented that they had "sold their birthright for a mess of pottage." This, of course, refers to the story in the Bible. Esau, the wild, unthinking brother, was the older one, and had, therefore, the rights of the first-born, to be honored and respected by the family. Returning, hungry and tired, from the hunt, he saw his brother Jacob cooking lentils, a "mess of pottage." For this one meal, Esau impulsively gave up his birthright, selling it to Jacob, saying, "What good will the birthright do me?"

"Thus," says the Bible, "did Esau despise his birthright."

Leopold Zunz showed that a Jew must react to the prejudice of others not by agreeing with them, or joining them, but with pride and dignity, with self-knowledge and self-respect. He would not allow others to continue in their mistaken belief that Judaism was inferior to the general culture. He set about to prove that Judaism had its own rich heritage.

Jewish science helped restore faith in themselves to young Jews who might otherwise have despised and rejected their birthright.

Abraham Geiger

1810-1874

"Liberty is a new religion, the religion of our age," said Heinrich Heine.

"We have no reason to give up the religion of our fathers," said Gabriel Riesser, "we have every reason to love it. We can find in it the highest ideals which humanity in our days can know."

"We shall not abandon the name of Jew, which, though much reviled, has been linked with the purest knowledge of God, the noblest freedom of spirit and refinement of morals," said Abraham Geiger, rabbi, scholar and friend of both these fighters for freedom.

It was a time of change. The days when the king and his nobles, with the support of the Church, ruled over the poor and ignorant farmers and workers had long passed. Thoughtful and cultured men had developed surprising new ideas: that all men were created equal; that governments were instituted among them not to drive them to war or to grow rich on taxes, but to protect their rights to life, liberty, and the pursuit of happiness. In the west, a new country had been founded on just those principles.

The French Revolution had made every country on earth realize that things were not going to remain as they had been. The soldiers of Napoleon had spread the ideas of Liberty, Equality and Fraternity to every state of Europe. The words had not always been followed by deeds; in truth, changes in law and customs came very slowly everywhere. Nonetheless, even after the defeat of Napoleon, the ideas remained and became the principles to which great numbers of people dedicated their lives.

Among those in the German states who eagerly awaited the equality they had been promised were the Jews of Berlin, Frankfurt and other large cities. Unlike the majority of Jews in the world, who lived separated from their neighbors in the towns of Eastern Europe, many of the privileged Jews of the

Memorial book of the Frankfurt ghetto, 1626 to 1900, bearing the names of departed members of the community.

German cities had done well in business and banking, and were able to send their children to high schools and universities. These comparatively wealthy, intelligent and educated Jews had one ambition: they wanted to be accepted as the equals of the non-Jewish Germans around them.

For many of these Jews, the home life and early childhood education they had been exposed to seemed poor and backward, compared to the glories of the universities. Their small synagogues, where pious worshippers wearing *talit* and *yarmulke* intoned the old Hebrew prayers, seemed to them to belong to the Middle Ages.

There were some, especially among the university graduates in Berlin, who decided it would be better not to be Jewish; for they knew that they would not be accepted as doctors, lawyers, professors, no matter how talented they were, if they remained Jews. The prejudice of their neighbors destroyed their spirit.

There were others who wished to remain Jews, and were proud of the ideals of justice and brotherhood that the prophets of Israel had taught to the world, but who also desired to remove what seemed to them strange and old-fashioned from Jewish worship and Jewish life.

Reasons for Reform

Many felt that making Jewish worship more modern would stop Jews from being ashamed of their religion, and would do away with a desire for conversion. They also felt that when the Jews showed they were loyal only to Germany, and much like the Germans in their ways, their neighbors would grant them full freedom.

During the short period of French rule, when freedom was in the air, Jews in Westphalia began to use an organ and a mixed choir in their services, just as in the Christian churches. Formerly no instrument had ever been played in the synagogue; and men and women had not sat together, much less joined in choral singing.

To distinguish this house of worship and later ones founded in Hamburg, Leipzig, Berlin and Vienna, from the old-fashioned synagogue, the leaders of Reform gave the name "Temple" to their congregations. In the temples, sermons were delivered in the German language. The new congregations varied in their practices, but most eliminated a good deal of the original Hebrew services, particularly references to Zion and the return to Jerusalem. German readings were introduced. Members did not follow ritual laws in their daily lives.

Reform Jews felt that in these ways they were adapting to modern life. They were Jews, but no longer distinguished from their fellow Germans by peculiar customs, a different language, or ties to other lands. They hoped to be accepted by the society around them as full and equal citizens.

"Not emancipation, but reform, is the leading issue of the day for the Jews," said Abraham Geiger.

Abraham Geiger.

Education of a Reform Leader

Abraham Geiger was raised by his father, Rabbi Michael Geiger, as a devout student of the Talmud. As had become customary among Jews in his city of Frankfurt-am-Main, he learned German and studied general subjects as well as Talmud; however, it is said that some of his relatives were shocked when he gave a talk in German as well as one in Hebrew on the occasion of his becoming a Bar Mitzvah.

Geiger wished to further his knowledge of Jewish history and tradition. At the great German Universities of Heidelberg and Bonn, he studied Arabic, philosophy, history and ancient Semitic languages, for these were subjects that had some connection with Judaism. At Bonn, Geiger won a prize for an essay written in Latin, on the subject: "What Mohammed Borrowed from Judaism." All of this happened before the "Science of Judaism" was heard of.

With some intelligent Jewish friends, among them a student named Samson Raphael Hirsch, Geiger studied Talmud and practiced preaching sermons.

"My association with these fellow students taught me more than the lectures of the professors," he later said.

At the age of twenty-two, the brilliant young man became rabbi at Wiesbaden, near his birthplace. He continued his studies, earning his doctorate the next year at the University of Marburg. He also continued research and writing in various fields of Jewish history, and began editing a "Scientific Journal of Jewish Theology."

Geiger soon became known as a leading scholar. He wrote a lengthy study of the Bible and of post-biblical times showing how there were different points of view concerning the law among different groups of Jews. The law, he wished to prove, had not remained the same through the ages.

In his position as rabbi, he turned his ideas into action, becoming a champion of Reform. Even those who opposed Reform saw that Geiger had a good background in Jewish learning, and that he had reached his ideas from knowledge and not from ignorance.

Rabbi Abraham Tiktin of Breslau, father of Solomon Tiktin.

Opposition to Reform

When Geiger was invited to become the second rabbi in the important city of Breslau, his reputation as a reformer went ahead of him. The Orthodox rabbi of the city, Solomon Tiktin, asked the government to stop the newcomer from preaching in German, since, as he said, "The law of the state does not allow Jews to change their customs of worship in this way." It was a year and a half before Geiger was permitted to become second rabbi in Breslau.

Rabbi Tiktin was right in his fears that the new young rabbi would express radical opinions. In his first sermon at Breslau, Rabbi Geiger pleased his followers, but shocked others, when he said: "Judaism is not a finished tale. There is much in its present form that must be changed or abolished. It can rise to a higher position in the world only if it will change itself."

Those who were opposed to Rabbi Geiger's teaching soon found some much more extreme ideas to contend with.

"Have you heard what the Frankfurt Reform Society has decided?" one Jew would ask another with amazement. "They have thrown out the whole Talmud! They say none of Jewish law, not in regard to dietary laws, or Sabbath, or marriage, or circumcision, has to be kept. In their prayers they say nothing about Zion or Jerusalem or restoring the Temple."

All this was true. The "radical" reformers in one sweeping stroke wished to wipe the board clean of all the ritual laws and customs of Judaism.

"All laws and ideas of Judaism which keep Jews separate and different need no longer be obeyed," said Reform Rabbi Samuel Holdheim. Challenged about the authority of the Talmud he replied, "The Talmud said what was needed in its time, and from that point of view it is right. I voice what is believed in my time, and from this standpoint I am right."

Rabbi Geiger, considered radical by many, did not support the Frankfurt Reforms. "I cannot expect everyone to look at Jewish tradition the way I do," said Geiger. "I am a historian." As a student of history he saw that ways of life must change gradually, and that the past cannot be destroyed at a single stroke.

As a scholar, Geiger well knew the value of the Talmud and traditional learning. "While in the dark ages bishops and knights were entirely devoted to ignorance," he wrote, "and the difficult art of reading and writing remained something foreign to them, the dispersed Jews still followed the goal of spiritual growth. I do not endorse every word of the Talmud, nor every idea of our teachers of the middle ages, but I would not give up any of it. Their great works show a keenness and a power of thought which fill us with reverence for the spirit of our ancestors."

That he believed strongly in change, however, there was ample proof. He regarded the ceremonies as "vessels" containing the idea. "Break the vessel and save its contents," he said. "When ceremonies no longer fulfil the purpose of strengthening our ethical sentiments, they become entirely worthless."

The Rabbis Meet

Geiger was the leader in calling together conferences of German Reform rabbis to discuss their problems and progress. The rabbis did not all think alike, though they all started with the belief that reform was proper and was needed.

At the conference of 1845, it was generally agreed that the use of Hebrew in the prayers was not necessary. Because of this, Rabbi Zechariah Frankel left the meeting, and from then on was counted as an opponent of the Reform group.

When discussion took place on changing the observance of Sabbath to Sunday, Geiger could not agree; though others, such as Holdheim, said, "Now Jews keep neither Saturday nor Sunday as a holy day. If they are to keep the principle of a day of rest at all, let it be a day they can observe." Not only did most men work on Saturday in those times; in most of Europe, the children had to go to public school on that day, as well.

Living Up to High Standards

All his life Rabbi Geiger followed Jewish laws, such as the dietary laws, even when he wrote that he did not consider them compulsory for Jews to follow. He did not want anyone to be able to say that he favored Reform just to make life easier for himself. This and his fine scholarship made him the most respected of Reform rabbis.

He was a friend of Leopold Zunz, who often exchanged letters with him. He continued, like Zunz, to study and write about the Jewish past; his output was second only to the master's.

Geiger's great hope was that Reform Judaism would be served by many rabbis of equal scholarship. He worked for the establishment of a seminary for rabbis in Breslau. Great

Sign of a kosher butcher-shop in nineteenth-century Germany.

was his disappointment when he was not asked to become the director. Instead, Zechariah Frankel, the conservative leader, was called to head the new Jewish Theological Seminary at Breslau.

In the last years of his life, Abraham Geiger was asked to be first teacher of theology at the Seminary for the Science of Judaism in Berlin. The time he spent teaching and lecturing on many aspects of Jewish history and literature was the time he enjoyed most of all.

Two statements were composed by Geiger to express his philosophy of life. They are:

"Through knowledge of the past to the understanding of the present; through comprehension to belief.

"To draw from the past, to live for the present, to work for the future."

Zechariah Frankel

1801-1875

It was the first day of the conference of Reform rabbis in Frankfurt, in the summer of 1845. The delegates had gathered with great enthusiasm, for in addition to their own earnest desire for reform, they had letters of support from twenty-two new congregations.

Among the letters was one from the Reform group in Breslau, asking the rabbis assembled to declare that the prayer service ought to be completely in the German language. This and other problems were going to be discussed during two weeks of meetings.

Rabbi Abraham Geiger, the leader of the conference, greeted his colleagues. He was pleased to see that a larger number had come than had attended the previous year's conference. At that time the rabbis had decided to abolish the *Kol Nidre* prayer, and had recommended following the law of the state, not Jewish law, in marriage and divorce. The fact that the decisions of that conference had been protested by over one hundred Orthodox rabbis had not kept any Reform rabbis away from this second meeting.

The Unexpected Delegate

One name came as a surprise. "Rabbi

Rabbi Zechariah Frankel

Frankel is here," came the report to Rabbi Geiger, who hastened to greet his acquaintance Zechariah Frankel, chief rabbi of Dresden.

Like many of the delegates, Rabbi Frankel was a highly educated European scholar. Born in the city of Prague, he had studied many years in the yeshiva there, and then had studied seven years, mainly in ancient languages such as Latin, Greek and Aramaic, at the University of Budapest. He received his degree of Doctor of Philosophy for his work on the Septuagint, the early translation of the Hebrew Bible into Greek, used by the Jews of Alexandria two thousand years ago.

Zechariah Frankel had applied to the government of the state of Bohemia for approval of his appointment as rabbi in the city of Teplitz, for all religious officials in the German states had to be passed on by the authorities. To show that he had enough learning to fit the position, he wrote his application in eight different languages, ancient and modern. He was immediately accepted.

Restrictions and Rights

Jews were still not given full rights in most of the German states. In many of the cities there were special taxes and special restrictions. Not till after the revolutions of 1848 were Jews allowed to hold state positions. Jews were criticized for not working in agriculture and the professions when, in fact, they were not allowed to enter these ways of life. There were discussions among serious citizens as to whether Jews were "civilized" enough to deserve freedom. Old prejudices had not died out.

Like Moses Mendelssohn in the previous century, Zechariah Frankel was recognized by the government as a fine person, despite the fact that he was a Jew. Like Mendelssohn, too, he remained an observant Jew, yet shared in the general life of the community.

The official in charge of education and religion in the kingdom of Saxony asked Frankel's advice on Jewish problems. Frankel explained to him the Jewish system of schools and synagogues. There was no guarantee of freedom of religion or freedom of speech for any group at that time, and the government was able to censor whatever it did not approve of, to close schools or to forbid worship. Frankel so favorably impressed the administrator that he granted new rights instead of taking away old ones.

In 1837, the government asked Frankel to become the rabbi in Dresden, capital city of Saxony. Dresden was not one of the most liberal German cities. Jews were not allowed to take part in any business except money-lending and dealing in second-hand items, although by Frankel's time they had cautiously begun entering other fields. Each adult Jew paid a special tax for the privilege of remaining in the city; relatives or other visitors had to register with the police and leave the city within a specified time. Police searched every Jewish home once a month to see that no residents had secretly come in. For Jews to marry, they had to get government permission and pay a special tax as well.

For centuries the Jews of Dresden were forbidden to build a synagogue. They were allowed to worship in homes, provided they "kept a proper silence" and did not let the sound of the prayers disturb the neighbors.

All these circumstances were not so unusual at that time as to discourage Rabbi Frankel from taking the position. His first effort after his arrival was to build a synagogue. Through appeal to the government, the learned rabbi was able to gain permission. The sound of worship did not disturb the neighbors, for he conducted a traditional service with order and dignity. Such reforms as a weekly sermon, and a boys' choir to lead the singing, were part of his program.

An old belief about the Jews, that they were not to be trusted in court, was responsible for a strange custom in Saxony and elsewhere. Because Jews would not swear lightly by the name of God, they were required to take a special oath before the Torah scroll in the synagogue before going to court as witnesses. The rule went out that in swearing allegiance to the state the Jews must take the special form of oath.

Here, once more, the value of a scientific study of Jewish history was demonstrated. Frankel wrote a learned essay on the sanctity of the vow throughout Jewish history. He was able to prove to the government that, far from being inclined to perjury, the Jews would hold to their given word as a holy duty. In Saxony, and soon thereafter in all the German states, the requirement for the special oath was removed, and Jews were permitted to be sworn as witnesses in court.

To show further the standards of Jewish law and justice, Frankel later wrote a complete history of Jewish law. His publications, like those of other historical writers, helped persuade the government—and Jews, as well—that Jewish institutions had always been on a high level of ethics and morality.

The Critical View

In all his works, Frankel showed that he was a "critical" student of Jewish tradition.

Tzedakah box, in which coins for help to fellow Jews were placed. The words read "For the sake of Zion I will not be silent."

He did not accept every word of Jewish tradition as being equally valid for all time. He believed that changes could be made in the prayer book and services, but with moderation.

When the Reform congregation of Hamburg put out its own prayer book, for example, there were different reactions from various groups. The new prayer book did not change the service completely, but it omitted the reading of the *haftarot,* and the entire *musaf* service. Wanting to show loyalty only to Germany, and not looking forward to a restoration of the Jewish state and the Temple in Jerusalem, the editors had eliminated all prayers about the land of Israel.

The strictly Orthodox rabbis, notably Isaac Bernays, opposed the new *siddur* for making any changes at all. Abraham Geiger proclaimed it a legal prayer book, since in the Talmud it is said that only the *Shema* and the *Amidah* (Eighteen Benedictions) are required prayers; but from his Reform point of view, he criticized the editors for not going far enough.

Zechariah Frankel was expected to speak against the prayer book. This he did, but not by saying, as did the Orthodox, that no one had the right to change the *siddur.* Jewish authorities have the right to change the prayers, he said, but the changes and omissions of the Hamburg group were not proper. "Public prayer is a matter that concerns the whole Jewish people. The removal of the hope for return to Zion, or of any reference to Jewish nationhood, is contrary to the very essence of Judaism."

The longing for Zion, said Frankel, does not make Jews poor citizens of the land wherein they reside. He mentioned the Greeks living in Austria who yet were workers for the freedom of Greece; for this they were respected and not reproached.

How will the Jews continue to exist, he

The old synagogue in Berlin.

asked, if they no longer keep their laws, and the feeling of being one people is no longer expressed? The Reform idea of the "Mission of the Jews," that they were to spread the idea of one God and righteous living among all the nations, was not sufficient, he felt, to keep the Jews a living force.

At the Frankfurt Conference

With this attitude, Frankel came to the second large conference of Reform rabbis. He came hoping to influence the Reform rabbis to moderate their zeal and to make their reforms constructive, instead of, as he saw it, destructive of Jewish survival.

Even among the many scholars at the conference, Zechariah Frankel stood out for his learning. More than any of the others, he had —besides those subjects that might be learned at the universities—a deep knowledge of traditional Jewish studies.

The conference opened. There was much to discuss. There were questions on marriage, circumcision, Sabbath observance. The most exciting issue at this time was, however, the question of Hebrew.

A great many members of the Reform temples did not understand, or, in many cases, even know how to read Hebrew. They felt that this use of a "foreign tongue" only made their services strange and outlandish. Some temples had already eliminated all Hebrew prayers except for one line of the *Shema*, and a few other selected passages.

Abraham Geiger himself wrote at a later time, "The significance of the prayers consists not only in their content but also in their traditional forms, in the words in which they have been handed down to us, hence, also, in the Hebrew language. This must remain, therefore, with few exceptions, the language of prayer."

At the conference, however, Geiger did not argue in favor of keeping Hebrew. "The content of the prayer and the feeling with which it is said is far more important than the form," agreed many of the rabbis.

When Rabbi Frankel rose to speak, the other delegates had a good idea of what he would say. This visitor to their conference was, like them, a modern, educated man who had made reforms in his own congregations. Yet they knew he would not go along with them in this.

"Hebrew," said Frankel, "is the historical chain which links all the dispersed parts of our people into one whole. If we drive it out of Jewish communal life in Germany, we destroy our unity, and become strangers to all other Jews."

"You are expressing a conservative opinion," said one rabbi. "This is a group dedicated to reform, not conservatism."

No attention was paid to Frankel's appeal. The majority of the delegates, on the third day of the conference, voted that "Hebrew should not be considered necessary as the language of prayer."

Zechariah Frankel rose and left the hall.

The Positive Historical School

Never again did Frankel try to join with the group that called itself Reform. Like that group, he believed in such changes as making the services more beautiful, emphasizing the meaning of rituals rather than the mechanical doing of them, studying tradition in a scientific way. Unlike them, however, he wished to conserve every bit of the Jewish tradition that could have any meaning or message. He could not approve the overthrow of so many of the forms and ideals of Judaism.

Certain changes must be made in Jewish life, he said, but "in accordance with the spirit of tradition and by means of that tradition." Above all, no Jewish group anywhere should cut themselves off from their past or from their people all over the world.

Frankel could not be counted among the traditional observant Jews, those who were given the name "Orthodox" by the Reform group. He did not agree with Rabbi Bernays, with Rabbi Hildesheimer, or with Rabbi Samson Raphael Hirsch, that the laws and customs of the Jews were in their perfect and eternal form; that all tradition was revealed or implied on Mount Sinai. He had made changes in practice that they could not condone.

Rabbi Frankel called his point of view the Positive-Historical attitude. He found his place in the center, between Orthodoxy and Reform. His headquarters eventually became the Jewish Theological Seminary at Breslau.

Frankel was called to head the new school in the year of its founding, 1854, and continued in this position till his death in 1875.

The Jewish Theological Seminary of Breslau.

need to improve the state of Judaism itself."

A sense of mission, a devotion to ethics and ideals without distinctive forms and ceremonies, will not keep Judaism alive, he taught. "Judaism is the religion of the Jews," was his seemingly simple yet profound statement. He believed in a Judaism that, while it adapted itself to needs of the modern day, remained clearly and distinctly the Jewish religion, with its own forms, its own ideas and hopes, its own fellowship with Jews of every land.

The appointment was a blow to Abraham Geiger, who had helped to found the Seminary by persuading one of his own members, Jonas Fraenkel, to leave money for the purpose. The directors of the Seminary made their choice of director in the hope that the institution would be devoted to historical, scientific learning, but not to either Reform or Orthodoxy.

Many scholars who later led congregations, or taught in other schools in Germany and in America, received their education at Breslau. An outstanding associate at Breslau was Heinrich Graetz, the best-known of Jewish historians, who wrote the first and greatest complete history of the Jews in a modern language.

Leopold Zunz, who remained a friend and correspondent of Frankel, had hoped through an objective study of Judaism to raise the Jews to the level of their neighbors. "The equalization of the Jews in life will result from the equalization of the science of Judaism with other studies," he had said.

Frankel did not quite agree. "We do not," he said, "try to obtain equality by parading our past literary glory. This is not the purpose. The motive for these studies is the

Jonas Fraenkel, whose wealth endowed the Seminary at Breslau.

Samson Raphael Hirsch

1808-1888

"My dear Naphtali," began the first letter; and it was signed, "Benjamin." There followed eighteen further letters, all of them written by Naphtali in answer to his friend Benjamin.

The "Nineteen Letters" appeared in a book in Hamburg in 1836. The author's name was given as "Ben Uziel." Unlike most letters, which are written for one person's eyes, these letters were read by thousands of people, and had great effect upon many.

Benjamin and Naphtali are old friends, perhaps from university days. Meeting for a short time after several years, Naphtali discovers to his grief that his friend Benjamin has become like many other educated young German Jews of the time. He has devoted himself to business and pleasure and the attempt to get along well in society, and has decided that Jewish law and tradition will only stand in his way.

"What else does it teach except praying and fasting and the keeping of holidays?" Benjamin asks in his letter. "Life itself be-

Samson Raphael Hirsch.

אגרות צפן

The Nineteen Letters

OF

Ben Uziel

Being a Spiritual Presentation of the Principles of Judaism

BY

Samson Raphael Hirsch

Late Rabbi of the Israelitische Religionsgesellschaft of Frankfort-on-the-Main

TRANSLATED BY

Bernard Drachman, Ph.D.

Rabbi of the Congregation Zichron Ephraim and Dean of the Jewish Theological Seminary, New York

TOGETHER WITH A PREFACE AND A BIOGRAPHICAL
SKETCH OF THE AUTHOR BY THE TRANSLATOR

Funk & Wagnalls Company

NEW YORK AND LONDON

Title-page of the English translation of the "Nineteen Letters."

comes nothing but prayers and ceremonies. What embarrassment in association with Gentiles, what difficulties in business!"

His friend Naphtali answers. It is not surprising that he takes eighteen letters to do so, for he has much to say.

The book appeared in the same year that the Reform rabbis of Germany met at Frankfurt; when at the Berlin temple the members asked to have the Shabbat transferred to Sunday; when most university graduates among the Jews were giving up the observances that made them different in any way from the non-Jews they associated with. To persuade a reader that a Jew must keep every Jewish law and ritual was a difficult task. To make the reader feel that it was a great privilege to do so was even more difficult.

The Author of the Letters

The writer who undertook this mission was not named Ben Uziel. His real name was Samson Raphael Hirsch. He was a young man of twenty-eight, the state-appointed rabbi of Oldenburg. He was not writing to a friend named Benjamin. He was writing to all the Jews of Germany. Most particularly, he had in mind the Jews who had studied with him at the University of Bonn and similarly educated German Jews who were now so largely forsaking Jewish law.

Samson Raphael Hirsch had been born and raised in Hamburg, and had received the early Talmudic training of most young Jews of his time. His family was a learned one, his grandfather a rabbi; his father, though also a scholar, was a merchant and expected his son to go into business. This the youngster might have done, if he had not, soon after he became a Bar Mitzvah, come under the influence of an unusual teacher.

Isaac Bernays, or Haham Bernays, as he preferred to be called in the Sephardic manner, was the first Orthodox rabbi who was also a university graduate. He gave instruction to his congregation in their own language, German, just as the Reform rabbis did; but at the same time he was completely traditional in his life, in his conduct of the services, and in his teachings. He showed that it was possible for a university-educated man to be loyal to Jewish law.

Under the teaching of Haham Bernays, young Samson Raphael was inspired to spend his life in learning and teaching Judaism. He devoted himself to Talmud study till he was twenty-one. Then he entered the University of Bonn. There he met a number of bright young Jewish students, eager to learn, full of new ideas, and ambitious for successful careers—which they knew were rarely attained by Jews in Germany.

The synagogue in the Frankfurt ghetto.

Friendship of Hirsch and Geiger

Among the fellow students was Abraham Geiger, two years younger than Hirsch. Both coming from traditional Jewish homes, both possessed of keen minds, both anxious to improve the lot of the Jewish people, the two became close friends. At Hirsch's suggestion they studied a tractate of Talmud together; with several other students, they practiced preaching sermons to each other.

"Thus," wrote Abraham Geiger, "a mutual love and esteem developed. I esteemed his great ability, his rigid virtue, and loved his good heart; he respected my talents, loved my frankness and my youthful cheerfulness."

As soon as the two friends left the university, they struck off in opposite directions. Geiger immediately became known as the champion of Reform. In his pulpit at Wiesbaden he conducted shortened German services accompanied by organ and choir. He announced that dietary laws and other Talmudic teachings were not binding.

Hirsch was called to be rabbi in Oldenburg. There he tried to inspire his people to remain faithful to Jewish tradition and wholehearted in the fulfilment of every Jewish rite. Speaking in the German language, as a man of modern culture, he tried to persuade them with every appeal to mind and heart that the intelligent modern man could also be a pious and observant Jew.

The fact that his friend Geiger had turned so completely to Reform saddened Hirsch greatly. It may be that much of the argument in the "Letters" of Ben Uziel was really addressed to Geiger.

To the modern young man, who sees in Jewish observance only separation and penalties, "Naphtali" appeals: "Do you believe you really understand the object which you are thus condemning? Have you acquired, by honest, earnest investigation, an actual understanding of a matter which, as the holiest and most important consideration of our life, should at least not be thoughtlessly cast aside?"

The Purpose of Judaism

In his "Letters" and in his later writings on the *mitzvot,* the laws and commandments of Judaism, Samson Raphael Hirsch speaks of the Jews as a people singled out by God for a special mission. This does not mean, says Hirsch, that God owes His love and care only to the Jews; but it does mean that the Jews owe all their love and loyalty only to God.

Service for Yom Kippur by Jewish troops in the German army encamped near the city of Metz in 1870.

God wishes to set apart one nation, not wealthy or great in any ordinary way, to be a holy nation, a kingdom of priests. This people, the Jewish people, is to train itself through every action of daily life to be priestlike, holy, separated and dedicated. Its mission is to proclaim through word and action that there is "One God, Creator, Lawgiver, Judge, Guide, Preserver, and Father of all beings; that all beings are His servants, His children; that all comes from His hand, and that this all is to be used only for the fulfilment of His will."

While so many follow the false gods of wealth and pleasure, the Jewish people throughout its history has had to stand apart, to choose "ethical isolation." When others forgot or rejected the "knowledge of God and human duty," this knowledge would be preserved in this people. It could not join in the doings of the other peoples in order that it might not sink to their level.

The sufferings of Israel in exile were sent

to help purify the people for its purpose. It is not that the Jewish people were more wicked than others, but that any failure or disobedience to God on their part had to be more severely punished. They had the mission of being perfect in obedience to God. "What God readily pardons in others, He would not forgive in us."

Attitude to Non-Jews

Hirsch answers some of the questions of Benjamin, which are really the questions of all those who believed in radical Reform. Benjamin fears that Jewish separatism shows hatred of other religions and prevents loyalty to one's country. Hirsch first gives his own explanation of Christianity: At the time of the exile of the Jews, the world was so evil that God desired a "branch to grow from the tree" of Judaism to bring enlightenment and knowledge of the one God to the pagan nations of the world.

The Jewish people are held together by Torah, he says, not by national loyalty; they can, therefore, be good citizens wherever they are. As for separation from their neighbors, some separation is necessary, and the Gentile will respect the Jew who respects his own tradition. The good Jew will be kind and just to every man. "He will carry out works of love for the world; he does not withdraw from its midst, but lives in it, with it, and for it. Israel's most cherished ideal is the universal brotherhood of man."

The "priests" or spiritual leaders of every group have always had special standards that they must live by. Activities and enjoyments that ordinary people may pursue are forbidden to this devoted class. Their way of life separates them and reminds them and others that they are dedicated to the service of God. In the Jewish people, said Hirsch, God has set aside the entire group as a "king-dom of priests," as witnesses and servants to Him.

The Influence of Hirsch

The writings of Samson Raphael Hirsch may not have had any influence on those Jews who had already given up Jewish observance as their way of adapting to life in a modern society. They had great influence, however, on many Jews who were teetering on the edge —who did not know whether or not to discard the laws and rituals they had been taught by their parents.

It was not only to those who were thinking of forsaking tradition that Hirsch wished to speak. It was also to those who kept every detail of the law, but did not always remember the significance of the law; who carried out ritual requirements, but were lacking in the righteousness and compassion that the law also demands.

The fame of Rabbi Hirsch as a modern spokesman for traditional Judaism took him to an important position as state rabbi in Austria. He was there five years when he was asked by a group of eleven men to come to the city of Frankfurt.

According to German law, the Jewish congregation of each city had to be supported by all the Jews living there. In Frankfurt, the major congregation had become Reform. The small group that separated from the congregation called themselves the "Israelite Society for Religion." The Society asked Rabbi Hirsch for his advice and help. Rabbi Hirsch not only came to Frankfurt; he remained, and raised the standards and the numbers of the modern Orthodox community. "The cause of truth," he said, "counts not the number of its adherents."

The Frankfurt Community

As Rabbi Bernays had done in Hamburg,

Founders of the Philanthropin, school for Jewish children in Frankfurt.

German-speaking Orthodox Jews. Even some men of wealth, who could have spent their time in the fashionable world of entertainment and pleasure, were inspired by Rabbi Hirsch to devote themselves to traditional living and observance. "A true Israelite," their rabbi taught them, "looks upon all his property as only a means to help him do what is pleasing in the sight of God. Children should be trained for bread-winning, but they should know that bread-winning is only a means, not the purpose of life. The value of life is to be judged by the goodness with which it is filled."

In other cities of western Europe, and in the new community growing up in America, there have been many who followed the teachings of Samson Raphael Hirsch. They are not those who keep apart from modern life and learning, who separate themselves from the outside world even in their language and their way of dress; who prefer to live in ghettos and to keep their children away from secular studies. On the contrary, they are cultured men, often outstanding in general fields, who feel that being observant Jews is the best way of life for themselves, as good citizens, as human beings, and as carriers of a divine mission.

The founders of Yeshiva University, which is an outstanding American institution of higher learning providing both general and Jewish studies, can be said to have followed the teachings of Hirsch.

Wherever such Jews live, they are examples of the type of life advocated by Rabbi Hirsch, who said, "The reform which Judaism requires is an education of the age up to the Torah, not a leveling down of the Torah to the age. The spirit of the age changes; the Torah remains."

Rabbi Hirsch established schools in Frankfurt where children received a general German education and also the teachings of traditional Judaism. The Reform group had already set up a Jewish general school called the Philanthropin, where religious observance was not stressed.

Hirsch influenced the government to allow the Jews to support, in their cities, the congregation of their choice, though this meant divisions in the community.

There soon developed, in Frankfurt, a strong community of modern, educated,

STATEMENTS BY JEWISH HISTORIANS

The first step toward liberty is to miss liberty; the second, to seek it; the third, to find it.

*   *   *

Equality for Jews in practice and life will result from the equality achieved by the Science of Judaism.

*   *   *

If there are ranks in suffering, Israel takes precedence of all nations; if the duration of sorrows and the patience with which they are borne ennoble, the Jews can challenge the aristocracy of every land; if a literature is called rich in the possession of a few classic tragedies—what shall we say to a national tragedy lasting for fifteen hundred years, in which the poets and the actors were also the heroes?

LEOPOLD ZUNZ

Israel is the people of Revelation. It must have had a native endowment that it could produce such heroes of the spirit.

*   *   *

We shall not abandon the name of Jew, which, though much reviled, has been linked with the purest knowledge of God, the noblest freedom of the spirit and refinement of morals.

*   *   *

Every reform is a transition from the past into a regenerated future. Such reform does not break with the past but rather preserves carefully the bond which connects the present with the past. It follows the law of historical development.

ABRAHAM GEIGER

Hebrew is the historical chain which links all the dispersed parts of our people into one national body. If we drive it out of Jewish communal life in Germany we destroy our national unity, and become strangers to all other Jews.

*   *   *

A people without a center or a government of its own can never attain to honor among the nations of the world. We must therefore demonstrate that the desire for rebirth still lives within us.

ZECHARIAH FRANKEL

The strength of Judaism consists in this, that as soon as one period of history comes to an end, another begins. A new idea replaces the old, fresh forces come into play, and the result is continuous progress.

NAHMAN KROCHMAL

A nation which has witnessed the rise and decay of the most ancient empires, and which still continues to hold its place in the present day, deserves the closest attention.

* * *

In its journey through the wilderness of life, the Jewish people has carried along the Ark of the Covenant, which breathed into its heart ideal aspirations, and even illumined the badge of disgrace affixed to its garment with a shining glory. Such a people, which disdains its present and has the eye fixed steadily on its future, which lives as it were on hope, is on that very account eternal, like hope.

HEINRICH GRAETZ

Join a community, by which alone your work can be made universal and eternal in its results.

* * *

The truly pious man is he who devotes himself in love entirely to the service of the Higher Power, who does not withdraw from the world, but lives in it, with it, and for it.

* * *

Israel's most cherished ideal is the universal brotherhood of mankind.

* * *

Be a Jew; be it really and truly; then will you be respected, not in spite of it but because of it.

* * *

The aim of our worship is the purification, enlightenment, and uplifting of our inner selves.

SAMSON RAPHAEL HIRSCH

UNIT THREE

MASTERS OF THE GOOD DEED

Lo ha-midrash ha-ikar elah ha-maaseh. "The important thing is not learning what to do, but the actual doing."

These words of *Pirkei Avot* ("Ethics of the Fathers") in the Mishnah, tell what Judaism has taught through the ages. Judaism asks its followers to do good, to help the needy, to establish justice and peace. Study and devotion are to lead to the goal of the good life, the life of helping others.

Those whom the Jews are supposed to serve include all mankind. The commandment given in the third book of the Bible, "Thou shalt love thy neighbor as thyself," does not mean that a person of a different nation is not to be loved. A few sentences later, the command is given, "Thou shalt love the stranger as thyself."

Yet it is no surprise that Jewish philanthropists, men of charity, have often given their largest contributions to Jewish causes; that Jewish fighters for freedom and justice have made special efforts to obtain justice and freedom for fellow Jews. One important reason for such loyalty is that Jews have so often been in desperate need of charity, justice, and liberty.

The nineteenth century was a period of revolution and reaction, when new industry and new empires grew up, when old prejudices were challenged by modern ideals of democracy. During this time of rapid change, there were Jews who helped their people and stood up to fight for their rights. At the same time, these leaders gave their best efforts to fight poverty and ignorance, and to help further justice at home and abroad. Patriots of their own nations, and loyal to their own faith, they worked for the good of all mankind.

Jews Without Rights

For hundreds of years, Jews had been a separate group, without legal rights, in every

Jews forced to listen to a sermon urging conversion, in Rome, 1829.

nation of Europe. They had often enjoyed a measure of self-government, taking care of their own religious life, their own schools, their own civil courts, their own charities. In truth, however, they were always subject to the king or ruling power.

They had to pay tremendous taxes; their property could be taken from them; they could be imprisoned; they could be forced to leave their homes or country—all without any appeal to the courts. During most periods, Jews could not own land or enter trades, so that they were forced into second-hand dealing and money-lending. In many places, the Jews were forced to live in ghettos and to wear special clothes or badges. They were made to listen to sermons that attempted to convert them to Christianity. Forced conversion, especially of children, often took place. Time after time, mobs rose against the Jews, plundering and killing. Finally, the Inquisition of the Catholic Church was able to forbid the Jews to live in many countries, both in Europe and in South America.

Through all the long darkness of the Middle Ages the Jews kept their belief that God was watching over them. In His own good time, they felt, He would send the Messiah to save them. If at times the Messiah seemed to be long overdue, they repeated the words of Maimonides: "Even though he delays in coming, despite all this, I believe."

It seemed impossible that help would come in any other way. Their neighbors, who so often turned against them, were also oppressed by the rule of greedy noblemen and war hungry kings. No ruler was going to give up any part of "the divine right of kings" in order to grant rights to his subjects.

The World Changes

In the sixteenth and seventeenth centuries, gradual changes came about which gave the "common man" of Europe a chance for a better life. The old feudal system of nobles ruling over serfs was breaking up. Commerce and trade between far-flung countries brought a new type of wealth. In the growing cities, merchants and freemen increased in number.

Money and skill in business became a source of power; one did not have to be a landed nobleman to enjoy wealth. Those engaged in commerce found that the nobles often wanted to borrow money from them. Banking and finance became important in the new prosperity.

A new class of educated men grew up. Culture instead of war and hunting began to be considered the civilized thing. There were other sources of education besides the church. People read books of philosophy. The idea spread that education could make all men into useful and happy citizens.

In the eighteenth century, the belief that all men are created equal helped bring about two revolutions, the American and the French.

Hope For Equality

Amid all this change, the Jews began to hope for emancipation. In reading about Jewish life in the past two hundred years, we see the longing of the Jews to be accepted as full and equal citizens. They dared to hope that the fine words about equality and brotherhood would come to apply to them as well as to their fellow-countrymen.

In Germany in the eighteenth century, Moses Mendelssohn proved that a Jew could be as cultured as any German intellectual. In France, as we have seen, the Revolution and the conquests of Napoleon brought the promise of full rights for the Jews. In return for the gift of emancipation, many Jews of Western Europe, such as those in the "Sanhedrin" called by Napoleon, felt they must become like the majority around them. Some felt they must give up their Jewish loyalties and become more German than the Germans, more French than the French.

We have seen that the fair promises of Napoleon's rule were quickly broken by the governments that returned to power in 1815. All over Europe, forces of reaction cancelled the rights that had been granted. Those Jews who had tasted freedom, who were educated and had hoped for good careers and a life in normal society were bitterly hurt. The truth was that the Jews were not then or later completely accepted by their neighbors. A long battle had to be waged for full citizenship in each country.

Progress and Prejudice

Throughout the century there were struggles between liberal or revolutionary forces and the ruling powers. Men like Heinrich Heine, converted to Christianity but proud of his Jewish origin, and Gabriel Riesser, Jewish newspaper publisher, joined the liberal movement and helped encourage the revolution of 1848 in Germany. Similarly, Jews in Austria, in Hungary, and in Italy joined the fighters for freedom. All were patriotic and worked to make their own countries unified and strong. Though the revolutions were put down, the goals the

A cartoon of Gabriel Riesser and other politicians.

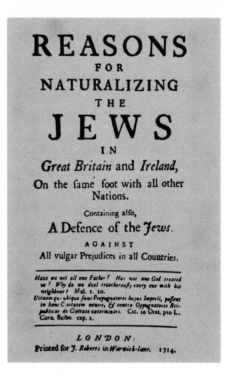

REASONS
FOR
NATURALIZING
THE
JEWS
IN
Great Britain and *Ireland,*
On the same foot with all other
Nations.

Containing also,
A Defence of the *Jews.*
AGAINST
All vulgar Prejudices in all Countries.

Have we not all one Father? Hat not one God created us? Why do we deal treacherously every one with his neighbour? Mal. 1. 10.
Utinam qui ubique sunt Propagnatores hujus Imperii, possent in bona Civitate venire, & contra Oppugnatores Reipublicae de Civitate exterminari. Cic. 10 Orat. pro L. Corn. Balbo. cap. 1.

LONDON:
Printed for *J. Roberts* in *Warwick-lane.* 1714.

Title-page of an early appeal for granting full rights of citizenship to the Jews, published in London in 1714.

revolutionaries had hoped for gradually came about in many countries.

The greatest progress was in England. Free business activity had been allowed to Jews since 1700; and in the nineteenth century, largely under the prosperous rule of Queen Victoria, step by step the Jews were allowed to assume rights in public life. In Russia, at the opposite end of the scale, the czars reigned supreme and rights for their subjects were forbidden to be discussed.

An anti-Semitic cartoon of an English Jew of the Stock Exchange, from the eighteenth century.

Those who were against rights for all the people were naturally even more opposed to rights for the Jewish minority. Those who feared that liberal ideas were upsetting all order in the world tried to strengthen the old order and the old prejudices.

During the nineteenth century there were many tragic events that proved that the anti-Jewish feelings of the Middle Ages still existed. Democratic governments on both sides of the Atlantic protested strongly against injustices to the Jews. Particularly active on these occasions, however, were certain Jews who had reached positions of influence and who tried to help their people. Adolphe Crémieux of France, the Rothschild family, and Moses Montefiore of England proved themselves valiant in the service of right.

The Shtadlan

In ancient Jewish history, we read of heroes

like Joseph and Esther who rose to high places and then helped their people. In the diaspora there was often similar need for help. No national government stood behind the Jews; no feelings of justice inspired the monarchs of the Middle Ages. Often great efforts were needed to keep a community of Jews alive and safe.

During the Golden Age in Spain, there were viziers such as Hasdai ibn Shaprut and Samuel ibn Nagdela in the courts of sultans. In the troublous times of wandering that followed the expulsion from Spain in 1492, Isaac Abravanel in the service of different Italian kings, and Joseph Nasi in the court of Turkey pleaded for their brethren. "Court Jews," advisers to kings in the German states, protected Jews against attack and expulsion. More often than not, though some of their efforts were successful, they lost their positions and their lives when they lost favor in court.

From the great Jewish community of Poland in the sixteenth and seventeenth centuries, an official delegate was sent to the capital city, to act as what we now call a "lobbyist" in favor of his people. The name given to this diplomat was *shtadlan*, the Hebrew word from the verb *l'hishtadel*, "to try." Having no real power, all the shtadlanim could do was to try to protect their people against evil decrees by bargaining and persuasion.

In modern Jewish history, the history of the past two hundred years, there have also been heroes of the good deed, men who used whatever wealth or influence they had for the good of their people. Inspired by ideals of prophetic justice, they devoted their lives to philanthropy and to the protection of their brethren.

The Few Who Became Wealthy

Names like Rothschild and Montefiore remind us that a few Jewish families in the world had risen to wealth while the great majority remained poor and without rights.

The Ghetto in Frankfurt, from a painting by Wilhelm van Hanno in the Frankfurt Historical Museum.

Living in cities, already engaged in trade and dealing with money, some Jews were able to become bankers early in the days when banking became necessary in the business life of Europe. In the city of Frankfurt, center of German banking, Jews for some time owned the largest investment houses.

The most famous family, the Rothschilds, received its start at the end of the eighteenth century through the friendship of Mayer Amschel Rothschild with a German prince, who asked him to safeguard and invest his fortune. The five sons of Mayer Amschel

William, elector of Hesse, friend of Amschel Rothschild.

Hebrew word for both "righteousness" and "charity." Montefiore spent a long life of one hundred years traveling the world in behalf of his people and dispensing funds where they were needed.

Baron Maurice de Hirsch, railroad magnate of Paris, was mindful of the Jewish tradition repeated by Maimonides: that it is better to raise a man to support himself than to hand out charity to him. Wishing to improve the situation of his people, he tried to endow schools in Russia. Upon the Czar's refusal, Baron de Hirsch continued his efforts, establishing schools in Galicia, in Turkey, and in the immigrant community of New York. His largest effort went into helping Jews settle in agricultural colonies in Argentina. He founded the Jewish Colonization Association and for many years supported the Alliance Israelite Universelle, which helps Jews every-

headed offices of the Rothschild firm in Frankfurt, Vienna, Naples, Paris and London. Each was able to do important service, through loans and exchanges, to his country. For example, the London branch enabled England to pay for the rights to the Suez Canal in 1875.

Lionel Rothschild became the first Jew allowed to take his elected place in the British House of Commons in 1858. Sir Nathaniel Rothschild was made a peer of England by Queen Victoria in 1885. Sir Moses Montefiore, the great philanthropist, was knighted as early as 1837. These individual outstanding men of wealth and integrity broke the taboos against their people.

Many of these Jews of wealth used their fortunes well, in the cause of *tzedakah*, the

The Great Synagogue, Duke's Place, London.

Baron Maurice de Hirsch.

where and supports schools in North Africa and the Near East. In all, his benefactions amounted to more than $100,000,000.

Baron Edmond de Rothschild, most generous of his charitable family, gave so much to found colonies and schools in Palestine that he is remembered in Israel to this day as *Ha-Nadiv*, the philanthropist.

Anti-Semitism and Tragedy

Food, medicine, education — all were needed by Jews in many lands, and these self-appointed foster-parents did their best to take care of such needs. All too often, however, the need was more crucial even than these; the lives and liberty of Jews were often threatened.

In 1840 an accusation was made against the Jews of Damascus in Syria that they had murdered a Christian monk in order to use his blood for Passover. This horrible lie had no proof behind it, but a number of Jews were arrested and tortured, two of them dying in

Mauricia, Jewish colony in Argentina founded by the Jewish Colonization Association of Baron de Hirsch.

prison. The world was shocked at this "blood libel." Adolphe Crémieux, leading lawyer of France, and Sir Moses Montefiore of England went on a joint mission to clear the Jews and to free the remaining prisoners. Crémieux was the director for many years of the Alliance, while he worked for liberal causes in the French government.

A still more shocking event was the kidnaping, in 1858, of a Jewish child of six from his home in Italy by the Catholic Church. The boy had been baptized by his nurse, and the Church insisted he therefore belonged to them, to be raised as a Catholic. Worldwide protests and the good offices of Moses Montefiore did not help. Edgar Mortara was never returned to his parents; he became a priest.

It could be seen in the second half of the nineteenth century that the prejudices of the Middle Ages had not died. They had become, in a way, even stronger. Throughout the Middle Ages, any Jew could have saved himself from persecution by becoming a Chris-

The degradation of Captain Dreyfus.

tian. By the middle of the nineteenth century, a new type of anti-Jewish feeling had grown up.

Together with the feeling against democracy and the fear of revolution went a hatred of the Jews. Ugly rumors about Jews trying to upset the governments of Europe and seeking to control the world were started. It no longer mattered whether a Jew was religious; as long as he was born Jewish, he could be a victim of anti-Semitism.

All the attempts to improve the culture and refinement of the Jew, to show him as a loyal patriot of his country, had no effect against the anti-Semite. This was dramatically proved by the Dreyfus affair. In 1894,

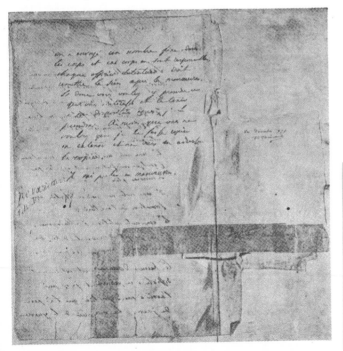

The document, later proved to be in the handwriting of Count Esterhazy, on the basis of which Dreyfus was falsely convicted of espionage.

Photograph of part of a letter Dreyfus sent to the Grand Rabbi from prison the day after he was found guilty.

Deuxième Année. — Numéro 87

Cinq Centimes

JEUDI 13 JANVIER 1898

Directeur
ERNEST VAUGHAN

ABONNEMENTS

PARIS..........
DÉPARTEMENTS et ALGÉRIE..
ÉTRANGER (Union Postale)..

POUR LA RÉDACTION
S'adresser à M.-A. BERTHIER
de la Rédaction

Adresse Télégraphique : AURORE-PARIS

L'AURORE

Littéraire, Artistique, Sociale

Directeur
ERNEST VAUGHAN

LES ANNONCES SONT REÇUES :
143 — Rue Montmartre — 143
AUX BUREAUX DU JOURNAL

Les manuscrits non insérés ne sont pas rendus

ADRESSER LETTRES ET MANDATS :
à M. A. BOUIT, Administrateur

Téléphone : 102-88

J'Accuse...!

LETTRE AU PRÉSIDENT DE LA RÉPUBLIQUE
Par ÉMILE ZOLA

LETTRE
A M. FÉLIX FAURE

Président de la République

Monsieur le Président,

Me permettez-vous, dans ma gratitude pour le bienveillant accueil que vous m'avez fait un jour, d'avoir le souci de votre juste gloire et de vous dire que votre étoile, si heureuse jusqu'ici, est menacée de la plus honteuse, de la plus ineffaçable des taches?

Vous êtes sorti sain et sauf des basses calomnies, vous avez conquis les cœurs. Vous apparaissez rayonnant dans l'apothéose de cette fête patriotique que l'alliance russe a été pour la France, et vous vous préparez à présider au solennel triomphe de notre Exposition universelle, qui couronnera notre grand siècle de travail, de vérité et de liberté. Mais quelle tache de boue...

[Text continues in columns — L'Accuse letter by Émile Zola]

The dramatic front page of the newspaper *L'Aurore*, in which the noted writer Emile Zola, under the heading "I accuse . . .! A letter to the president of the Republic," demanded justice for the falsely convicted Alfred Dreyfus.

---

a loyal French Jewish army officer was accused of spying for Germany. He was convicted amid cries of "Down with the Jews!" After years of solitary confinement on Devil's Island, Dreyfus was finally released through the efforts of his family and of brave and liberal Christians, among them the novelist Emile Zola.

The Dreyfus affair showed once again how unsure the Jews were of their hard-won civil rights. It also showed, however, that joining with the Jews in their efforts to win freedom and justice were decent and humanitarian Christians of every land.

Totalitarians, those who wished to deny rights to all, began with the Jews. Those who loved democracy knew that equality and justice for the Jew were necessary if the country as a whole was to be just and free. In the rights of the smallest minority was the test of the true worth of each society.

The reinstatement of Captain Dreyfus.

Interior of the Portuguese synagogue in Paris.

Sir Moses Montefiore

1784-1885

Sir Moses Montefiore.

Seven days out on the Mediterranean Sea, two of the passengers on the ship *Leonidas* saw a pirate ship sailing towards them. They had been warned of this danger, but had insisted on the journey. In a few minutes, however, the British warship *Gannet* came into view behind them. The pirate craft set sail in the opposite direction; the *Gannet* pursued. The rest of the voyage to Alexandria was made in safety.

Ten years later, the same two travelers again arrived in Egypt. This time the worst danger was in the trip overland where bandits lay in wait for wayfarers. Travelers moved in groups, and all were given guns. Even the lady, though she was sure she would never be able to use a weapon against anyone, was persuaded to carry two loaded pistols in holsters suspended from her waist. With watchmen standing guard each night on the road, they arrived safely in Jerusalem.

A sleigh drawn by horses jolted through the snowy wastes near the northwest border of Russia. It was eight years later, and the couple who had dared the lawlessness of the Near East now braved another road. The howling of wolves was heard, sometimes far off, sometimes frighteningly near. The passengers took turns beating a gong; their driver assured them that the noise would make the beasts keep away. Finally they arrived at the capital city of St. Petersburg.

These heroic travelers were not international spies or reckless adventurers. Their names were Moses and Judith Montefiore. At the time of the first journey they were already middle-aged. They were a fine English couple, wealthy and respected, faithful to their religion, devoted to their relatives, interested in books and study. They could have spent their days busily enough on their two estates, in London and in Ramsgate, visiting with friends, serving in honored positions in synagogue and local community affairs.

What caused them to go on such journeys was the desire to do good deeds. "Justice, justice, shalt thou pursue," were words from the Bible that they tried to follow. Sir Moses and his lady not only lent their names to good causes, and wrote checks as many wealthy men have done; they sacrificed them-

View of interior of the Ramsgate Synagogue.

selves, their time, their comfort, and their safety in order to help the poor and the oppressed.

The Successful Financier

The grandfather of Sir Moses had come to London from Italy in 1744. Moses was born, however, in Leghorn, Italy, where his parents were on a business trip. The boy grew up in London. At first apprenticed to an importing firm, young Moses became interested in banking. Handsome, six feet three inches in height, at one time a captain in the county militia, Moses Montefiore was a favorite of all his relatives.

The young man's uncles joined together and for 1,200 pounds sterling—the equivalent then of $6,000—bought permission for him to practice as a broker on the Stock Exchange in London. Only twelve Jewish brokers were allowed to be licensed at that time. It was some years later that this restriction on Jewish brokers was removed.

Though it can be seen that Jews as yet did not have every civil right in England, there was much freedom for them, more than in any other country of that time except the new United States of America. Moses Montefiore was able to do well in his career. He was associated with other leading financiers, the chief one being Nathan Rothschild.

In 1812, Montefiore married Judith Cohen, the sister of Mrs. Rothschild. The future Lady Montefiore was his faithful and helpful wife for more than fifty years.

Both Moses Montefiore and the Rothschilds lent large amounts to European governments during and after the wars of Napoleon. His own projects included two that were considered new and full of risk: the development of railroads, which were just beginning to be built in England and Europe; and the installing of gas-lighting, which became and remained for many years the

Lady Montefiore when young, copied from an oil painting in the Montefiore College, Ramsgate.

method of lighting used in all cities of the world. He was not discouraged by scientists who said that neither of these new-fangled inventions was safe or sensible. In 1836, the Royal Society of England, dedicated to the furthering of science, elected him to membership for his foresight and daring.

The same qualities made Moses Montefiore prosper in every thing he did. At the age of forty, he saw that his wealth and his investments were sufficient to give him a fine income for the rest of his life. He had no children. He turned to his good wife and asked her if she would be happy if he retired from business.

"Let us thank God, and be content," said wife Judith.

From that time forth, Moses Montefiore was able to devote himself to the activities

FERRIERES.

An Austrian caricature of 1862, showing Napoleon III (right) receiving bags marked "Loans" from Baron James de Rothschild.

respectfully. Both he and his wife kept the dietary laws at home and abroad; often at dinners or receptions they would eat nothing, or a few permitted items.

On the road, at inns, or on shipboard, Moses Montefiore would put on his tefilin and pray every morning. His wife would light the Sabbath candles, and all travel would cease, wherever they were, for the day of rest. A scroll of the Torah accompanied them on every journey, by land or sea.

The first arrival of the Montefiores in Jerusalem was a great event for the inhabitants of the city. Lady Montefiore wrote in her diary, "Many were the solemn thoughts which rose in our minds on finding ourselves in this Holy Land: the country of our ancestors, of our religion, and of our former greatness, but now, alas! of persecution and oppression. We hear from every one of the

which were really dear to him.

Travels to the Holy Land

A major step soon after his retirement was the first visit of the Montefiores to Palestine. This was the year 1827. What air travel can now do in a few hours required months in those days. It took three months to reach Malta; and seven weeks more to reach Jerusalem. It was on this crossing that the encounter with the pirate ship was recorded.

The difficulties of travel never caused any change in the pious habits of the Montefiores. At home, Sir Moses tried to attend synagogue every morning, to pray with a *minyan*, the group of ten men required for public prayer. Friends liked to tell how he had chanted the entire Hebrew grace after meals at a state dinner where Lord Nelson was also a guest; the others, including the Admiral, waited

Sir Moses Montefiore in middle-age.

extortions that are levied, and that there is no means of support."

The Montefiores resolved on this first visit to devote themselves to the well-being of the Jews living in Palestine. They wished to see them improved in health and education; they wished most strongly to see them occupied in farming or other constructive activities, so that they would not depend for support on charity collected from Jews all over the world.

On six more occasions did Sir Moses make the long journey to Jerusalem, each a time of crisis. He visited during times of smallpox and cholera epidemics, and at times of war. During the visit of 1838, the country was, according to their guides, "alive with brigands." Since it was known to all that they were carrying large sums of money to give to the poor, they knew they were in danger of attack. All members of the group, including Lady Montefiore, were armed with pistols.

The ship Judah Touro, named after the philanthropist; from an old print in the Peabody Museum, Salem, Massachusetts.

The Touro Infirmary, endowed by Judah Touro, New Orleans.

In 1855, a crop failure and severe winter in Palestine, and the stoppage of contributions from Poland because of war, left the land destitute. In addition, smallpox broke out. Montefiore raised funds and prepared to go. Then came the news that a Jew of New Orleans, whom he had never met, had died and had left $50,000 for Sir Moses to use in Palestine as he saw fit.

Judah Touro, born in Newport, Rhode Island, willed his entire fortune to charitable and religious institutions. Every synagogue in the United States at that time received a bequest. Orphan asylums, hospitals, benevolent societies of every denomination, received

Judah Touro, from an early photograph (daguerreotype) in the files of the American Jewish Historical Society.

large endowments. The largest single gift was made "to ameliorate the condition of our unfortunate Jewish brethren in the Holy Land," in such manner as Sir Moses Montefiore "may advise as best."

With this bequest and other funds to distribute, Sir Moses set out once again. In the suffering city of Jerusalem, besides distributing alms, he laid the foundation of a hospital, ordered the building of a windmill for the grinding of grain, opened a girls' school and an industrial school, and established the Touro Houses, dwellings for low-income families, to fulfill the American bequest. The section he built up near the windmill is called *Yemin Moshe,* his own first name being, of course, Moshe in Hebrew.

Montefiore's great wish was for the Jews in Palestine to return to the cultivation of the soil. He established agricultural colonies at Jaffa, Safed, and Tiberias, but there was not to be great success in farming in Palestine until the next century.

The windmill and Yemin Moshe in modern Jerusalem. Much new building has taken place since the time of this photograph.

Damascus Delegates

Persecution of Jews anywhere aroused Sir Moses to help. When Jews in Damascus were falsely accused of the crime of murder in 1840, he joined Adolphe Crémieux of France on a mission to the Near East. Montefiore's previous knowledge of the area and his friendship with Mehemet Ali of Egypt helped win the freedom of the unfortunate prisoners.

The Montefiores then journeyed on to Constantinople to persuade the Sultan to grant Jews equal rights and to abolish torture

Interior of the Spanish-Portuguese Synagogue, Shearith Israel, in New York.

Medal struck in honor of Sir Moses on his hundredth birthday. The Hebrew words on the obverse read: "Happy is everyone who fears the Lord, who walks in His ways." The places listed on the reverse are those to which Sir Moses traveled in service of his people.

לכבוד אחינו ב"י, הא לכם מכתב יקר מכבוד השר וגדול בישראל
כקש"ת מהו' ר' **משה מונטיפיורי** נ"י שהשמיע"ו סיו
העליונה, וראיתי בזה תועלת גדול לכל ישראל בכל מקומות מושבותם

לכן אחלק בעקב ואמצו בישראל:

[Hebrew letter text]

משה מונטיפיורי

A letter of Moses Montefiore sent to the Jews living in lands of the Ottoman Empire.

Sir Moses Montefiore speaking to Czar Nicholas I in 1846 in St. Petersburg.

as a means of obtaining confessions. On the triumphal return from this trip, Sir Moses spoke of his wife's help: "To Lady Montefiore I owe a debt of gratitude; her counsels and zeal for our religion and love to our brethren were at all times conspicuous. They animated me under difficulties and consoled me under disappointments." It was, indeed, a remarkable thing that Lady Montefiore, at a time when fine ladies were supposed to be delicate and to remain obediently at home, accompanied him on his most dangerous journeys.

Into Darkest Russia

Perhaps the most daring journey undertaken by the Montefiores was the one to Russia in 1845. Czar Alexander II had decreed that all Jews living near the border must move inland. Hundreds of thousands were to be uprooted from home and livelihood. Like other humane people everywhere, Sir Moses was distressed; like many other Jewish and liberal leaders, he asked his own government to help, and sent messages of appeal to the Czar. Unlike others, Sir Moses chose to go directly to the court of Russia, at whatever cost or hardship, to intercede for his people.

At the time of this difficult journey, the Montefiores were in their sixties. Winter snows still covered northern Europe, and there were wolves along the way. Nonetheless, they undertook the mission.

Montefiore was received by the Czar as a representative of the British government, for the good wishes of Queen Victoria and of Parliament had gone with him. The conversations between Jew and Czar had some positive results. The decree was revoked. The Czar promised to help the Jews gain education and enter trades.

The promises of the Czar were worth little. The fact, however, that Montefiore had been

Drawing by Moritz Oppenheim of the kidnapping of Edgar Mortara.

took him to far-flung parts of the world; he stood before many rulers in many lands.

The powerful government of England favored most of his activities. As president of the Jewish Board of Deputies, Montefiore was not able to obtain all the civil rights he worked for; he himself, despite much urging by leading Englishmen, was never appointed to the House of Lords. His missions, however, were regarded with sympathy and respect by all of England. In reward for his noble deeds, he was knighted and named a baronet by the queen.

Testimonial of respect presented to Sir Moses and Lady Montefiore by their Jewish brethren in the United Kingdom.

able to visit and speak with him, and later to visit several Jewish communities of Poland, gave hope and confidence to the downtrodden Jews of Eastern Europe. They looked to Moses Montefiore as Prince and Father of his people.

An Attempt Ends in Failure

A journey to Spain and Italy was made necessary by a tragic event which Montefiore, and indeed all the governments of the world, could not counteract. A six-year-old child, Edgar Mortara, was kidnapped from his Jewish parents in 1858 in the Italian city of Bologna. The Catholic Church claimed that a nursemaid had baptized the child and that therefore he belonged to them. He was hidden from searchers; no court brought any action against the Church; and all efforts and outcries against this deed brought no results. The boy was raised in the Church and became a priest in Belgium; his family never saw him again.

This was one attempt by Montefiore which failed, and there were others. He remained, however, the greatest example in Jewish history of the shtadlan, the "one who tries," who does his utmost for his people. Sir Moses went far beyond most such men because his efforts

Joy in The Torah

A scene far different from the ones which opened this chapter was a typical one in the lives of the Montefiores. Not only braving the seas or standing in a sultan's court, but also at home in England at the Hebrew schools of London, Lord and Lady Montefiore showed their love of Judaism and their people.

Every year at Purim, the classes of the Hebrew schools would assemble, dressed in their best, to sing for the Montefiores and to receive prizes and presents from them. Every child would be called up to receive a coin from Sir Moses, and to shake his hand. Lady Montefiore, who never was blessed with children, would take some of the younger ones on her lap and kiss them.

The love for Jewish education, for Torah, was the leading passion in the lives of both Montefiores. They were founders of the Jews' Free School, the Hebrew National Schools, and Jews' College for higher studies in London. They gave large sums also to institutions of general education, such as the College of London.

Judith Montefiore died on the eve of Rosh Hashanah in 1862, after a marriage of fifty

Jews' College, Queen's Square, London.

Interior of the sukkah of the Montefiores.

Coat of arms of Sir Moses Montefiore.

Montefiore College, Ramsgate, named after Judith, Lady Montefiore.

years. In her memory her husband gave donations to every synagogue and orphans' home in the British empire, founded a rabbinical college at Ramsgate and a Nursing Home at South Norwood. Thus her interests in both education and healing were honored.

"I am no great man," Sir Moses once said to an admirer. "The little good that I have accomplished, or rather that I intended to accomplish, I am indebted for it to my never-to-be-forgotten wife, whose enthusiasm for everything that is noble and whose religiousness sustained me in my career."

Love of All Mankind

Montefiore's love of justice and concern

Drawing of Sir Moses Montefiore in his old age.

for the poor and oppressed were not confined to his own people. He gave to the movement to abolish Negro slavery. He distributed alms to all the poor in every city he visited. When sending money to a stricken area, he instructed, "If there are others who are more needy than the Jews, see to it that they are helped first." He appealed for funds to help Christians oppressed in Syria.

At the time of the Russo-Turkish war, a relief committee for refugees was set up in England. Sending a contribution, Sir Moses also telegraphed: "Should my presence in Constantinople or Adrianople be deemed in any way beneficial to the sufferers, I shall be ready to proceed there without delay." A

The Montefiore mausoleum in Ramsgate. The inscription reads: "Into His hand I commend my soul, when I sleep and when I awaken."

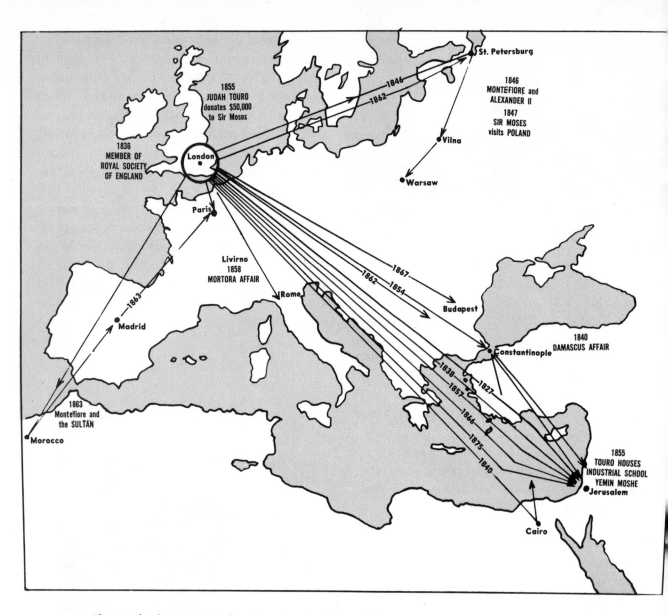

The travels of Moses Montefiore to protect the rights of the Jews. Note the seven trips to the Holy Land.

remarkable offer this was, since Sir Moses was at this time ninety-eight years old!

A Century of Life

The hundredth birthday of Sir Moses Montefiore was celebrated by services of thanksgiving all over the Jewish world. The early Zionist group, "Lovers of Zion," held an international conference in his honor. Sir Moses had seen so much of the suffering of fellow-Jews in the diaspora that he felt strongly that there must be a Jewish homeland. "Palestine must belong to the Jews, and Jerusalem is destined to become the seat of a Jewish Empire," he had stated.

Dearly loving his own country of England, he had no doubt that loyalty to that democracy and loyalty to the Jewish people's strivings for freedom went hand in hand. Among thousands who sent him birthday greetings was Queen Victoria herself, who offered congratulations on "a century of loyalty and philanthropy." To her he represented the highest type of Englishman.

Active to the last in the fulfillment of religious duties and the practice of *tzedakah,* Sir Moses died in his hundred and first year. To this day he is loved, honored and remembered by his people for a lifetime of good deeds.

Front page of a book written in Hebrew about Moses Montefiore.

Isaac-Adolphe Crémieux

1796-1880

The elegantly dressed ladies and gentlemen at the banquet turned to the head of the long table. "A toast to our honored guest!" called the host. "A toast! Long life! Health and prosperity to Master Crémieux!" came the answer. Crystal wine goblets were raised; smiles and admiring eyes turned toward the distinguished guest.

From his seat of honor at the right hand of his host, Adolphe Crémieux rose. All were still; the great man was known above all as a speaker, and all wished to hear his words.

Before he could open his mouth, there came a shout from outside one of the tall windows of the banquet hall. A face was pressed against the pane; someone had pulled himself up to the windowsill from outside, in order to see into the hall. "He's getting up! He's standing!" the onlooker cried out.

From the street below came an answering roar. Hundreds of people, crowding the narrow avenue before the building, echoed the

A caricature of Cremieux by his countryman, Honore Daumier.

toast that had just been offered. "Long live Adolphe Crémieux!"

Tears in his eyes, Adolphe Crémieux for a moment could not speak. His tongue had ever been ready; he had shrunk from no debate. No opponent in court had escaped the quickness and biting irony of that tongue. The slightest insult to him or his people had brought forth answering fire. He had advised and reproved kings; he had inspired and stilled revolutionary mobs. Only this, the outpouring of the gratitude and love of his people, could so overwhelm him that, briefly, the great advocate stood silent.

Declaration of Ideals

What had he done to deserve such applause? This French lawyer, returning from Egypt to Paris at the end of the year 1840, was greeted by cheering and weeping crowds at Corfu, Venice, Trieste, Vienna, Frankfurt, every stop on the way.

He had done only what he had to do, said Crémieux. When he was able to speak, when the sound of the crowd outside had lowered for a time, he made his modest statement:

Isaac Adolphe Cremieux

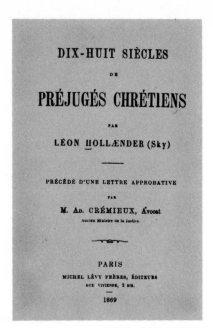

Title-page of a pamphlet on prejudice, with a preface by Cremieux.

"I am a lawyer, and I saw that there were unfortunates to be saved; I am a Jew, and I saw religious persecution to be fought; I am a man, and I saw the barbarity of torture to be abolished; how could I have hesitated without myself committing a crime? I fulfilled my duty. I defended my own hearth, and the principle of freedom of worship. . . . I felt within myself the strength of right: woud not my silence have been shameful cowardice?"

In this statement Adolphe Crémieux described the motives and actions of his whole life. What he was specifically referring to was his role in the Damascus affair, one of the sad events of the nineteenth century that showed that vicious ignorance and anti-Jewish prejudice still lived in the modern world.

The Damascus Affair

In the city of Damascus in Syria, a Catholic priest, Father Thomas, had disappeared. He was never found. It was suggested to the police that it must have been the Jews who had killed him for the monstrous reason that they needed Christian blood to celebrate Passover.

Similar incredible charges had been made against the Jews during the Middle Ages. Strangely, the false charge of using human blood had also been made against the early Christians by the Romans. Jews have always hated murder and valued life; our laws forbid us even to eat "the blood which is the life" of animal flesh. Nonetheless, the blood libel came up frequently, and one pope after another had to warn his followers not to believe such harmful nonsense.

It was not to be expected that in the modern world any sensible person would dare to accuse any group of such a thing. Yet the sad fact was that it was not even fanatic Moslems or grieving churchmen who made the charge at Damascus; it was the consul representing the highly civilized country of France, Ratti Menton by name, who said the Jews must be responsible.

Eight leading Jews, and after them scores of others, including many little children, were arrested. With all sorts of tortures the Moslem police finally got two of the Jews to "confess" that they had seen the murdered man on his last day. They took back their confessions as soon as the tortures stopped, but the people wanted to believe that the Jews were guilty. One old man and one young one died under torture and whipping. Others were blinded or had their teeth pulled out. One Jew agreed to convert to Islam so as to escape further torture.

When a Jew from Austria was arrested, his own consul came to his defense. For the other Jews there was no defender. Consuls of other leading countries of Europe, though they were shocked by the happenings, kept silent in order not to antagonize the rulers of the Near East.

The news reached the press of Europe. Incredibly, some newspapers of France, conservative and Catholic in outlook, presented the charges as true. There were meetings of Jews in many cities, including New York and Philadelphia. This was the first time that the Jewish community in the United States had united to confer and take action together. In every western country, thinking men expressed dismay at the events in Damascus. Protests were sent to the governor of Syria and to the viceroy of Egypt, who controlled Syria; and to the Turkish sultan, whose power extended over the whole Near East.

In France, the outstanding defense lawyer and liberal leader, Adolphe Crémieux, appealed to King Louis Philippe and to Adolphe Thiers, Minister of Foreign Affairs. The king answered vaguely. Thiers defended his consul, Ratti Menton, as "an agent faithful to his duty," and accused the Jews of using pressure to thwart justice.

A meeting was called in London, which Crémieux attended. His first words were, "France is against us." It was decided that the English philanthropist Sir Moses Montefiore should go, together with Crémieux, on a mission to the scene of the atrocities. With their wives, and accompanied by Dr. Solomon

A French rabbi of the nineteenth century.

Adolphe Thiers, French Minister of Foreign Affairs.

Munk, an expert in the languages of the Near East, these leading Jewish citizens of Europe started on the long journey.

Queen Victoria sent good wishes to the delegates, and offered the use of a British ship for the first part of the journey.

In the city of Alexandria, then capital of Egypt, the delegates asked the viceroy in vain for permisssion to go to Damascus. He claimed such a trip would be too dangerous. Meanwhile messages came from the governments of England, Austria and other countries; the president of the United States wrote of his "surprise and pain," and asked for the victory of "justice and humanity."

Only the French consul-general at Alexandria, and the French government at home, to Crémieux's distress, seemed to be giving support to Ratti Menton's slander and its terrible results.

Finally the sultan in Constantinople gave his support to the mission. The viceroy of Egypt issued orders for the release of the remaining prisoners and for the clearing of the names of the accused.

"What a miracle is this return to life!" rejoiced Adolphe Crémieux. He and Sir Moses, however, were not content. The Englishman went on to Constantinople to try to persuade the Sultan to forbid the use of torture in the prisons of the Near East.

Crémieux's first interest had always been in the raising of all groups, particularly his fellow Jews, to a high level of education and worthiness for citizenship. He gathered the Jewish leaders of Alexandria and with their help, and his own large contribution, founded schools for the Jewish boys and girls of Egypt. In the Crémieux schools, the children were to learn Hebrew and religious teachings, as well as modern languages and skills.

On Crémieux's homeward journey, not only did the Jews of all the cities on the way hail him; not only did the Rothschilds of Frankfurt give him banquets, and the rabbis of the east honor him with the title of *Morenu,* our teacher. Even the governors and mayors, the consuls of great nations, Prince

Prince Clemens von Metternich, Austrian statesman.

Metternich of Austria, came out to show him honor. All gloried in the fact that another step had been taken in the cause of human rights.

A Jewish French Citizen

The life of Adolphe Crémieux was a continuing battle for the rights of man. Born and raised in a silk-merchant's family in the southern French city of Nimes, he had been named Isaac Moses. In 1808, at the age of twelve, he came to the Imperial Lyceum, the state school at Paris, adopting the name Adolphe for school registration.

The young Jewish student from the small town was delighted to be accepted among other French youngsters from all over the country. He stood out for his keen mind and power of speech; he was called even then "the lawyer." No anti-Jewish feeling existed at the school, though he had often suffered from it at home. "How many fistfights I used to have as a boy in Nimes!" he recalled.

Young Adolphe, like his friends, adored Napoleon, who was then at the height of his glory, having won most of Europe and having been proclaimed emperor of France. Liberty, Equality, Fraternity, the ideals of the French Revolution, which Napoleon avowed, were the ideals of the students.

Unlike Napoleon, who exercised absolute power, and unlike many Frenchmen who wanted to stamp out all freedoms after Napoleon's downfall, Adolphe Crémieux served these ideals throughout his life. It was as a lawyer, defending the innocent, asking equal justice for all, pleading in court for the rights of free speech and free press, that Crémieux was able to carry on his battle for human dignity.

At the time of his admission to the bar, Crémieux stood up for Jewish rights. He was asked to take the oath *more judaico,* in the special Jewish way. He refused. "Am I only

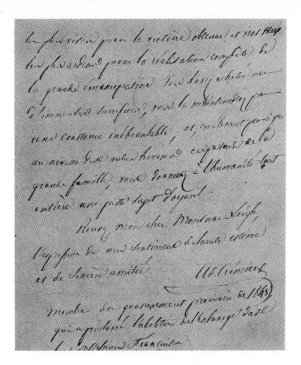

Part of a letter of Adolphe Cremieux congratulating America on the emancipation of the slaves.

A caricature of the 1848 Revolution, showing the king, the Church, and the Jews, in league with the devil. Jews were most often victims of king and Church, rather than co-workers.

a Jew? No, I am also a French citizen. Therefore I take the oath of a Jewish French citizen." Allowed to swear in the customary way, he entered immediately upon his career, soon becoming the outstanding defense lawyer in France.

France in Upheaval

During the century following the French Revolution of 1789, France underwent many changes of government. When Napoleon fell, King Louis XVIII was asked to rule, and Charles X followed him, just as though the "divine right of kings" had never been challenged. Crémieux was obliged to defend three young men whose crime was that they sang the forbidden French anthem of the Revolution, the *Marseillaise*. His appeal to the patriotic memories of the jury saved his clients from prison.

When revolutions overthrew the despotic King Charles, Crémieux helped to restore order. He supported the choosing of Louis-Philippe as king, and served as a deputy in

the National Assembly during his reign. Though Crémieux was on the side of the liberal revolutionaries in 1848, he helped the old king to escape from his palace and from the threatening mob.

Crémieux was named Minister of Justice in the next government. He helped Louis Napoleon, the general's nephew, to rise to power; when he saw the dictatorial ambitions of the man, he broke with him, and was imprisoned for a time. In 1870, Prussian troops defeated the French armies and took control

Louis Napoleon, nephew of the emperor, on his return from Germany in 1871.

Jews praying for the welfare of the state and for Louis Napoleon at the installation service for the Chief Rabbi of Paris.

of Paris, the capital city. Crémieux, though an old man, was head of the French government outside of Paris, trying to keep law and order in the provinces as the new republic came into being.

Freedom and Dignity

All freedoms were dear to Crémieux. He defended newspapers and their reporters at times of censorship, upholding a free press as the basis for a good society. He never took any fee for such cases.

Crémieux fought continually against capital punishment, which was imposed for even minor crimes. During his term as Minister of Justice, he was able to abolish the death penalty. He was also able to put through rulings that Jews and other minority groups, including Negroes, in the North African colonies, were citizens of France.

Upholding human dignity for all, Crémieux abolished the punishment of "public exhibition," when a convicted criminal was tied to a pillory in a public square to receive the insults of passersby. In all these campaigns he was true to Jewish tradition, which holds that human life is sacred; and that the human

dignity, even of a criminal, must be respected, "lest thy brother appear vile in thy sight."

Work for His People

With greatest zeal, Crémieux fought for his brethren, the household of Israel, appealing to the Czar of Russia, the Sultan of Turkey, and his own fellow-legislators when their rights were threatened. What are the faults of the Jews? he asked the anti-Semites of his own land, who accused the people of being crafty money-lenders, not engaging in useful work. They are "the vices which your persecution gave them, which have disappeared since the dignity of man has been restored to them."

It was Crémieux's concern not only to obtain rights for the Jews, but to be sure they were educated to use those rights well. "Schools! Increase the number of schools!" he exclaimed in a speech towards the end of his life. "Let all Jewish children, without exception, attend them! Jewish mothers who hear me, make your children understand the value of school. Tell them that education is life. Teach them that they must raise themselves to the level of their fellow citizens of other faiths, and that they must raise themselves to the highest ranks."

Crémieux delivered this talk at the celebration of his tenth anniversary as president

Library of the teachers' institute sponsored by the Alliance Israelite Universelle near Paris.

Schools supported by the Alliance in Beirut.

Elementary school in Jerusalem also supported by the Alliance.

of the Alliance Israelite Universelle. The aims of this international Jewish organization, which was founded after the tragedies of the Damascus and Mortara cases, were:

1. To work everywhere for the emancipation and spiritual progress of the Jews.
2. To lend effective aid to those who suffer because they are Jews.
3. To encourage all publications likely to lead to this result.

The Alliance established schools all over the Near East, the Balkans, and North Africa, including the first agricultural school in Palestine, and has helped Jewish refugees and victims of war and famine on many occasions. Crémieux, founder and moving spirit of the Alliance, gave great sums in its support for many years, as did Baron Maurice de Hirsch.

Servant of France

Crémieux's love for his fatherland was be-
yond question. "Jewish French citizens!" he proclaimed. "To France our boundless devotion, our unlimited love!" To some young Jews of North Africa he wrote in a letter: "As Jews, you are the first sons of God; as Frenchmen, you are the sons, the citizens of France. What a splendid position! What noble duties to fulfill!"

The words Crémieux had spoken at the funeral of Abbé Gregoire, the noble French churchman who had advocated Jewish rights during the Revolution, could also have been said of Crémieux, when he died at the age of 85 after a lifetime of fiery service in the cause of liberty:

"Freedom shall proclaim thee one of its most faithful servants."

Edmond De Rothschild

1845-1934

High in the hills of Galilee in the land of Israel grow the gardens of the *Nadiv*. To this beautiful spot come tourists from every land in the world, and busloads of children from nearby schools. The visitors look at the stone map which pictures the surrounding country-side; they raise their heads and look over the countryside itself, the cultivated fields and sturdy houses of the Galil, as far as the Great Sea. Then they walk through the gardens, under the overhanging branches of the carob trees, till they come to the stone building. Inside, in the cool cavern, they pause at the simple stone vault, the final resting-place of *Ha-Nadiv Ha-yadua*, "the well-known bene-factor," whose name no one needs to ask.

Everyone in Israel knows that the Nadiv, the "Benefactor," was Baron Edmond de Rothschild. Though he died in his home city of Paris in 1934, his coffin and that of his wife Adelheid were brought twenty years later to be enshrined in the gardens of Zikhron Yaakov.

Baron Edmond de Rothschild.

The Rothschild Family

The family of Rothschild has made its name known throughout the world. It has played a part in the growth of industry, the expansion of empires, and the whole history of modern Europe.

The founder of the family business and fortune was Mayer Amschel Rothschild, a dealer in second-hand goods in the crowded ghetto of Frankfurt in the eighteenth century. With a little experience in banking, and an interest in old and rare coins, pious Mayer Amschel was able to do some business with William, Prince of Hanau. Gradually the Prince gave over the care of his fortune to the able coin-dealer. Mayer Amschel became the agent in loans to other governments of

Mayer Amschel Rothschild.

A draft for a loan by Mayer Amschel Rothschild, now in the Frankfurt library.

The Rothschild family's original house in the ghetto of Frankfurt-am-Main.

the Near East. Parliament was closed and no official bank could lend the four million pounds needed. Disraeli was able to seize the chance by accepting the tremendous loan from Lionel Rothschild—with whom he was dining when the message arrived.

A Seat in the House of Commons

The Rothschild family was honored in Europe. Its members were given titles like Baron, and called by the aristocratic-sounding names of *von* Rothschild in Austria, *de* Rothschild in France. In England, where offi-

Solten von diesen schönen Münzen, welche um billige Preiße zu haben sind, und daraus verlangt werden, so beliebe man sich an den Eigenthümer zu addressiren, welcher noch mehr seltene Cabinets-Münzen, wie auch Antique-Seltenheiten und Alterthümer zu verkaufen hat.

Adresse

Mayer Amschel Rothschild

Hochfürstl. Hessen-Hanauischer Hof-Factor, wohnhaft in Frankfurt am Mayn.

Title-page of a Rothschild coin catalogue, 1770-1780, now in the Frankfurt library.

Europe, in helping rulers to redeem the losses of war. He began to earn his own fortune by investments and loans through all of Europe.

By the time the founder died in 1812, the five sons of the family had established headquarters in five important cities, Frankfurt, Vienna, Paris, Naples and London. They were able to carry on business involving large fortunes all over the world.

The English branch of the firm was one of the most active. On a Sunday evening in November of 1875, the Prime Minister of England, Disraeli, received a telegram that it might be possible to buy the Suez Canal from Egypt before France claimed it. Both countries wanted this strategic waterway in

cials were elected by democratic vote, Lionel, grandson of Mayer Amschel, was the first Jew elected to Parliament.

Twice Lionel Rothschild was elected by the City of London to a seat in the House of Commons. Twice he was told that a Jew could not take a seat. Determined to do so, Lionel entered the house of Parliament on a July day in 1850 and walked forward to take the oath of admission. The clerk rose with the usual book, the Christian Bible.

"I desire to be sworn on the Old Testament," said Lionel.

The House was in an uproar. After much debate, the members allowed the newcomer

Baron Lionel de Rothschild, in top hat, takes his seat in the House of Commons, 1858, as shown in a magazine drawing of the time.

to swear on his own Bible. The next day, however, he was required to take a second oath, ending with the words "upon the true faith of a Christian." This he refused to do. "Baron Lionel de Rothschild," announced the chairman, "you may withdraw."

Six times Lionel was reelected by the City of London. Each time he entered the House, walked towards the Table, and was ordered to leave. Violent arguments went on about the lawfulness of a Jew taking part in the government of England. The Liberals introduced a bill allowing the oath to be taken in a different form. It was passed in the Commons, but the House of Lords defeated it ten times.

Nathaniel Mayer Rothschild, first Jew to become a peer of England.

The eleventh time, the House of Lords passed the bill. Lionel again entered the House. He walked forward to the Table. With his head covered according to Jewish law, he took the oath in his own words and then went to his seat.

In 1885, thirty-five years after his father had first attempted to take his seat in the lower House, Nathaniel Mayer de Rothschild took the oath as a peer of England and a member of the House of Lords, with his head covered and with his own Hebrew Bible under his hand.

Philanthropy

It was not only in compelling respect for themselves that the Rothschild family helped

Chief Rabbi Nathan Marcus Adler, religious leader of English Jewry during the reign of Queen Victoria.

their people. The Rothschilds were, one and all, proudly Jewish. They refused to lend money to the czars, because of their anti-Semitic decrees. Certain cities on the continent were inspired to treat their Jews more fairly in order to gain credit with the firm. Philanthropists, often in secret, for every worthy humanitarian or cultural cause, they gave freely to Jewish causes. No one went away empty-handed from an interview with a Rothschild.

Memorial to Baron de Rothschild in Israel.

Rabbi Samuel Mohilever.

The greatest in philanthropy was Baron Edmond de Rothschild, the son of James, who had founded the House of Rothschild in Paris. He and his wife Adelheid, a cousin, were interested in art and culture. Their religion was very dear to them.

All the Rothschilds helped immigrant Jews, refugees who came to their countries from Eastern Europe. It was Edmond who chose to be more than a giver of temporary

Grand Rabbi Zadok Cahn of France.

charity; who tried to rebuild the lives of the Jews and give them new status in Palestine, the Land of Israel.

A Visitor Makes an Impression

One day in the fall of 1882, the chief rabbi of France brought a visitor to Baron Edmond's office. The Baron knew the visitor would ask for money; he knew that the vicious May Laws in Russia, crowding the Jews into small areas and preventing them from earning their living, had created many new refugees. He took out his check book and dipped his pen, prepared to give whatever was asked.

The stranger, however, would not let Rothschild give until he had spoken his message. For some time he held the attention of the multi-millionaire. It was this man, Rabbi Samuel Mohilever, founder of the Lovers of Zion in Poland, who spoke in Yiddish to Edmond de Rothschild, and persuaded him that the land of Palestine was the one place for the persecuted Jews of Eastern Europe.

The Zionist movement had not yet been organized. Though hope for the return to Zion was expressed daily in the prayers of millions of Jews, there were few who thought that Jewish settlers could redeem the land. Rabbi Mohilever was one of the few at that time who worked for the actual building of farm colonies in Palestine. He came now to

Conference of the Hovevei Zion in Odessa, 1890.

gain Rothschild's help, as he had gone also to Baron Maurice de Hirsch, to save the struggling farm settlements of northern Palestine.

He spoke so well that Edmond de Rothschild, instead of giving a few thousand francs to the old gentleman and then forgetting him, became a lifelong supporter of Jewish colonization in Palestine. It was his money that saved the early settlements of Rosh Pinah, Petah Tikvah, Rishon le Zion, Zikhron Yaakov; and that founded Tel Hai and Kfar Gileadi.

Saving the Settlements

The pioneer settlers from Eastern Europe had known nothing of farming, even in the Russian climate. In the less temperate land of Israel, where the neglect of centuries had left deserts and swamps, they could hardly scratch any crops from the soil. Plagued by malaria, malnutrition and thirst, many died; many gave up the struggle and moved to cities or left the land. As yet the Jewish world as a whole had not risen to the support of their efforts.

Rothschild's first contribution saved the colonies from bankruptcy. The settlers did not know who had given it. The name they were told was *"Ha-Nadiv Ha-yadua."* Like his relatives, Edmond did not want his name to be used. "Publicity is a very dangerous thing," he had said. "Great things can best be done in private."

His name, however, was soon guessed. Who else but a Rothschild, one settler asked another, could give so lavishly?

It was the money of the Nadiv that provided experts and equipment to help the settlers to drain swamps, to develop irrigation, to plant vineyards and to build wine-cellars. During the forty years of his life that remained, he gave in excess of fifty million dollars to the farm colonies of the Palestine.

The Reward of Giving

At his first visit to the land, in 1887, Edmond de Rothschild could see the results of his giving, in secure villages with well-constructed housing and good water supplies. This visit and four later ones were made on his private yacht, which had a kosher kitchen and a synagogue; every door had a *mezuzah*.

In Palestine this fabulously wealthy man went about inspecting factories and cowsheds, fertilizer storehouses and irrigation ditches. Everywhere he was met by settlers who came miles to see him. Children offered him flowers and sang to him. The Nadiv could not remain anonymous.

A view of Petah Tikvah, early agricultural colony.

Coat of arms adopted by the Rothschild family in 1817.

The Nadiv, like all Rothschilds, had a mind of his own. It was his idea to encourage grape-growing and the making of wine in the colonies. His experts told the people what to do. When the culture of the vine did not prove profitable, he bought up the crop himself, year after year, at a higher price than the market would give.

He gave money for archeological expeditions, to dig up famous Bible sites. He helped form the Palestine Electric Corporation, the Nesher Cement works, the Palestine Salt Company; and started the planting of tobacco, almonds, and other crops.

The People Take Over

The fact that he was giving charity was brought home to Baron de Rothschild many times. Zionist thinkers, notably Ahad Ha-am, criticized him for making the colonists dependent upon him, instead of letting them decide on their own way of life and stand on their own feet. It was the Jewish people who should support the settlement of Palestine, not a few generous millionaires.

By the year 1900, the Baron handed over the care of the colonies to the Jewish Colonization Association, a group directed by Jews of England, Germany and Belgium, which had been founded by Baron de Hirsch to settle Jews in new lands. Baron Rothschild's funds and interests were later transferred to PICA, the Palestine Jewish Colonization Association; and then to the State of Israel when it was founded in 1948.

It was better, Baron Rothschild knew, for a group or a country to take care of its own problems. However, when the Baron first came to the aid of the settlements, there were no funds and no supporters. All would have been lost and would have had to be started again.

The Interest Continues

Other Rothschilds have also given support to Palestine, and, since its founding, to projects in the state of Israel. A Rothschild group, including Edmond's son, has financed archeological "digs," developed modern Caesarea, paid for the *Knesset* building in Jerusalem center, and given generously to the Weizmann Institute of Science.

None of the Rothschilds have called themselves Zionists. They did not directly support

The Jewish Agency building in Jerusalem.

Theodor Herzl and his political activities leading towards a state. Their interest was in helping Jews who had settled in the Land of Israel. Yet there was surely, on the part of Edmond, and probably on the part of others in the family as well, a special devotion to Israel that grew out of their Jewish pride. Tears filled Edmond's eyes when he saw the Western Wall, all that remains of the ancient Temple. In Tel Aviv he said sadly, "Never before did I regret so much as now that I cannot speak Hebrew."

Branches of the Rothschild family still live and still enjoy their wealth and position in France, in England, and in America. Various Rothschild estates, such as the unused one in Vienna, have been turned into government residences, museums, and public parks. Of Baron Edmond's holdings, twenty thousand engravings from his art collection are displayed at the Louvre, greatest art museum of France. His home at Number 41, rue de Faubourg St. Honore in Paris, is now the United States Embassy.

Rothschild contributions still go out to thousands of endeavors, from hospitals to modern dance troupes. The family's business of international finance is carried on with dignity and with never-failing profits.

Of all the family of the Rothschilds, with all their wealth, none has created a more lasting monument than Baron Edmond de Rothschild's, on the soil of Israel.

SELECTIONS FROM JEWISH HUMANITARIANS

With God's blessing: Rise, say prayers at 7 o'clock. Breakfast at 9. Attend the Stock Exchange, if in London, at 10. Dinner 5. Read, write and learn, if possible, Hebrew and French, 6. Read Bible and say prayers, 10. Then retire.

Monday and Thursday mornings attend the Synagogue. Tuesday and Thursday evenings for visiting.

* * *

I shall, please Heaven, on my return to England, form a company for the cultivation of the land and the encouragement of our brethren in Europe to return to Palestine. Many Jews now emigrate to New South Wales, Canada, etc., but in the Holy Land they would find a greater certainty of success; here they will find wells already dug, olives and vines already planted. By degrees I hope to induce the return of thousands of our brethren to the Land of Israel. I am sure they would be happy in the enjoyment of the observance of our holy religion, in a manner which is impossible in Europe.

* * *

I have great cause for thankfulness. Since I was here in November last, I hope that, by divine blessing, I have been of some use to my fellow-creatures, both Jews and Christians, and, I believe I may add, Moors. To God alone, who helped and sustained me, be honour and glory. I believe that my dear Judith would have approved my conduct and, sure am I, had it pleased an all-wise Providence to have spared her, she would have shared my fatigue and dangers, but it was otherwise ordained, and I can only submit with humble spirit to the decree of Heaven.

Diary excerpt, 1864.

MOSES MONTEFIORE

On lighting the candles in the evening with my mother, according to her wish and what is taught us, I experienced a new sensation of devotion and solicitude to act right. I trust that God Almighty will direct us to perform that which is most pleasing to Him. I do not know any circumstances more pleasing to me than to perceive that my dear Monte is religiously inclined. It is that sort of religion which he possesses that in my opinion is most essential—a fellow-feeling and benevolence.

Diary excerpt, 1812, two days after marriage.

*   *   *

What the feelings of a traveller are, when among the mountains on which the awful power of the Almighty once visibly rested, and when approaching the city where he placed his name; whence his law was to go forth to all the world; where the beauty of holiness shone in its morning splendour; and to which, even in its sorrow and captivity, even in its desolation, the very Gentiles, the people of all nations of the earth, as well as its own children, look with profound awe and admiration—Oh! what the feelings of the traveller are on such a spot!

On approaching Jerusalem.

JUDITH MONTEFIORE

Gentlemen, all the liberties are sisters, and all persecutions walk hand in hand. Persecute, and you create slaves; proclaim equality for all, and you create citizens.

*   *   *

I fulfilled my duty . . . I defended my own hearth, and the principle of freedom of worship, a great and noble principle which joins heaven to earth in allowing each man to offer God the homage of his love according to his faith. I took pen in hand when slander cast venom against the Jewish religion. I called to my aid all the sympathies of noble men. But I felt within myself the strength of right, and strength of spirit: would not my silence have been shameful cowardice?

*   *   *

Believe it, this world is governed by an admirable Power, The Creator and Protector of this vast universe. And why not tell you all my thought? God, who sees all, who presides over all, extends His protection here below to the mortal man who does good on earth, and He rewards in Heaven his immortal soul. Yes, God and the immortality of the soul, this is my religion.

ADOLPHE ISAAC CREMIEUX

UNIT IV

BUILDERS OF ZION

"Next year in Jerusalem!"

For centuries this wish has been expressed by Jews twice a year, at the end of the Passover Seder and at the close of the Yom Kippur fast. In the dark days of exile, in every country of their dispersion, the hope of return to their own land of Israel kept the Jews from despair. They prayed three times daily for the gathering of the scattered children of Israel, for the rebuilding of the Temple and for the return of God's presence to Zion.

Roman conquests in the years 70 and 135 exiled many Jews from their land. From the fourth century on, Christian influence made life difficult for those Jews who remained. Later, Moslem overlords controlled the land, until the Crusades brought war and a new period of Christian rule. Moslem armies eventually drove out the European invaders.

Theodor Herzl.

The castles built by the Crusaders, like much of the land around them, fell into disuse and decay.

Through the centuries, in small groups in Safed, in Tiberias, in Hebron, in occasional villages such as Pekiin (which is said to have had a Jewish settlement ever since the first Exile), some Jews continued to live in Palestine.

During every age, a few brave travelers and pious pilgrims returned, finding the land for the most part desolate and despoiled. Heroes of faith such as Judah Ha-Levi and Moses Maimonides crossed the Mediterranean to seek the stony hillsides of their ancestors. Refugees from persecution in Europe made numerous attempts to reach Palestine. Some were successful, while many failed in the difficult journey.

Following the exile from Spain in 1492, a notable group of scholars made their home in the city of Safed, studying Kabbalah in the Holy Land. A large immigration of Hasidim around the year 1800 was followed by smaller groups from time to time, during the next two centuries.

Palestine in Modern Times

In the year 1841 Syria and Palestine came under the rule of the Ottoman or Turkish Empire. The Sultan, who ruled from Constantinople, the capital city, had little control over his far-flung territories, where local sheiks tried to keep their own power. The slow-moving methods of Near Eastern governments, with a tradition of graft and bribery, did nothing to build up the land of the Bible.

Centuries of neglect, the wars of the Crusades, and the grazing of Arab flocks, had destroyed trees and left the land of Israel desolate. Once life-giving springs of water had spread to form swamps breeding malaria-carrying mosquitoes. Hills which had borne vineyards now showed only the stones of ancient terracing. The greater part of the land, both north and south, was rocky and barren.

About thirty thousand Jews lived in Palestine in the year 1881. A small number lived in farm colonies. Most of the Jews lived piously but in poverty in crowded sections of Jerusalem, Jaffa, Hebron, Safed and Tiberias. They had neither the ability nor the desire to become farmers, to go out and build up the country.

Since talmudic times, Jews of the world had been happy to send money to maintain scholars in the holy cities. *Halukkah*, or distribution of charity, supported many of the Jews of Palestine in the nineteenth century. In every pious Jewish home of Eastern Europe stood a coin-box into which the mother of the family would put her small contribution on Friday afternoon before lighting candles for Shabbat. Special messengers would come each year from Palestine to collect the funds. These *meshulahim* would be eagerly welcomed and asked for news. "How goes it with our brothers in our land?"

Unrest in Russia

The year 1881 is an important one from

Early halutzim ploughing in a Palestinian farm settlement.

which to reckon not only developments in the land of Israel but also the growth of Jewish

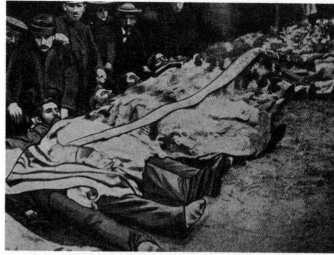

Victims of anti-Jewish pogroms in Russia.

communities in America and all over the western world. In that year, Czar Alexander II was assassinated by a revolutionary group. Unrest spread through Russia. Newspapers began to print articles against the Jews, and pogroms—riots and attacks against Jews and their property in hundreds of Russian towns —followed. The police did nothing to help, and the rioters believed that the government was with them.

Finally, order was restored. The new czar, Alexander III, was ashamed of the image the world had gained of his country. Investigations, however, blamed the Jews for the hatred they had aroused. In May of 1882, under the influence of advisers who believed in one unified Russia with one religion (Russian Orthodox), Alexander passed laws restricting Jewish life.

Known as the May Laws, the new decrees provided that Jews could not buy property, or renew leases; could not keep their stores open on Sunday to make up for the loss of income they sustained in keeping their own Sabbath; could not live on farms or outside towns; could not visit another city, or move to a new home, or remain in their old homes unless they had been specially registered. Jews were expelled from Moscow, from all border areas, and from several provinces.

For years enemies of the Jews had said they should become farmers, or artisans, or professional men, instead of tradesmen as so many of them were. Now all these jobs were closed to them. Jewish farmers and craftsmen were forced to leave the farms and towns where they worked. The number of Jews to be admitted to military academies or to universities was restricted to a tiny percentage.

Already struggling to make a living, and dismayed by the pogroms, the Jews under Russian rule now found life nearly impossible.

Governments of the world protested. A meeting called by the Lord Mayor of London sent a message to the Czar, deploring "the renewed sufferings of the Jews in Russia," and reminding him that "religious liberty is a principle which should be recognized by every Christian community as among the natural human rights."

The Czar claimed that Jews were likely to join revolutionary movements. Cardinal Manning of England wrote: "How can citizens who are denied the right of naturalization be patriotic? How shall a homeless and exiled race love the land which disowns them?"

Jewish leaders, such as Baron Horace Gunzburg, head of the Jewish community of St. Petersburg, and the great Rabbi Isaac Elhanan Spektor of Kovno, appealed for their people. A government commission was set up to discuss the "Jewish problem." The rabbi defended Judaism and the Talmud from vicious charges made by the Russian members. He spoke of efforts to educate and spread "enlightenment" among the Jews. The Commission, however, had no effect in improving conditions for the five million Jews under Russian rule.

Jewish political prisoners from Bialystok in Siberia, 1897, with their Russian guards.

Exodus from Eastern Europe

The Jews began to leave Russia in large numbers. Without funds or any knowledge of the western world, they fled across the border. They wanted to go to free lands where they knew fellow-Jews had already settled. They longed for life where there was a promise of freedom for them and education for their children.

The Alliance Israélite Universelle sent representatives to the border city of Brody, where thousands of refugees gathered daily. Funds of the Alliance and of relief committees everywhere, often supported by Christians as well as Jews, were collected to help the travelers.

Baron Maurice de Hirsch was a great benefactor at this time. He established the Jewish Colonization Association with a grant of ten million dollars (which grew to forty million) "to assist and promote the emigration of Jews from any parts of Europe or Asia, and principally from countries in which they may for the time being be subjected to any special taxes or political or other disabilities, to any other parts of the world, and to form and establish colonies in various parts of North and South America and other countries for agricultural, commercial, and other purposes." The ICA particularly encouraged settlement in Argentina.

Many Jews went to England, South Africa

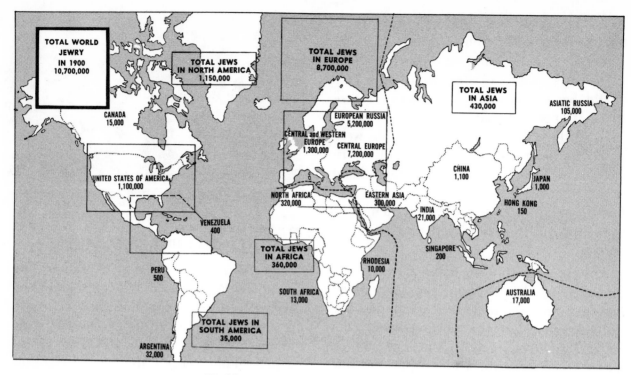

World Jewish population in the year 1900.

and Canada. The greatest number, however, went to the United States. From the year 1880 to the year 1920, two and a half million Jews entered the land of liberty. The majority settled in the cities of the eastern seaboard, the largest number by far in New York.

America was free and wealthy, a land of opportunity. It is no wonder that it seemed "the golden land" to the Russian refugees. Tiny Palestine was neither free nor wealthy, and the Turkish sultan did not welcome immigrants. Yet, in the year 1882, seven thousand Jews from Eastern Europe entered Palestine. The modern *Aliyah*, the "going-up to the land of Zion," had begun.

Preparing the Way

The modern Zionist movement, devoted to restoring the land of Israel to the people of Israel, grew up in the nineteenth century. Nationalism was a strong force among all nations at that time. Germans, Frenchmen,

Italian, Russians—each group became proud of its national traditions, trying to unify and build up its nation. The Jews also loved their native lands, often trying to give up their own differences so as to be like the majority group. They found, to their heartbreak, that the strongest nationalists wished to exclude the Jews among them from the rights of citizenship. The Jews were considered by many to be outsiders, foreigners, no matter how many generations their families had lived in the land. Anti-Semitism grew all over Europe.

One of the first who said that the Jews must reestablish their own nation was Moses Hess (1812-1875). In his book *Rome and Jerusalem,* printed in 1862, he wrote that every people that can make a contribution to the world should be allowed to live and fulfil itself. Christian culture is represented by Rome. Jewish culture, in order to flourish, should establish itself once. more in Jerusalem. Hess hoped that liberal France would help build Palestine into a Jewish homeland.

Rabbi Zvi Hirsch Kalischer (1795-1874) believed that the Jews should start the work of settling the land of Israel immediately, when the need was so great. In his book *Derishat Tzion (Seeking Zion)* he urged the founding of agricultural colonies. It was partly his influence that made the Alliance Israélite found the colony of Mikveh Israel in 1869.

The Hebrew author Peretz Smolenskin (1842-1885) was a strong believer in Jewish education and culture. He did not see value in the Jews trying to excel in the culture of other nations; he felt they should appreciate and strengthen their own great intellectual heritage. Jewish ideas would then enrich the world, and the Jews would have proper pride in themselves as a people.

Peretz Smolenskin.

Christian Friends of Zion

The idea of a Jewish return to Zion was popular among many Christians, especially those who loved the Bible. Lawrence Oliphant was an Englishman who visited Palestine and spent much effort trying to persuade the Sultan to allow Jewish settlement. Other Englishmen were moved not so much by the words of the Prophets, foretelling the return of Israel, as they were by political considerations. They wished to see Palestine ruled by a friendly people rather than by the Turks, so that England could keep up its shipping and other interests in the Near East.

The novelist George Eliot (pen-name of Mary Ann Evans) glorified the hope of return to Zion in her book *Daniel Deronda,* published in 1876. Her character Mordecai speaks these words: "Our dispersed people in all the ends of the earth may share the dignity of a national life which has a voice among the people of the East and the West. Our race shall have an organic center, a heart and brain to watch and guide; the outraged Jew shall have a defence in the court of nations. I seek nothing for the Jewish nation but the good which promises good to all nations. Our national life was a glowing light. Let the central fire be kindled again, and the light will reach afar."

Lovers of Zion

Rabbi Kalischer had inspired many young people to work for the revival of Jewish culture and national feeling. In many towns of Eastern Europe groups of Jews calling themselves *Hoveve Zion,* "Lovers of Zion," came into being. Rabbi Samuel Mohilever (1824-1898) founded the first of these groups in Warsaw in 1881.

The pogroms and the May Laws inspired a physician of Odessa, Leon Pinsker (1821-1891), to change his earlier idea that Jews

Dr. Leon Pinsker.

The original group of Bilu pioneers, in their later years.

could assimilate into Russian society. He now saw that Russia would not accept the Jews, and that no government would give them freedom and status. In a stirring essay called *Auto-Emancipation,* he declared that only through gaining self-respect could the Jews earn the respect of others.

Inspired by Dr. Pinsker's call, and by the terrible situation in Russia, the members of Hoveve Zion met for an international conference in the German city of Katowitz in 1884. They sent greetings to Moses Montefiore on his hundredth birthday, hoping for his support, and gained encouragement from the Alliance and Baron de Rothschild. The idea of returning to build up a Jewish homeland was becoming a living force.

The Bilu-im

Of the seven thousand Jews who entered Palestine in 1882, few really thought about rebuilding a Jewish nation. Most went to settle in the cities. The most idealistic group, the one that became a legend to inspire future *halutzim,* pioneers on the land, was the *Bilu.*

Twenty university students, out of a much larger group that had started out, arrived in Palestine from the city of Kharkov in Russia. They took their name from the initial letters of their motto: *Bet Yaakov, l'khu v'nelkha,* "House of Jacob, come, let us go!"

Their hope was to set an example for other Jews all over the world. They were to become cooperative farmers on the soil of Palestine. On their way, they sent out a Hebrew message to their fellow Jews. It read in part: "We want a home in our country, at least as a state within a larger state. We hope that everyone, rich and poor, will give his best labors to the holy cause. Hear, O Israel, the Lord our God, the Lord is one, and our land, Zion, is our only hope."

Unskilled in farming, the new young colonists faced a long struggle. They survived only through help from funds set up by Montefiore and Rothschild. They had gone before the Zionist movement was organized; before the Jews of the world would support their efforts. They are remembered as the

Halutzim reaping a harvest.

first *halutzim*, true pioneers whose example was to inspire thousands more.

Theodor Herzl

The ideal of rebuilding the land of Israel was already cherished by Jews in every land, especially those in Eastern Europe. The creation of political Zionism, the actual effort to establish a Jewish self-governing nation, however, was largely the work of one man, Theodor Herzl (1860-1904).

A popular reporter and writer in Vienna, knowing nothing of the ideas already held by Jews of the eastern lands, Herzl at the age of thirty-five was fired with the thought that the Jews must have a state of their own. The anti-Semitism he saw in France at the time of the Dreyfus Affair helped convince him. He put forth his ideas in a book called *Der Judenstaat (The Jewish State)*.

With tremendous determination, Herzl carried his dream forward. In answer to his call, the first Zionist Congress, with delegates from all over the world, met at Basel, Switzerland,

in 1897 and proclaimed: "Zionism seeks to establish for the Jewish people a publicly recognized, legally secured home in Palestine."

Zionism became an organized movement throughout the world. The Jewish National Fund was set up to purchase land in Palestine, paid for and belonging to the whole Jewish people.

Though he spoke to the Kaiser and the Sultan, and impressed officials of England and other countries, Herzl did not see any political results before his early death. He had, however, united Jewish efforts for the Zionist cause throughout the world.

Zionist Viewpoints

Many who worked for Zionism had different points of view. The noted writer Asher Ginzberg (1856-1927), whose pen name was Ahad Ha-Am ("One of the people"), called to the Jews to revive the spirit of Judaism before reviving the land of Israel. He founded *B'nei Moshe*, a group of leaders of Hoveve Zion whose knowledge and ideals made them work for a Zionism with cultural as well as political aims. They hoped that the restored

Theodor Herzl speaking to Kaiser Wilhelm II on the road to Jerusalem.

land would be the cultural center of a renewed Jewish people.

Most Reform Jews opposed Zionism because they believed Jews had a mission to spread their beliefs throughout the world, not to become once more a separate nation. There were Orthodox Jews who objected to the attempt to restore Zion by human means before the coming of the Messiah.

Most Orthodox Jews, however, had been in sympathy with Zionism for many years. Rabbi Isaac Jacob Reines and other disciples of Mohilever organized the Religious Zionists, called Mizrachi, in 1901. The name is an abbreviation of *Merkaz Ruhani*, "Spiritual Center," for they wished the coming Jewish state to be ruled by Jewish religious law.

"Mizrachi" also means "To the East," for Jews through the ages faced eastward in prayer, to direct their thoughts toward Jerusalem.

There were some, Jews by birth, who opposed Zionism because they were in favor of assimilation, becoming part of the people around them. Others, like the historian Simon Dubnow, felt that in the diaspora Jewish communities could survive as they had for so many years, with new ones taking the place of those that died out. There were some Jews, particularly among the well-to-do in western countries, who above all else wanted to be accepted by their own countrymen as full citizens. They were embarrassed and disturbed by the idea that a Jew was supposed to have ties to any other land.

Among Russian Jewish thinkers, there were some who were socialists. Russia was a police state, ruled by an absolute monarch, the czar. Only a small number of aristocrats and men of wealth enjoyed power and privilege. The majority of the people lived in poverty and with no hope for the future. The socialists, many of whom were followers of Karl Marx, wished to change society. They worked for a revolution to overthrow the

Ahad Ha-Am, philosopher of Zionism and Jewish rebirth.

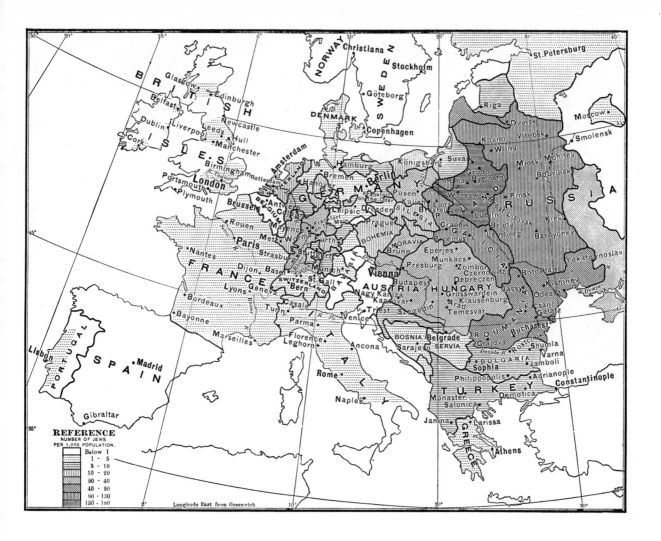

Map showing the comparative density of Jewish population per 1000 in Europe, 1900.

government. It was their goal to have the state own all the wealth, and for all the people to receive equal income for their work. Like Marx, these socialists were against religion and did not believe in working for any Jewish causes.

There were those, however, who believed in Zionism as well as in some of the socialist ideals. They wished to build Palestine as a state based on the dignity of labor, where all would share equally. Nahman Syrkin (1867-1924) and Ber Borochov (1881-1917) organized the Labor Zionist party, *Poale Zion,* in

1901. An outstanding leader was A. D. Gordon (1856-1922), who demonstrated his belief in the "religion of labor" by becoming, after a life of comparative ease in Russia, a farm worker in Palestine at the age of forty-eight.

Gordon was part of what was called the Second Aliyah, the second large wave of immigration to the land of Israel in modern times. Pogroms took place in Kishinev and in Homel in 1903. An attempted revolution against the czar was cruelly put down in 1905. These events and the hardships they brought

Aaron David Gordon, prophet of labor.

Members of a Zionist group preparing to go to Palestine. In the center is young David Ben Gurion.

caused many Jews to leave Russia. Among other idealistic Zionists who went to Palestine during this Aliyah were David Ben-Gurion, later to be first Prime Minister, and Izhak Ben Zvi, later to be President, of the State of Israel.

World War and Revolution

The year 1914 marked the beginning of World War I. This war, which brought destruction to so much of Europe, caused untold suffering to the Jews of Eastern Europe. Russian and German armies battled back and forth across the territories where the greatest number of Jews of the world lived. Intense nationalism and hatred for aliens, easily stirred up in time of war, brought about an increase in anti-Semitism.

In 1917, in the midst of World War I, the Russian Revolution broke out. The czar's government was overthrown. At first the Mensheviks, the moderate socialists, took over.

The Bolsheviks, more violent in their aims, fought against them. The Jews of Russia were the greatest sufferers in the civil war, famine and oppression which followed.

Meanwhile, over 600 Jews from Russia, Palestine and other lands led by Joseph Trumpeldor (1880-1920) and Vladimir Zev Jabotinsky (1880-1940), formed the Zion Mule Corps and the Jewish Legion which fought bravely against Turkey. The Ottoman Empire, together with the great powers of Germany and Austria-Hungary, fought against the Allies which included England, France, Russia and the United States. The

The 39th Battalion, in which Jews fought for the liberation of Palestine under British command during World War I, camped outside Jerusalem.

Joseph Trumpeldor, hero of Jewish defense, who fell at Tel Hai under Arab attack.

An ardent worker for Zionism in England was Chaim Weizmann (1874-1952), a Russian-born Jew who had become a loyal British citizen. As a brilliant chemist, he had helped develop explosives for the English navy. His influence with members of the War Cabinet, and the urging of American officials, including the leading American Zionist, Justice of the Supreme Court Louis D. Brandeis (1856-1941), helped to bring about a declaration in favor of Zionism.

On November 2, 1917, Arthur James Balfour, British foreign secretary, issued a letter beginning with the words: "His Majesty's Government view with favor the establishment in Palestine of a national home for the Jewish people."

Great rejoicing on the part of Jews all over the world greeted the declaration. Large numbers resolved to leave the exile and return to the homeland. Even Jews who were not interested in an actual Jewish state now became more interested in developing Palestine as a cultural center and as a refuge for

Central Powers headed by Germany were finally defeated.

The Balfour Declaration

While war was still raging, statesmen of Great Britain were discussing how to distribute the territories of the Central Powers after victory. They planned to break up the Ottoman Empire. The territory of Palestine was important because it was close to the Suez Canal and could be a base to safeguard British interests in the whole Near East.

Many English leaders felt that supporting the Zionist cause would be a wise move. Under British control, Jewish settlers could be counted on to remain friendly and keep the land well-governed.

Justice of the Supreme Court Louis Dembitz Brandeis, outstanding American jurist and dedicated Zionist.

persecuted brethren. These "non-Zionists" included many philanthropists in America and England, such as Louis Marshall, Jacob Schiff and Lord Edmund Rothschild.

Under the British Mandate

After the war, as had been planned, territories that had belonged to defeated Germany and Turkey were distributed among the victorious nations. The new League of Nations gave England the Mandate, or temporary rule over Palestine. England's task was to be to protect the country, to build it up, to encourage immigration, to aid in setting up the forms of government, and eventually to allow its independence.

The British had control of all national affairs, such as defense, police, money and

Lord Balfour, British Foreign Secretary.

DOCUMENT 1.
THE BALFOUR DECLARATION.

Foreign Office,
November 2nd, 1917.

Dear Lord Rothschild,

I have much pleasure in conveying to you, on behalf of His Majesty's Government, the following declaration of sympathy with Jewish Zionist aspirations which has been submitted to, and approved by, the Cabinet.

"His Majesty's Government view with favour the establishment in Palestine of a national home for the Jewish people, and will use their best endeavours to facilitate the achievement of this object, it being clearly understood that nothing shall be done which may prejudice the civil and religious rights of existing non-Jewish communities in Palestine, or the rights and political status enjoyed by Jews in any other country"

I should be grateful if you would bring this declaration to the knowledge of the Zionist Federation.

The Balfour Declaration in full.

post office administration, control of trade and immigration. The *Yishuv,* or Jewish community of Palestine, established its own inner government as far as it was able to do so. It set up schools, hospitals and welfare institutions, built colonies, and developed industry and transportation.

Representatives of the Yishuv, democratically elected, took care of many of the duties the government and legislature of a free country would ordinarily assume. Thus, leading figures of the Yishuv such as David Ben-Gurion, Izhak Ben Zvi, Moshe Sharett and Golda Meir, were later able to take over the reins of the Israeli government without hesitation.

The Jewish National Fund, headed by

David Ben Gurion in the Jewish Legion.

Menahem Ussishkin (1863-1941), and the Palestine Foundation Fund bought land and invested in projects to develop the country. Funds were collected from Jews all over the world.

The Jewish Agency, set up in 1929, helped and trained Jews everywhere, and coordinated all aid to immigration into Palestine. It was the spokesman for world Zionism until the establishment of the State of Israel. With the encouragement of the Israeli government, and supported by the United Jewish Appeal, it has continued its overseas work and its help to new immigrants.

The Culture of the Yishuv

The culture of the Yishuv, strengthened by increasing immigration, proved to be on a high level. The most amazing development, according to many historians, was the bringing back of Hebrew as a modern language, after it had been used primarily for prayer and study for nearly two thousand years. The most important fashioner of this miracle of revival was the compiler of a new dictionary, Eliezer Ben Yehudah (1858-1922), who insisted on speaking Hebrew with his family even when it meant he had to invent new words to describe such modern things as railroads and telephones.

Leading Jewish poets and thinkers such as Hayyim Nahman Bialik (1873-1934) and Ahad Ha-Am settled in the growing country. Many professional men of Europe became farmers and builders in Palestine.

Nazi persecution, beginning with Hitler's coming into power in Germany in 1933, caused outstanding German Jewish scientists, doctors, lawyers and other intellectuals to flee to Palestine. World-renowned professors such as Martin Buber (1878-1965) were added to the already brilliant faculty of the Hebrew University in Jerusalem. Under its first president, Dr. Judah Magnes (1877-1948), the university quickly became one of the leading institutions of learning in the world.

Together with Hadassah, the women's

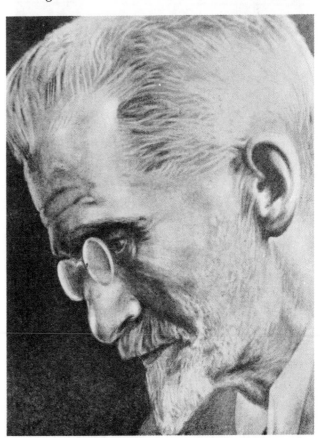

Eliezer Ben Yehudah, father of modern Hebrew.

Scientists at work at Rehovot.

Zionist organization founded by Henrietta Szold, the university sponsored a great hospital and medical school.

In Rehovot, the scientific research institute established in honor of Chaim Weizmann (who also was its first director) conducted studies in all branches of modern science. In Haifa, the Technion became the leading engineering school in the Near East.

Riots and Retractions

The task of building the land, of draining swamps, irrigating fields, conquering disease, educating newcomers, building roads and factories and cities was a tremendous one. Jews paid high prices for whatever land they purchased from Arab families. They brought in modern farm machinery, books and newspapers, health services, good schools and higher wages. Jewish settlers brought to the Arabs of Palestine more freedom, better education, and a higher standard of living than enjoyed by their fellow Arabs in any countries of the Near East.

Some of the Arab landowners began to fear the changes which the Jews were bringing into the land. In a modern democratic country the Arab sheik could not keep his power or his old way of life. Some Arab leaders were able to arouse their followers with the claim that the Jews were taking away their country and would destroy the holy places of Islam. Time after time they succeeded in inciting riots against the Jewish settlers.

British officials and police often did little to stop the riots. Indeed, Jews who fought back were often arrested; and farm colonies were searched to make sure that the Jews were not able to store weapons for self-defense. In the countries of the Near East, in all the lands around Palestine, some fifty million Arab Moslems dwelt. England was not so anxious to protect the rights of a few hundred thousand Jews as she was to appease the Arab world.

Bit by bit, the British administrators began to back away from the promises of the Balfour Declaration and the Mandate. In decrees called White Papers, issued by the British government, the number of Jews allowed to enter the land was cut down. Arab leaders, in particular the Mufti of Jerusalem, demanded that the Jews be prevented from ever becoming a majority in Palestine.

The most tragic result was that at the time Hitler was taking over Europe, Jews who might have escaped to Palestine were forbidden to do so. Still, great numbers of Jewish refugees managed to reach Palestine. The *Haganah,* underground army of the Yishuv, and indeed all Jews, did all they could to help the so-called "illegal" immigrants to enter

An illegal ship filled with immigrants seeking to enter Palestine.

the land. In 1939, just when the Jews of Europe were being sent to concentration camps where six million were murdered, Great Britain issued a new White Paper which ruled that during the next year Jewish immigration was to be completely stopped.

Leaky ships packed with refugees who, in the midst of war, had traveled for months to come within sight of the shores of Palestine, were actually turned away to sink or be destroyed on the high seas.

News of the Holocaust

The terrible events of the years of World War II in Europe were hardly believed when they came to the world's notice in 1945, after the defeat of Germany. The fortified walls, barracks, gas-chambers and furnaces of the concentration camps stood as evidence of six million Jews who had been systematically herded together, humiliated, tortured, and put to death. Survivors who looked like living skeletons came forth from the camps to tell the story. The insanity of Nazi hatred had brought about the greatest and most ruthless slaughter in human history.

When asked where they wished to go, the survivors of the holocaust had one answer:

Jewish displaced persons in a makeshift shelter on the island of Cyprus.

"To Palestine." Yet England still refused to allow immigration. Members of the Haganah and volunteers from every nation, inflamed at this injustice, set about to help the "Displaced Persons" of Europe to break through the British navy's blockade and enter the Promised Land.

Many ships were stopped within sight of the port of Haifa, and were forced to proceed to the island of Cyprus. There the passengers, who had barely escaped death in the Nazi concentration camps, found themselves again imprisoned behind barbed wire.

The Partition Plan

The conscience of the world, which had done so little to help the Nazi victims, began to be aroused. England was criticized and, in answer, offered to set up committees to "investigate" the situation. Members of the Yishuv, who had controlled themselves for so long and had fought bravely on England's side during the war, now refused to submit to British decrees. Small terrorist groups, defying the authority of the elected representatives of the Yishuv, began to harass British troops and bomb their installations in Palestine.

Finally, England had to agree to let the question of Palestine come before the United Nations. It had been suggested before that the land might be divided, part of it to be a Jewish and part an Arab state. The Jewish Agency Executive, headed by Chaim Weizmann, the Zionist Organization of America, and the majority of the people of the Yishuv expressed their willingness to go along with the Partition Plan. Though it provided only for a small Jewish state, it would finally be a fulfilment of the desperate hopes of the Jewish people.

On November 29, 1947, the Partition Plan creating an independent Jewish state was approved by the United Nations Assembly. There was joy and dancing in the streets of Tel Aviv and New York. The British prepared to leave Palestine, the people of the Yishuv prepared to take over their own government, and the Arabs began to attack the Jews.

The State Emerges

Daily, Arab military action against Jews increased. As the British vacated fortified sta-

The complete Declaration of Independence of the State of Israel, issued May 14, 1948, the fifth day of Iyar 5708.

Secretary General Trygve Lie of the United Nations (left) checks the vote of the General Assembly delegates on the Palestine Partition question on November 29, 1947. Dr. Oswald Aranha of Brazil, president of the Assembly, awaits their verdict on the crucial vote which was 33 to 13 to set up independent Jewish and Arab states in Palestine. From the Zionist Archives.

The Arabs refused to admit that Israel was there to stay. They continued to boast for many years that they would destroy the Jewish state. Fear of Israel's strength, proved again in 1956 during the Sinai campaign, have kept them from a full-scale attempt to fulfil their threat. And, to this day, the Arab states refuse to sign a peace treaty with Israel.

But a true Jewish state now exists, one that has welcomed a million more immigrants in the first ten years of its existence. The tiny country stands as the fulfilment of the dreams and hopes of two thousand years.

A soldier of Israel.

tions they would turn them over to the Arabs. The armies of the surrounding Arab nations mobilized at the borders. Most of the world thought the new state would never come into being.

On May 14, 1948, as the British Mandate ended, the new State of Israel was declared. David Ben-Gurion was elected prime minister by the Provisional Council, and Chaim Weizmann was named president.

Full-scale war immediately broke out. The armies of Egypt, Iraq, Jordan, Saudi Arabia, Syria and Lebanon all took part. Arab radio announcers urged the half-million Arabs in Israel to leave the country so that the Jews might be totally destroyed. Then, said the announcers, the Arabs would return to take over.

Secretly trained, poorly armed, but fired with idealism and courage, the young fighters of Israel proved themselves to be true descendants of the Maccabees. At great cost, the War of Independence finally ended in an heroic Israeli victory and an uneasy truce.

Theodor Herzl

1860-1904

Lieut. Colonel Dreyfus during the First World War.

One reporter, Theodor Herzl, correspondent for the Vienna *New Free Press*, left the scene shaken and trembling. Where was this outcry taking place? Not in some backward village of Asia or Africa, as he later wrote, but in France, "in republican, modern, civilized France, a hundred years after the Declaration of the Rights of Man. The French people do not want to extend the rights of man to Jews. The edict of the great Revolution has been revoked."

Until that day, Herzl revealed, "most of us believed that the solution of the Jewish problem was to be patiently waited for as part of the general development of mankind. But when a people which in every other respect is so progressive and so highly civilized can

At nine o'clock in the morning on January 5, 1895, the great court in front of the Military Academy of Paris was lined with five thousand troops in square formation. To the center of the square was led a tall captain, pale and tense, holding his head high. A general on horseback looked down on him with disgust.

"Alfred Dreyfus," said the general, "you are unworthy to be a soldier. In the name of France I degrade you from your rank." A roll of drums began. The officer of the guard began to tear insignia and buttons from the convicted man's uniform. Alfred Dreyfus raised his right hand and cried out, "I swear that you are degrading an innocent man! I am innocent! Long live France!"

The falsely-condemned man was led in his disgrace around the parade ground. As he passed a group of reporters he stopped and cried out to them, "Tell all France that I am innocent!"

From the massed troops and from the crowd of onlookers outside the fence came cries of "Traitor! Death to the traitor!" And then other mutterings became louder and louder. "Down with the Jews!" "Death to the Jews!"

Theodor Herzl.

The family of Theodor Herzl.

reasons for Jewish holidays; his family, though not very observant, celebrated Passover, and the story of the Exodus from Egypt impressed him greatly. He knew little of Hebrew texts, or his people's history. His great interest, like that of his parents, was to know German culture and become a successful professional man. Very early he desired to be a writer.

When Theodor was eighteen, following the sad death of his only sister, the Herzl family moved to Vienna. There the young man attended the university and studied law. He joined the students' cultural organization which had as its motto: "In the temple of knowledge all worshippers are equal."

Such liberal ideas were popular in the Austro-Hungarian Empire, of which Vienna was the capital. At the same time other ideas, such as extreme nationalism which claimed

take such a turn, what are we to expect from other peoples?"

A Jew of Western Europe

Theodor Herzl had seen anti-Semitism before. And though at times he had almost forgotten that he was a Jew, events had always arisen to remind him.

As a child of well-to-do parents in Budapest, Theodor Herzl had grown up in an atmosphere of freedom. He had gone to a Jewish-sponsored elementary school, then to the Technical High School, and then to the Evangelical High School to prepare for the university. He received the small amount of Jewish education, ending with Bar Mitzvah at the age of thirteen, which was usually given to the children of emancipated families in his city. He studied Bible stories and knew the

Herzl as a schoolboy.

that all minority groups were inferior, and the rising doctrine of anti-Semitism, appealed to many.

Anti-Semitic speakers were welcomed at the university. Following one talk, the student cultural organization disbanded. Herzl joined a fraternity that seemed liberal, and became active in duelling, debates, and writing for the group's paper. In 1883, a meeting in which the fraternity took part turned into an anti-Semitic riot. Herzl knew he must resign.

The young man was bitter about such happenings. He sometimes felt that the Jews ought to assimilate, forgetting their religion and becoming just like the majority around them. Yet he realized that this was neither possible nor honorable. In *The New Ghetto,* a play he wrote in 1892, he argued: "If you become untrue to yourself, you mustn't complain if others become untrue to you."

Almost forgetting his Jewishness for some years, Herzl devoted himself to playwriting and composing travel notes and articles for newspapers. Then, as correspondent in Paris for the *New Free Press,* he attended the Dreyfus trial.

The Idea of a Jewish State

The reaction of the crowd to Dreyfus's conviction showed Herzl that all Jews were condemned for the apparent guilt of one. And Dreyfus, who was later proved innocent, had only been suspected because he was a Jew. Herzl saw the Jews as a group unprotected and subject to attack. And suddenly, a light seemed to ignite in his mind. Like a flash, he saw what must be done. From that time until his death, a single great idea, the idea of a free and sovereign state as homeland for his people, demanded every minute of his time, every bit of his energy.

"The Jewish question exists," he wrote. "It would be stupid to deny it. It is a national question. We are a people. The ancient prejudices against us are rooted deep. The situation will not change for the better, but rather for the worse. There is only one way out: into the promised land."

With boldness and vigor, Herzl sought out the wealthy men who could help in his project. He first went to Baron de Hirsch, saying, "Until now you have been only a giver of charity. I want to show you the way to become something more." He next addressed a long letter to the Rothschilds, asking that they lend their wealth to the great endeavor. "I have the solution to the Jewish question," he wrote. "I know it sounds mad; and at the beginning I shall be called mad more than once—until the truth of what I am saying is recognized in all its shattering force."

A Doctor's Diagnosis

A friend of Herzl, Dr. Emil Schiff, visited him and was troubled to see the elegant journalist looking as though he had not changed his clothes or slept for days. "Sit down, Emil; I want to read you something," said the writer. With passionate feeling Herzl read his entire letter to the Rothschilds.

The library of Dr. Herzl.

As he read, he noticed the doctor's face changing, expressing some deep emotion. At the conclusion, Herzl waited for his friend's comment. The doctor had tears in his eyes. He looked sadly at his friend Theodor.

"My dear Herzl," said the good doctor, "you are in a bad way. You have been working too hard and your mind is under strain. You need a rest and medical attention."

"I am not out of my mind!" Herzl exclaimed. He started to tell of his plans to see the German Kaiser, to get his help in influencing the Sultan of Turkey to agree to grant the Jews a territory of their own.

"Give up this idea," pleaded Dr. Schiff. "You will destroy yourself and your parents. You are making yourself a figure of ridicule. If you have any regard for the opinion of the world, throw away this whole idea."

Herzl was depressed but not defeated. Though Baron de Hirsch would not support his plan; though the Rothschilds did not answer him, nor did the German leader Bismarck; though his friends turned from him in dismay, he continued to work for the cause. When the millionaires refused him, he stated, "Finally, and above all, there is the mass of the Jews, to which I shall know how to find my way."

Herzl put forward his ideas in a book called *The Jewish State*, published in 1896. Through the book his name and his ideas became known to Jews in every country who were already interested in Palestine settlement.

"Think of it!" they exclaimed. "A Jew of the western world, a graduate of the university, an emancipated man, a writer for a great newspaper of Vienna, a friend of aristocrats, who believes as we do!"

Though Moses Hess, Leon Pinsker and others had written books advocating a Jewish national revival, it was Herzl's call to action that united Zionists all over the world.

The World Zionist Congress

"The Jewish question must be removed from the control of the benevolent individual," said Herzl. "There must be created a forum before which everyone acting for the Jewish people should appear and to which he should be responsible."

Against all odds, Herzl set out to create such a forum. He issued an appeal for a world Zionist Congress. Leading Jews of Europe, as different as Dr. Max Nordau, a brilliant critic who had almost left Judaism, and David Wolffsohn, a Lithuanian timber merchant who had worked for Palestine for years, joined Herzl in his efforts. The vast bulk of the work, however, was carried on by Herzl himself.

He founded a newspaper to spread Zionist ideas, not only writing most of the articles but using his own money for publishing expenses. He traveled to England, speaking to the Maccabean club, to author Israel Zangwill, and to British statesmen. He pleaded with Baron Edmond de Rothschild to give his money to gain a charter for an independent state, not just to support small colonies. He sought out every way to approach rulers of the larger countries.

Zionist leaders: Dr. Bodenheimer, Herzl, Max Nordau, and David Wolfssohn.

Delegates to the fifth Zionist Congress. Herzl is in the center with his mother to his left, Israel Zangwill to his right.

The call to the first Zionist Congress was a thrilling one to the Hoveve Zion (the Lovers of Zion) of Eastern Europe, to Russian Jewish students in Berlin and Vienna, to pious Jews who believed in the prophets' promises of return to Zion—though not to some of the leading Jewish citizens of the West. Many of them were afraid that their rights—in France, in Germany, in Austria, in England—would be endangered.

The Congress gathered in Basel, Switzerland, on August 29, 1897, with 197 delegates present. They had come from every country where a good-sized Jewish community lived. Three represented Zionist clubs in the United States. Everyone was formally dressed as though for a session of parliament. A flag bearing the colors of the *talit*, the Jewish prayer-shawl, had been made up, with two blue stripes and a Star of David on a white field. The session opened with the traditional Jewish blessing of *Shehehiyanu,* said on occasions of celebration and gratitude: "Blessed art Thou, O Lord our God, King of the universe, who has kept us alive and brought us to this day."

When Herzl arose, a dignified figure with a black beard like one of the ancient prophets, wild applause broke out. For fifteen minutes the delegates could not be quieted. The Hebrew writer Ben Ami wrote: "The dream of two thousand years was on the point of realization; it was as if the Messiah confronted us; and I was seized by an overpowering desire, in the midst of the storm of joy, to cry out, loudly, for all to hear: 'Hail to the king!' "

Herzl remained standing calmly. He felt the applause was not for him, but for the cause. He now represented Zion to all the world. For the first time since the destruction of Jerusalem, a Jewish statesman had arisen.

His first words were, "We are here to lay the foundation stone of the house which is to shelter the Jewish nation." The colonies in Palestine were a small beginning. Now there must be legal recognition that the Jews had a right to their own land. "The basis can be only that of right; we have had too much experience with toleration."

The Congress issued a declaration which was called the Basel Program. It stated: "Zionism seeks to secure for the Jewish people a publicly recognized, legally secured homeland in Palestine." It went on to advocate encouragement of settlement; organization of Jews into local Zionist groups; strengthening of Jewish national consciousness; and "the obtaining of the consent of the various governments necessary for fulfilment of the aim of Zionism."

Bronze medal struck in honor of the second Zionist Congress at Basel. The quotation, from the book of Ezekiel, tells of God's promise to bring the children of Israel from among the nations to their own land.

Herzl and the Zionist delegation to Kaiser Wilhelm, returning from Palestine.

In the Courts of Kings

Now carrying a great burden of work as president of the World Zionist Organization, Herzl devoted himself above all to the last point of the program. His hope was to persuade the Sultan of Turkey to give a charter to the Jews to rule Palestine. The Sultan ruled the whole Near East, though his Ottoman Empire was in danger of falling apart. Herzl had the ambitious idea that Jews could pay the national debt of Turkey, and gain the charter in return.

In hope of influencing the Sultan, Herzl first reached the Kaiser, the Sultan's best friend in Europe. In Constantinople and later on a trip to Jerusalem, Herzl spoke to the German ruler, who listened but did nothing. Herzl finally had an interview with the Sultan, who spoke politely and vaguely. He was not willing to let Jews buy land or settle in large numbers in Palestine.

The pogrom in the city of Kishinev in 1903 aroused Herzl to go to Russia. "Think of it," he said. "Seven million outlawed human beings who have again begun to tremble."

In St. Petersburg, Herzl pleaded for support of Zionism before the anti-Semitic Russian Minister of the Interior, von Plehve. On his homeward journey, Herzl stopped in Vilna, where the Jews, though they had been forbidden by the police to assemble, turned out by the thousands to greet him as "the greatest son of the Jewish people." Not wishing to antagonize the authorities by another demonstration, Herzl left the city at one o'clock in the morning. Nevertheless, all the Jews of the city were awake to see him off; and the police broke up the gathering. Shaken by the poverty and the oppression he had seen, and by the great faith the people placed in him, Herzl turned with even more dedication to his task.

On further journeys, Herzl spoke to ambassadors and ministers of every great nation. He visited the King of Italy, and the Pope, who refused to consider the return of Jews to Palestine. Herzl suffered from a serious heart condition, but he refused to stop his work for a Jewish state.

The delegation to the Kaiser, in Jerusalem.

Max Nordau.

The Offer of Uganda

In England, Herzl was well received by various statesmen. England would have been glad to see the Turkish empire divided. Although no one was able to promise Palestine to the Jews, one definite offer was made. Joseph Chamberlain, the Colonial Secretary, suggested that the British protectorate of Uganda, in East Africa, could be opened to Jewish settlement.

A letter from the Foreign Minister of England was read at the Sixth Zionist Congress. The greatest government in the world was making an offer directly to the Jewish people, showing faith that the Jews could be trusted to set up their own government. Max Nordau explained that Uganda would not be a substitute for Palestine; it would be temporary, a training ground, a "shelter for the night." The Kishinev pogrom was fresh in everyone's mind. "Let us save those who can still be saved," Herzl pleaded.

The proposal to investigate the offer was passed, but it could not win the hearts of the delegates. Those from Russia, the most dedicated to the love of Zion, walked out of the Congress Hall.

Herzl wished to ignore the protesters; then he was told that they were weeping, overcome with grief at the betrayal of their hopes. He went out to speak to them, and with great effort persuaded them not to leave the Zionist movement.

The incident proved that only the land of Israel itself, for whose rebuilding prayers had been said through the centuries, could rally the Jewish people and keep their loyalty.

The Last Days

During the debates and troubles of this time, Herzl's health became poorer, yet he did not spare himself. He continued to negotiate with officials of Russia, Austria, Germany and Turkey. He wrote to the New York philanthropist, Jacob Schiff, for help in appealing to Russia. He was able in April, 1904, to gather together the Greater Actions

The meeting place of the Zionist Congress.

Theodor Herzl with his father and mother, and his three children.

Committee of the Zionist Organization and to persuade the members to work in harmony.

Herzl's doctors, listening to his heart, told him he must rest. Even at the health resort where he was persuaded to go, he continued to write letters and instructions, staying up all night till five-thirty in the morning to prepare documents for a friend to take to St. Petersburg. "Is this how you expect to restore your health?" the friend asked. "Yes, yes," answered Herzl. "You know there is no time to lose. The last weeks, or days. We must hurry."

Herzl's condition became worse. Pneumonia set in. His wife and his oldest daughter were with him. He begged that his mother and his two younger children be called. On Sunday, June 3, they arrived and spent a short time at his bedside. "It will soon be over," he told them.

That same day, Theodor Herzl died. He was only forty-four, and had spent just eight years on the great project of his life. In those eight years, he had become the organizer of a worldwide movement, the giver of hope to millions, the founder of a nation. Six thousand mourners walked in his funeral procession.

No Longer a Dream

At the end of the First Zionist Congress in 1897, Theodor Herzl wrote these words in his diary: "If I were to sum up the Basel Congress in a single phrase I would say: In Basel I created the Jewish State. Were I to say this aloud I would be greeted by universal laughter. But in any case, certainly fifty years from now, everyone will realize it."

The prophecy came true. It was fifty years later, on November 29, 1947, that the Jewish state was voted into existence by the United Nations.

In the midst of all the mighty endeavors the new State of Israel undertook in its first years—years of heroic defense, of bringing in a million new citizens, and of rebuilding the land—there was one duty that had to be fulfilled.

In his will, Herzl had asked for a simple funeral. With perfect faith that his lifework

The ship Theodor Herzl on its maiden voyage.

would be successful, he instructed that his coffin should remain in the Vienna cemetery "until the Jewish people transports my remains to Palestine."

As the children of Israel had carried father Jacob from Egypt to the land of Israel, so the people of the new state did for their patriarch. In the year 1954, fifty years after Herzl's death, his remains were brought to the city of Jerusalem. The tomb of Theodor Herzl now stands on Mount Herzl, overlooking Jerusalem, in the old-new land he had foreseen.

The tomb of Herzl on Mount Herzl, Jerusalem.

Hayyim Nahman Bialik

1873-1934

A little boy ran free in the fields and forests around the village of Radi in Volhynia. Hayyim Nahman, eighth child of Bialik the timberman, a strange child, lost in daydreams, chasing the sunset: ". . . gentle I was, tiny and lonely," wrote the man later. All of nature, sunrise, sunset, trees, clouds, wind, were marvels to him. "Wonder caught me, circled me about, closed over my little head; it widened my eyes and deepened my heart."

At six, the child sat in *heder* in the town of Zhitomir, where his father kept an inn. Behind the counter the father studied Mishnah, slow to leave his book to fill the orders of the peasants. In the heder the boy followed his imagination instead of listening to the teacher. To Hayyim Nahman, each of the Hebrew letters had its own nature.

"The *lamed* strode erect with outstretched neck and upright head, as much as to say, 'Just have a look; I stand head and shoulders taller than you all.' Meanwhile the little *yud* would come scurrying up, a tiny creature, and how my heart went out to it! I was always afraid that it was so small it might be lost, or trodden underfoot."

Hayyim Nahman Bialik.

Then his father died, and Hayyim Nahman, an orphan at the age of seven, found himself in the house of his stern old grandfather. His childhood was gone. Study was now to be his life, under strict and impatient teachers. All the relatives said that no good could come of the boy, for he was active and mischievous; and many were his punishments.

Books and the Outside World

How grateful he was for the bookcase full of Hebrew books in the grandfather's home! In reading legends of King Solomon, discussions of holiness from the Kabbalah, wonderful tales of the hasidim, the youngster found escape from his harsh surroundings. He wrote a poem dedicated "To the Agadah," to the legends of his people. "In you," he wrote, "my soul finds soothing from its woes."

Even some works of the Haskalah, modern non-religious writings in Hebrew, came his

The mother of Hayyim Nahman Bialik.

way. Shalom Abramowitsch, called the father of modern Hebrew and Yiddish writing, lived in Zhitomir. Young Bialik read his volumes on science and natural history, and his stories about the sad life of the Jews in the Russian Pale of Settlement. Mendele Mocher Sfarim, Mendele the Bookseller, was the name used by Abramowitsch in his books. Little did the eager boy realize that in later years he would often be mentioned together with "Mendele." They were two pioneers in reviving Hebrew as a language of the people.

In his reading and in his life, the boy saw that there was much to learn in the world outside the ghetto; and that there was much, so much to be improved in the life of the Jewish people. "Poverty is my father; bitter Exile is my mother," he wrote as a young man. "But it is not the wanderer's staff, nor the beggar's bag I fear; for seven times more cruel, more terrible than these is life itself,

the life that knows no hope, no radiance; the life of a hungry dog, fettered to its chain."

A Choice of Paths

At fifteen the boy was able to go to Volozhin, to the great yeshivah inspired by the Gaon of Vilna. He did well in the study of Talmud, as his grandfather had hoped. There Hayyim Nahman saw students who spent their whole lives doing nothing but study Talmud, who started when they were younger than he, slept little, ate black bread, and never lifted their eyes from the book long enough to see the world outside their window. He spoke of such students in his long poem *Ha-Matmid*:

The old men linger and commend his choice,
And pray within their hearts a silent prayer:
"Happy the son who gives his life to Torah

Four Hebrew writers. From right to left: Bialik, Ben-Ami, Shalom Aleichem, Abramowitz.

A view of Bialik Street.

And happy those who brought up such a son!"

To Bialik, these students who cut themselves off from the world were wasting their lives. "On what were all these lives, these powers spent?" he asked. He felt that their brilliance could have been used to teach others, to improve their people's lot, to brighten the world in some way.

My fate has not decreed that I with you,
Unhappy ones, should lose myself. I left
you,
Forsook your company, transgressed for
bread,
And walked and lost myself in other paths.

The "other paths" that Bialik wished to follow became clear to him at Volozhin. With a group of other students he decided to learn Russian and German, modern science and literature; and to devote his life to working for the Jewish people. They read the essays of Ahad Ha-Am, demanding that the Jews rouse themselves to rebuild their nation and their culture. They wanted to give their talents to awakening the pride of their fellow-Jews, helping them learn how to build their own future.

Many such students, forsaking the traditional study of Talmud and leaving the yeshivot, gave up all loyalty to Judaism. Often converting to Christianity, they became professors, writers, artists and scientists accepted in Russian, German and French society. To Bialik this was sad treason. He wrote later of such lost Jews, speaking of these bright young men as artists who created only for strangers, like the children of Israel in Egypt, who built for their oppressors:

You pour your spirit into alien marble,
And in the stranger's rock entomb your
soul.
While still the vampire's teeth are in your
flesh,
Your soul too shall you offer him for food.
And you shall build him cities, Pithom,
Ramses,
With living bricks, your own and children's
children.

With his friends at Volozhin, Bialik vowed not to leave his people or ever try to assimilate among the Gentiles. The group hoped that Bialik would grow up to be a great writer, who would arouse his people from their hopelessness.

The Life Work Begins

At seventeen, Hayyim Nahman managed to travel, without telling his grandfather, to the Russian city of Odessa, where several Jewish writers lived. To the young man's delight, he was able to meet Asher Ginzberg, well-known under the pen name of Ahad Ha-Am. The philosopher not only welcomed him; he read some of his poems, and saw to it that one, *El Ha-Tzipor*, was printed in a Hebrew magazine. The poem tells of the hope of return to Zion. In it, the poet speaks to a bird who has migrated from sunny Palestine to his cold northern city, bringing news that brethren in the land of Israel are

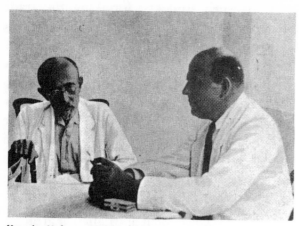

Hayyim Nahman Bialik with the famous Hebrew writer, Ahad Ha-am.

working for the future.

The young man hoped to go west to Berlin, free of the cruel laws of the czar. There he would be able to study, become educated so that he might be a leader of his people. This dream could not yet come true. He learned through friends at Volozhin that his grandfather was ill.

Bialik returned to Zhitomir to comfort his grandfather's last days. He married and set up a home. For some years he worked in the timber business, and then became a teacher. Many of his early poems, on nature, on his own lost childhood, on his deep love for his people, on his grief for the hard lives of his parents, were written during these years. Published in Hebrew journals, these poems made his name known in the Jewish world.

When the First Zionist Congress was called, Bialik dedicated a poem to the delegates. "Woes of your people summon you from far corners of exile, and their bitter cry has roused you, pioneers of our return," he wrote. His heart leaped to greet them, "bless from far the hour you meet."

After ten years away from his friends and the interests of his youth, Bialik returned to Odessa. In company with Ahad Ha-Am and Mendele, he became a leader in Jewish literature and thought. He was editor of the He-brew magazine *Ha-Shiloah,* and founded the publishing house of *Moriah,* to produce Hebrew books. With Joshua Ravnitsky, he compiled *Sefer Ha-Agadah,* rewriting Jewish legends and midrashim so that students of all ages could enjoy them.

The Kishinev Pogrom

Russian law, quotas and restrictions oppressed the Jews all through this time. In 1903 there occurred an event that shocked the world. A mob attacked the Jews in the city of Kishinev, destroying thousands of homes and leaving dead and injured on every street. That such a thing could happen in the twentieth century was unbelievable to civilized people. The czar's government and police were condemned for not protecting the victims.

The feelings of the Jews of Eastern Europe can be shared by all who read Bialik's poems, for it was he who put those feelings into powerful words. "My heart is dead," he wrote. "Cursed be the man who demands vengeance! Vengeance for this, the blood of little children, has not yet been invented by Satan."

It was forbidden to criticize the Russian government. Crying out against the Kishinev pogrom implied blaming the czar. Bialik wrote his strongest poem, calling it at first "Lament in Nemirov," pretending that he wrote of the massacre that took place in Nemirov in 1648. "In the City of Slaughter" tells how the poet walked through the streets of Kishinev, describing the horror of ruin, torture and death that met his eyes.

Weeping for the cruel slaughter of innocent people was only part of the poem. A new note entered. Bialik spoke forth like a prophet of old against the Jews themselves, for allowing themselves to live such dark and bitter lives, to die such deaths for nothing. The victims had cowered, not trying

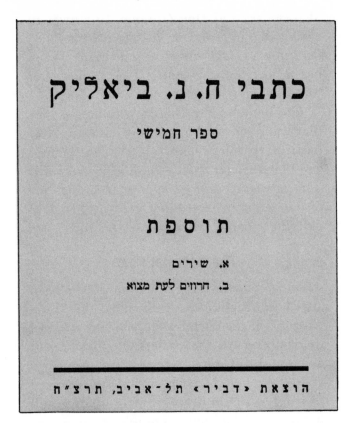

כתבי ח. נ. ביאליק

ספר חמישי

תוספת

א. שירים
ב. חרוזים לעת מצוא

הוצאת ״דביר״ תל-אביב, תרצ״ח

Title page of a book containing some of the writings of Bialik.

to fight back. The survivors now begged charity, still not daring to stand up as men, to strengthen themselves for the future.

Great is the shame, and great too is the anguish;
But which is greater, say thou, son of man!

The call of the poet aroused the Jews as nothing else had. Jewish young men organized themselves into self-defense units. Thereafter, pogroms met at least some resistance. Later in Palestine, some of the same defenders formed the *Shomer,* the corps of watchmen who guarded the new settlements and upheld Jewish pride. Like their ancestors who returned from Babylon to rebuild the land of Israel almost 2500 years before, they built with one hand and defended themselves with the other.

Awakening the People

Yet Bialik had not only meant that Jews should take up weapons against their enemies. He meant that they should raise their heads and live with dignity. Often he lamented the lack of hope and ambition that afflicted his downtrodden people. "Surely the people is grass," he wrote, using the words of the prophet Isaiah. "They are dried up like straw; they fade and wither."

Lo! when the voice of their God thunders about them forever,
This is a people that moves not, a people that stirs not nor trembles.
When the great trumpet resounds, then, when the banner is lifted,
Then shall the dead arise, the dead stir out of their slumber?

Perhaps the greatest work describing the lifelessness of the Jewish people is "The Dead of the Desert." Bialik chose an old legend, telling how the people of Israel who left Egypt but were not worthy of entering the Promised Land lie eternally in a death-like sleep in the wilderness, mighty in appearance but forever asleep. No one knows their place. No storm or wild beast can hurt them. Yet they are said to rise, no one knows when, to shout defiance and proclaim: "We are heroes! The last generation of slaves, the first generation of free men!" Then they sink once more into their trance. Their power is unused, and the desert remains barren.

The challenge to the people of Israel was clear. The words of Bialik helped inspire many of them to become active in the cause of their people. Zev Jabotinsky wrote: "There are few examples in history of poetry influencing a generation so deeply and so directly. The shomrim movement in Palestine, even the Jewish Legion which fought for the Holy Land in 1918—they are all Bialik's children."

161

Bialik's house.

Joining His Brethren

It could not be too long before the poet joined his brethren in Palestine. The Russian Revolution overthrew the czar in 1917. After devastating war, the Bolshevik party took control and the Communist dictatorship began. Bialik soon found that the new regime forbade freedom of speech and press. Communist censors destroyed the Hebrew plates he had set up for printing a book of poems by Shlomo ibn Gabirol.

Leaving Russia was not easy, but Bialik and his wife Manya managed to cross the border. In Berlin, they set up the Hebrew publishing house of *Devir*. Finally in 1924, they became permanent residents of Palestine, settling on the street in Tel Aviv that was called Bialik Street.

The poet now devoted himself to providing Hebrew literature for the new Hebrew-speaking population of Palestine. He produced textbooks, storybooks, translations of Shakespeare and *Don Quixote*. In answer to worldwide greetings on his fiftieth birthday, he wrote a poem whose refrain went: "I am not a poet nor a prophet; I am a hewer of wood."

The home of the Bialiks became a center that was open to thousands of visitors. Most particularly on Shabbat afternoon, groups would gather for discussion and joyous song. The very words *Oneg Shabbat*, meaning "joy of the Sabbath," were first used by Bialik to describe a happy gathering of this sort.

The National Poet

Beloved as few other men have ever been anywhere, Bialik was often called the "First Citizen" of the Yishuv. He was the pride of the country. All the settlers felt that he had given soul and spirit to the Hebrew language and to the new Hebrew nation. He rejoiced to see Jewish children growing up free and happy, as he had not been able to do, enjoying the beauties of nature and looking forward to helping with the upbuilding of their own land. The people he loved was flourishing once more.

While yet young, Bialik had written a poem called "After My Death," in which he asked the reader to say

The honor guard around the coffin of Hayyim Nahman Bialik.

162

Ah! Pity, for he had yet one song more,
And now that song is lost, and lost forever.

The songs of Bialik, the contributions he was able to make to the growth and to the happiness of the Yishuv, were not completed when he died at the age of sixty. The whole country mourned. His home was later turned into a museum, so that admirers might still visit and learn something of the man.

In England a Poet Laureate is appointed by the government. He is to be the official poet of the country, to write of great events, to express the feelings of the people, to put their joy and sorrow into words. Hayyim Nahman Bialik was the Poet Laureate of the Jewish nation even before the nation came into being. He was appointed not by any government, but by the will and love of the people.

Henrietta Szold

1860-1945

A quiet woman of forty-nine and her seventy-year-old mother toured Palestine in November of the year 1909. The daughter and the widow of Rabbi Benjamin Szold, distinguished scholar of Baltimore, the two American ladies were taking a trip to Europe and the Near East as a much-needed vacation. Their devotion to Judaism made them look forward especially to four weeks in the Holy Land.

Through the desolate countryside and the old sections of Jerusalem and Jaffa they traveled. They walked on the sandy roads of the new suburb that had just been named Tel Aviv. In Jerusalem and in the colonies, Miss Henrietta Szold wrote her friend Alice Seligsberg, they found "life coupled with misery, poverty, filth, disease"; yet there was also "intellectual life, coupled with idealism, enthusiasm, hope." They saw the valiant work being done in schools and settlements by heroic men and women. "If only they could be more intelligently supported by the European and American Jew!"

At Jaffa the tourists came to the Jewish Girls' School. As they walked towards the building, Henrietta later reported, she and her mother were horrified to see children "with a wreath of flies around their eyes." Inside the school, all the children had clean faces and healthy eyes. In response to Mrs. Szold's question, the principal told them what caused the difference; why the pupils in school would grow up without suffering the affliction of trachoma or other eye ailments. "That is simple; we have a physician who visits us twice a week and a nurse who comes daily, and we take care of the eyes." As they left the school, Mrs. Szold turned to scold her daughter. "That is what your group ought to do. What is the use of reading papers and arranging festivals? You should do practical work in Palestine."

Henrietta Szold.

Henrietta Szold did not answer. The work of her women's Zionist club in New York did seem rather unimportant when she saw how much there was to be done in the land itself. The same thought had gone through her mind before her mother spoke of it. She was, however, nearly fifty, tired of years of intense study and literary work. "If I were twenty years younger," she had written from Jerusalem, "I would feel that my field is here."

Henrietta Szold felt with some reason that she deserved rest and perhaps retirement after decades of study and service to Judaism. In the great twelve-volume Jewish Encyclopedia published four years earlier, there was an article about her as a distinguished American scholar and editor. She was already known as someone who had made an important contribution to Jewish life and learning.

The Young Teacher

At seventeen, young Henrietta Szold of Baltimore was a teacher in high school, and a writer for magazines. Under the pen-name of "Sulamith" she wrote articles for the New York *Jewish Messenger*, criticizing American

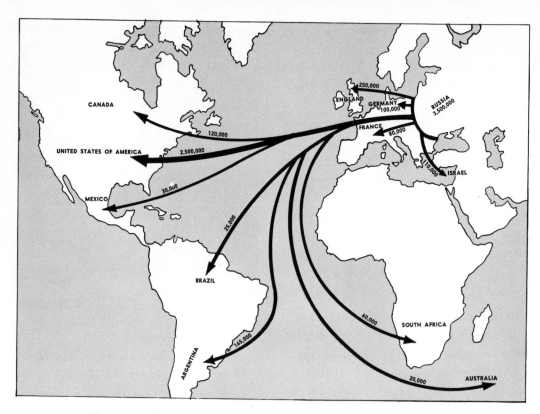

The stream of Jewish immigration from Eastern Europe, 1881-1932.

Jews for not knowing their tradition, and for forgetting culture in their pursuit of wealth and pleasure. She taught both children's and adults' classes in her father's religious school, and was active in study groups, including a botany club and a literary club. At home, as the oldest in a family of daughters, she helped her mother in housekeeping and in the care of the younger sisters. She also studied with her father and helped him in his research as a son might have done.

When Henrietta was twenty-one, news of the May Laws in Russia aroused concern in the American Jewish community. Soon began the great immigration of poor and persecuted Russian Jews to America. Those who docked at Baltimore found a friend in Rabbi Szold. Henrietta was impressed with the Hebrew knowledge and high ideals of the newcomers. For them she founded the first night schools in America, classes for immigrant adults who

worked during the day but who wanted to learn English and to become good American citizens. For years young Miss Szold directed such schools, raised money for them, found rooms, and employed teachers. She was heartbroken when some of the ambitious immigrants were turned away for lack of space.

"The eagerness of the pupils was often painful to witness, and nothing more pathetic can be imagined than the efforts made by men well advanced in years to crook their work-stiffened fingers around a pen," Miss Szold recorded. By the time the city of Baltimore took over the support of the night schools, and the idea had spread to other cities as well, 5000 pupils, including many Christians, had been educated under Miss Szold's direction.

Editor and Scholar

At the age of thirty-three, Henrietta Szold

166

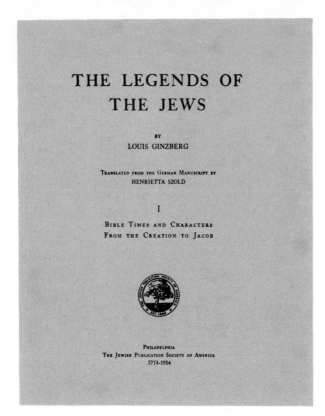

Title-page of "The Legends of the Jews" translated by Henrietta Szold.

entered a new career, which required her to leave teaching. She became secretary and editor of the Jewish Publication Society of America, located in Philadelphia. In this role, among many other editorial tasks, she translated Heinrich Graetz's *History of the Jews* and Professor Louis Ginzberg's *Legends of the Jews,* both great scholarly works. As a hard-working historian she edited the American Jewish Year Book for many years.

All this was done by a woman who never went to college, for hardly any girls at that time enjoyed the privilege of higher education. Her learning, however, was far greater than that of a typical college graduate. "My father had raised me for Jewish scholarship," she said.

When the beloved Rabbi Szold died in 1902, the daughter and the widow went to live in New York for the sake of Jewish learning. Henrietta Szold became at forty-three the only woman to attend rabbinic classes, particularly in Talmud, at the Jewish Theological Seminary of America. She became a friend of Solomon Schechter, the new director of the Seminary, and other students and scholars of that institution.

If Not Zionism, Nothing

Henrietta Szold had been a Zionist for years. It seemed a natural part of her love for Judaism and her concern for the Jewish people. "I became converted to Zionism," she wrote, "the very moment I realized that it supplied my bruised, torn and bloody nation with an ideal—an ideal that is balm to the self-inflicted wounds and to the wounds inflicted by others."

When she left for her first trip to Palestine, friends had warned her that seeing actual conditions in the Holy Land might make her lose her faith in Zionism. On the contrary, she came back "more than ever convinced that our only salvation lies that way." She realized, however, that it would be more difficult to build up the Jewish homeland than she had thought. "If not Zionism, then nothing," she wrote after leaving Palestine. "Then extinc-

Henrietta Szold and other Zionist leaders.

tion for the Jew."

Henrietta did not answer her mother directly when Mrs. Szold cried out about the need for practical health work in Palestine. A determination, however, grew within her. At the age of fifty, not giving up other work she had promised to do, she became the hardworking secretary of the Federation of American Zionists. As her mother had suggested, she returned to her little study group of young women and urged them to support health work among the women and children of Palestine.

The Founding of Hadassah

On Purim, February 24, 1912, a group of thirty-eight women met at Temple Emanu-El in New York. They decided to call themselves the Hadassah Chapter of a national organization to be known as the Daughters of Zion. They were to further Zionism and Jewish loyalty in America, and support health work in Palestine. Professor Israel Friedlaender of the Seminary gave them a motto, from the book of Jeremiah: "The healing of the daughter of my people."

The name Hadassah was the Hebrew name of Queen Esther, and has always been a favorite name for a Jewish heroine. At the first small national convention of the Daughters of Zion, held in Rochester, New York, in 1914, the name Hadassah was given to the entire organization.

There was no question as to who was the leading spirit of Hadassah. It was Miss Szold who traveled the country, speaking to small groups and founding new chapters. She it was who inspired Nathan Straus to contribute to the first Medical Unit to be sent to Palestine. Two nurses, Rose Kaplan and Rachel Landy, were sent to Palestine by Hadassah in 1913.

General Allenby entering the city of Jerusalem.

Mission to Palestine

The outbreak of the war in 1914 meant a halt in Hadassah's work, and indeed stopped all progress that was being made in the Jewish settlements of Palestine. British armies led by General Allenby, and joined by the Jewish Legion of volunteers under Zev Jabotinsky, fought against the Turks throughout the land. Yet the "American Zionist Medical Unit" was still in existence after the war. The Zionist Commission asked Miss Szold if she would go to Palestine—for two years—to help establish needed health services all over the land.

"I don't mind difficulties and hardships, if I could be sure that my being in Palestine would contribute even in the smallest measure to the resolving of the chaos that now exists there," Henrietta Szold wrote at the time. She worried that her Hebrew was not as good as her English; she feared the influ-

A Jewish nurse treating an Arab child.

ence she could have would be very small. "But it is right, nevertheless, that I go—even if I fail utterly."

In her sixtieth year, Henrietta Szold left the United States for Palestine, to begin there a new life and a tremendous new responsibility that ended only with her death, a quarter century later.

The Great Adventure

The problems Miss Szold faced in Palestine were of many kinds. Beginnings are always difficult. The land was poor and had been devastated by war. There were conflicts with Arabs and with unsympathetic British authorities. There was a large immigration (The Third Aliyah) of halutzim from Europe who wanted to work for the new Jewish homeland that had been promised by the nations of the world.

"Immigrants and malaria!" Henrietta Szold wrote. "Not hospitals are needed, but preventive, educational, sanitary work." Wherever Hadassah was able to set up clinics and teach the people about protecting themselves from mosquitoes, the rate of malaria went down. Through the land Miss Szold traveled, in broken-down cars, in wagons, on donkeyback, seeing the growth of new hospitals, health

centers, school lunch programs, clinics to advise mothers on how to take care of their babies. Arabs as well as Jews were treated and cared for.

The two years she had intended to stay became longer. Trips to the United States to speak for Hadassah were brief. She always returned to Jerusalem.

Despite all the hardships, Henrietta Szold was able to write to her sisters: "I am on the great adventure of my life. The Jews are ready to work—they are working. The movement as a whole is a miracle. And the country? It too is a miracle. Full of faults, but so beautiful. It too must be conquered, its stones, its climate, its swamps, but it is worth, oh! so worth the struggle."

When Henrietta Szold was elected by the World Zionist Organization to be one of the three governors of Zionist affairs in Palestine, she felt it was a shame that at this difficult time "the great Zionist movement had no one else to turn to but a tired, worn-out old woman of sixty-seven." Yet this same "old woman" still had before her one of the greatest tasks ever undertaken by any woman, anywhere.

Henrietta Szold digging the first shovel of earth for a health center in Israel.

Henrietta Szold at a reception center in Israel with "her children."

Saving the Children

A disbelieving world saw Hitler take over the rule of Germany in 1933. The Nazi campaign of hate and death against the Jews began. To escape persecution and the threat of worse to come, many German Jews fled to Palestine. Many others could not. Most countries of the world restricted immigration. The British authorities in Palestine also limited the number of Jews allowed to enter.

Henrietta Szold determined that she would do her utmost to save as many innocent victims as she could. She went to a London conference on the German situation, and agreed to work to save the children. She twice visited Germany itself, to see the growing horror of anti-Semitic propaganda. Youth groups and Jewish organizations were preparing teen-agers to leave Germany. Miss Szold comforted their parents, who could not leave.

"My new job, the organization of the transfer of the children from Germany to Palestine, is growing under my hands from day to day. It deals with children; it is not child's play. The responsibility is great. If and when I carry it through, I think I should let my active life come to an end with it."

At the age of seventy-three, Henrietta Szold had become director of a new project, Youth Aliyah. Years before, she had written, "Deep down in my heart I have always held that I should have had children, many children." Now her children began to come home.

Every time a ship docked at Haifa harbor with a group of Youth Aliyah children aboard, Henrietta Szold was there to meet them. Every one of them was greeted by the great lady of Hadassah. Miss Szold spoke to them in their own language, guided them to the medical offices, helped them get their possessions. She stayed with them until they were, as she wrote, "tucked away in their beds" in the schools, villages, *kibbutzim* or reception centers which had arranged to take them. Their health, their problems of adjustment, their education for the future, all were her concern.

In the years 1933 to 1945 that Henrietta Szold was head of Youth Aliyah, 30,000 youngsters who would otherwise have been killed in concentration camps were saved.

A young kibbutznik.

Such an Old Age!

The love and respect which Henrietta Szold earned from all who knew her and her work never failed to surprise her. Hearing herself praised at the cornerstone-laying of the Hadassah-Hebrew University Hospital in 1935 seemed to her like attending her own funeral. Yet she admitted that "It really is next to incredible that a person of my age can keep going at such a pace. Such an old age! And when I was a little girl I expected a serene old age." One explanation she often gave for her ability to do so much was that she always kept the Sabbath faithfully, as indeed she kept all of the mitzvot. Resting on Shabbat gave her strength for the week.

In her eightieth year she wrote, "I wonder whether I shall survive these eightieth anniversary celebrations of which rumors reach me day after day. They probably will introduce me as the heroine, because they don't

Scroll recording establishment by the University of scholarships for Youth Aliyah students in the name of Henrietta Szold on her eightieth birthday.

believe that eulogies are distasteful to a person who has never considered herself as a public character." In honor of her birthdays, one gift she would allow was donation of sums for a life-saving or educational project.

The Hadassah Hospital, a living memorial to Henrietta Szold.

Three modern day Maccabees who saved Israel from the Arab invaders.

Not By Might!

Much heartbreak came to Henrietta Szold in her years of service. Like all violence, the riots of Arabs against Jewish settlers filled her with dismay. She felt that the British were encouraging such acts so that they could claim a Jewish state was impossible; they did not wish to give up their rule of Palestine. Miss Szold wished for a state where Jews and Arabs would live together in peace.

"The Jew and his cause have persisted through the ages not by the might of the fist, not by the power of brute force, but by the spirit of divine law and love," she wrote.

World War II and disorders in Palestine marred her last years. Much as she had seen, she was spared the worst. She did not live to hear the full story of the murder of the six million in Nazi Europe. She did not see Arab armies invade the new State of Israel. She did not suffer through the battles in which so many of the heroic Maccabees of modern Israel fell—many of them her own Youth Aliyah children.

Her Last Year

Henrietta Szold's last year was spent largely in a hospital bed. The eighty-four-year-old patient mourned that she could not travel to Haifa to meet another boatload of incoming children. She lamented also that for the first time she could not hand out diplomas to the graduating class of Hadassah nurses—the very year, she said, that she could really appreciate the devoted work of nurses. The class in its white uniforms and caps marched in her honor beneath her hospital window.

At her funeral on a chill February day in 1945, as a nation wept, a fifteen-year-old-boy, Simon Kresz, stood up to say the *Kaddish*. This prayer is offered, when possible, by a son of the deceased. In a very real sense, this was one of her children, for he had been saved from certain death in Poland by Youth Aliyah.

Perhaps this act meant more than all the eulogies spoken throughout the world, calling her heroine, paragon and prophetess. Above all, she was a mother in Israel. God had made her childless, so that she might be the mother of thousands.

Henrietta Szold attends an Israeli cabinet meeting. Seated to her left is David Ben Gurion.

Chaim Weizmann
1874-1952

Chaim Weizmann as a young man.

World War I was raging through Europe. The Allies, including Great Britain, France, and the newly-joined United States, were holding the line against the Central Powers of Germany, Austria-Hungary and Turkey. On this morning of November 2, 1917, the highest officials of the British government were holding an important meeting.

The Prime Minister, David Lloyd George, the Foreign Secretary, Arthur James Balfour, and all the members of the War Cabinet were discussing the future of the Near East. The Turkish (Ottoman) Empire, they felt, would surely fall; its many Arab lands were divided among themselves, and had no loyalty to the Sultan in Constantinople. When Turkey was defeated, the British leaders hoped, England would be called on to protect and rule in the vital area near the Suez Canal. Keeping this area friendly to England would safeguard the route to India and the well-being of the British Empire.

Outside the Cabinet Room waited a distinguished scientist, a dignified, black-bearded man, well known to the members of the government for the great contribution he had made to the war effort. The secretary, Mr. Kerr, knew that this man, professor of chemistry at the University of Manchester, had developed the method of producing acetone for ammunition for the big guns of the British navy. "Have patience, Dr. Weizmann," he said. "Don't worry. Everyone is on your side."

Young Jews of Russia

Though born in Russia, Chaim Weizmann had transferred his allegiance from his pogrom-ridden homeland to free and democratic England. Not allowed to enter the university in Russia because of the small Jewish quota, he had become one of the many Jewish students who struggled to gain an education in the western universities. He had left his small town near the city of Pinsk to study in Germany and Switzerland. He and his friends often went hungry, living in strange cities and working when they could to earn money for their tuition.

The young Russian Jewish students knew that they could not return to live under the cruel rule of the czars. Many of them joined revolutionary clubs, hoping to help overthrow the Russian government. They

A cartoon showing the relationship of the Russian government to the Jews.

175

dreamed of establishing a democracy in which all men, including the Jews, would enjoy civil rights. They did not foresee that a new dictatorship would spring up after the Revolution.

Chaim Weizmann argued with those who saw the coming Revolution as the greatest good. They thought he was narrow in working for a Jewish cause. "They could not understand why a Russian Jew should want to be anything but a Russian," Weizmann wrote; while he was "moved by the fate of his people and by a love of its history and tradition." Influenced by Ahad Ha-Am, he believed in rebuilding the Jewish people through knowledge of its own culture and ideals. He aroused many other students to dedicate themselves to Zionism instead of to revolution.

Theodor Herzl's book *The Jewish State* was published when Chaim Weizmann was a student of twenty-one. "It was like a bolt from the blue," Weizmann later wrote. "We had never heard the name Herzl before."

Apparently Herzl had never heard of them either. He knew nothing of the already active Zionist movement, *Hibbat Zion;* he had never read the works of Hess or Pinsker, whom the Zionist students followed. Yet the book inspired them. Here was a western Jew, at home in Paris and Vienna, whose ideas led him to Zionism. He was a man of action, to whom they could look for leadership.

The Brilliant Scientist

Though Chaim Weizmann spent much time in Zionist work, he did well also in his university studies. He was a brilliant research chemist, and was able to sell the rights to several new discoveries he made in dyeing and other chemical processes. While continuing his Zionist work in England, he continued his scientific career as well.

In the role of a scientist helping the war effort, he had become a friend of many of

Dr. Chaim Weizmann.

Britain's top leaders. They all knew of his deep interest in the cause of a Jewish state. He had also called on American Zionists, headed by Louis D. Brandeis, to appeal to the officials of the American government. Brandeis, who was appointed Justice of the Supreme Court by President Woodrow Wilson, was able to report the approval of the United States government for a future Jewish state.

The Declaration Is Made

Now, outside the door of the Cabinet meeting, Chaim Weizmann waited for the result of his efforts. As in an important chemical experiment, he had studied every aspect, planned and worked for years, before expecting to see results. He now waited to see if his hopes, and the hopes of his people, were to be fulfilled.

The door of the room opened. Out came

Sir Mark Sykes, his close friend and Secretary of the War Cabinet. Before him he held out an official document. Signed by Lord Balfour, the minister in charge of foreign affairs, it read:

His Majesty's government view with favor the establishment in Palestine of a National Home for the Jewish people, and will use their best endeavors to facilitate the achievement of this object, it being clearly understood that nothing shall be done which may prejudice the civil and religious rights of the existing non-Jewish communities in Palestine or the rights and political status enjoyed by the Jews in any other country.

For the first time, a great world power had committed itself to the idea of a Jewish state in Palestine. Twenty years after the First Zionist Congress, it seemed that the hopes of the Jewish people were finally to be fulfilled.

Rejoicing greeted the declaration among Jews in Russia, where the second stage of the Revolution was beginning; in America, where many of the Jewish community were supporters of the Zionist Federation; in Palestine itself, where the hundred thousand Jewish residents had been much reduced by the sufferings of war. For those Jews in England, France and Germany who feared that a Jewish state would make their loyalty to their own countries suspect, the last statement of the declaration had been purposely included. For those who thought that the Revolution was the answer to all problems, the declaration had no appeal; indeed, as soon as the Soviet government was set up, Zionism was outlawed in the Soviet Union.

To Chaim Weizmann, of course, the Balfour Declaration was a cause for celebration. "I telephoned my wife," he wrote in his autobiography, *Trial and Error,* "and went to see Ahad Ha-Am."

Weizmann's wife Vera, the first one to whom he spoke, was a practicing physician and a devoted co-worker for Zion. They had met while both were at the University of Geneva. Through the years of their marriage she had raised their children, continued her medical work, and kept their home open as the headquarters for Zionist friends.

A Cultural Center

The second one to whom Chaim Weizmann reported was the sage of the Jewish awakening, then living in London. He had always emphasized that the Jews must build up their own spirit and revive their culture before building up an actual state. He had worked, however, for this political goal. Both men hoped that the Jewish state in the making would be both a political reality and a cultural center.

Dr. Weizmann's devotion to culture and education was immediately proven. The English government sent him as one of a Commission to survey the situation in Palestine. There he spoke with General Edmund Allenby, still engaged in driving the Turkish and German armies from Palestine. In the midst of war, Dr. Weizmann approached General Allenby with the request that he allow foundation stones to be laid for the Hebrew University to be built on Mount Scopus near Jerusalem.

The general was astounded. "But we may be rolled back any minute!" he exclaimed. "What is the good of beginning something you may never be able to finish?" Weizmann replied: "This will be a great act of faith—

An Israeli stamp in honor of Chaim Weizmann.

A Keren Hayesod booth.

faith in the victory which is bound to come, and faith in the future of Palestine." The ceremonies were held, while the distant sound of guns on the northern front could be heard. Later, in 1926, General Allenby went back as a guest at the actual dedication of the University.

The British Mandate

As he had waited outside the door of the Cabinet meeting in 1917, so in April of 1920 Chaim Weizmann waited for the San Remo Conference to make up its mind about what was to happen to Palestine. The victorious Allies decided that the mandate for the former Turkish territory should be given to England. The League of Nations, in giving the Mandate, instructed England to protect and guide the land until its inhabitants were ready to rule themselves.

Visit To America

Chaim Weizmann, now head of the World Zionist Organization, intensified his work as a political and practical leader of Zionism. To raise funds for the *Keren Ha-Yesod*, the Palestine Foundation Fund, and for the Hebrew University, he made his first visit to America. With him went Menahem Ussishkin, lifelong Zionist worker, and Albert Einstein, already world-famous as the discoverer of the theory of relativity.

Since the ship docked on the Sabbath, the delegates remained aboard till evening: Jewish law requires that one does not begin or end a journey on the Sabbath. Jews by the thousands walked from the limits of New York City to the dock to greet the arrivals. In the evening, when the travelers intended to proceed straight to their hotel, "the whole of New York Jewry," Weizmann later wrote, seemed to surround them. Even with the help of mounted policemen to direct traffic, it took hours to reach the hotel.

The enthusiasm shown by American Jews at this time was only a sign of the important

Albert Einstein.

Menahem Ussishkin.

The Jewish Agency

The Mandate for Palestine included the statement: "An appropriate Jewish agency shall be recognized as a public body for the purpose of advising and cooperating with the administration of Palestine in such matters as may affect the establishment of the Jewish National Homeland." It was Chaim Weizmann who in 1929 created the Jewish Agency. It included, at his suggestion, several "non-Zionists," who did not wish to work for a political state, but who were willing to help the Jews of Palestine. Weizmann believed in getting the help of all who could possibly support Zion in any way.

Dr. Weizmann was first head of the Jewish Agency. He started it on its work of helping hundreds of thousands of Jews to enter Palestine. To further understanding of the Jewish tradition and the Zionist cause, the Agency set up programs, promoted tours, and published educational aids. (The Jewish Agency has continued its work of teaching and immi-

role they were going to play from then on in Zionist affairs. Most American Jews, sharing America's love for justice and brotherhood, followed the belief of Justice Louis D. Brandeis, who had said: "Every American Jew who aids in advancing the Jewish settlement in Palestine will be a better man and a better American for doing so. There is no inconsistency between loyalty to America and loyalty to Jewry. The Jewish spirit is essentially modern and essentially American. Indeed, loyalty to America demands that each American Jew become a Zionist."

American wealth and influence became important in building the Jewish state. Among those who worked closely with Chaim Weizmann on his many visits to America were thoughtful leaders such as Louis Lipsky, the great orator Rabbi Stephen S. Wise, and philanthropists such as Felix Warburg and Louis Marshall.

Rabbi Stephen S. Wise and Louis Lipsky.

Chaim Weizmann with King Faisal of Transjordan.

gration in cooperation with the government of Israel.)

Dr. Weizmann's work in the Yishuv included the founding of the Weizmann Institute of Science, leading research center of the Near East. For some years he was its active director.

The English Administration

As leader of world Zionism for most of the years between two World Wars, Weizmann suffered many setbacks. His beloved England, which had promised to support the Jewish state, failed him again and again. England seemed afraid of antagonizing the large Arab countries that surrounded Palestine. Jews brought progress, health and education to the land; but Arabs, fearing change and loss of their power, could easily be aroused by their leaders to riot against the Jews. After each riot, British officials lowered the number of Jewish immigrants to be allowed, and cut down the amount of land that could be bought by the Jews.

It is useless to try to guess how many vic-

tims of the Nazis might have been saved if Palestine had been open to all who wished to enter. Yet Chaim Weizmann led the Yishuv in supporting England's war effort in World War II. As he said, "What else was there for us to do?"

Partition and the State

The revelation after the war that six million Jews had been killed seemed to bring about a strong world opinion in favor of a Jewish state. England, still ruthlessly forbidding Jewish immigration into Palestine, finally realized that the situation was beyond her control. Although the Jews had hoped for "Palestine undiminished and undivided," Weizmann with most other Zionist leaders now agreed to work for the Partition Plan, which was presented to the United Nations Assembly in 1947. It provided that two states be authorized, one Jewish and one Arab, in the territory covered by the Mandate.

Dr. Weizmann's inauguration as first President of Israel Feb. 17, 1949. The President and Mrs. Weizmann near the Jewish Agency building.

Once again Chaim Weizmann represented his people in dealing with a great government. He spoke with President Harry S. Truman, who admired the elder statesman and his dedication to the ideals of the Hebrew prophets. President Truman's interest helped to keep the United States delegation faithful in its support of the Jewish state.

The Partition Plan was passed, in a dramatic roll-call vote, on November 29, 1947. The Jewish state was to be a reality.

Rejoicing turned to doubt as Arab disorders rose in Palestine and the British planned to withdraw. As British troops left on May 15, 1948, they handed over many of their military stations to the Arabs. They seemed to feel that the Partition Plan would never be carried out, for they expected the Jews to be driven into the sea.

The representatives of the Yishuv assembled in Tel Aviv to proclaim the new State of Israel. Six Arab armies immediately invaded. It seemed that only by a miracle could the new State survive.

America Shows Its Faith

Only a few minutes after David Ben-Gurion had read the proclamation of Israel's independence, a declaration came from the White House: "This government has been informed that a Jewish State has been proclaimed in Palestine, and recognition has been requested by the Provisional Government itself. The United States recognizes the Provisional Government as the *de facto* authority of the new State of Israel."

THE PALESTINE POST

JERUSALEM
SUNDAY, MAY 16, 1948

PRICE: 25 MILS
VOL. XXIII. No. 6714

STATE OF ISRAEL IS BORN

The first independent Jewish State in 19 centuries was born in Tel Aviv as the British Mandate over Palestine came to an end at midnight on Friday, and it was immediately subjected to the test of fire. As "Medinat Yisrael" (State of Israel) was proclaimed, the battle for Jerusalem raged, with most of the city falling to the Jews. At the same time, President Truman announced that the United States would accord recognition to the new State. A few hours later, Palestine was invaded by Moslem armies from the south, east and north, and Tel Aviv was raided from the air. On Friday the United Nations Special Assembly adjourned after adopting a resolution to appoint a mediator but without taking any action on the Partition Resolution of November 29.

Yesterday the battle for the Jerusalem-Tel Aviv road was still under way, and two Arab villages were taken. In the north, Acre town was captured, and the Jewish Army consolidated its positions in Western Galilee.

Most Crowded Hours in Palestine's History

Between Thursday night and this morning Palestine went through what by all standards held among the most crowded hours in its history.

For the Jewish population there was the anguish over the fate of the two hundred Haganah men and women in the Kfar Etzion bloc of settlements near Hebron. Their surrender to a fully equipped superior foreign force desperately in need of a victory was a foregone conclusion. What could not be known, with no communications since Thursday morning, was whether and to what extent the Red Cross and the Truce Consuls would secure civilized conditions for prisoners and wounded, and proper respect for the dead. Doubts on some of these anxious questions have now been resolved.

On Friday afternoon, from Tel Aviv, came the expected - announcement of the Jewish State, and its official naming at birth, "Medinat Yisrael"—State of Israel, with the swearing in of the first Council of Government. The proclamation of the State was made at midnight, coinciding with the sailing from Haifa of Britain's last High Commissioner. Within the hour, President Truman announced in Washington that the Government of the United States had decided to give de facto recognition to the Jewish State, with

JEWS TAKE OVER SECURITY ZONES

The Battle for Jerusalem, which began when the British forces withdrew on Friday morning, continued all day Friday and yesterday. The crackle of small-arms fire and explosions of mortar shells were still being heard in the early hours of this morning as the battle entered its third day.

Repeated efforts on Friday evening and again on Saturday by the U.N. Truce Commission to bring about a "cease fire" were brought to nought when the Arab representatives failed to agree within the specified time limit.

On Friday morning, Jewish forces entered the Russian Compound and Zone C to re-occupy the buildings requisitioned from Jews last year. This operation was almost bloodless, but beyond the western edge of Zone C, Arabs engaged the Jews in Jaffa Road. The Arabs were forced back and the Barclays Bank area was taken.

In other parts of the city fighting flared up. Jews overran one area after another as the areas evacuated by the British. By last night, the quarters and

der of Jewish settlements in North-Eastern Galilee.

The Security Council met yesterday in a special session to consider action on the invasion of Palestine by member states of the U.N.

In the afternoon, Jerusalem was subjected to shelling from the northwest.

Haganah forces throughout the country continued mopping up, and Jewish sources claimed most of Western Galilee safe against attack. Naharayim, near Jisr el Majamie, inside Trans-Jordan.

2 Columns Cross Southern Border

By WALTER COLLINS
U.P. Correspondent

CAIRO, Saturday. — A com-

Egyptian Air Force Spitfires Bomb Tel Aviv; One Shot Down

Kol Israel, the Tel Aviv broadcasting station, reported at 2 o'clock yesterday afternoon that Tel Aviv had been bombed three times in the previous evening and morning, and that one plane had been shot down and its Egyptian pilot taken prisoner.

In the first raid, four planes attacked from a height of 300 feet. Two dropped bombs, while the others strafed the city. Little damage was caused. In the second attack two hours later, the airport to the north of the city was bombed, and an Air France plane parked there by plane for Haifa. The third raid was launched shortly before midday, but the planes were driven off without causing any damage.

Two settlements in the Negev had also been attacked from the air, the radio report ed

Etzion Settlers Taken P.O.W.

Fighting in the Kfar Etzion bloc continued throughout Friday, after Kfar Etzion it-

A country-wide blackout was ordered by Air Raid Precaution Headquarters in Tel Aviv.

U.S. RECOGNIZES JEWISH STATE

WASHINGTON, Saturday. —Ten minutes after the termination of the British Mandate on Friday, the White House released a formal statement by President Truman that the U.S. Government intended to recognize the Provisional Jewish Government as the de facto authority representing the Jewish State.

The U.S. is also considering lifting the arms embargo but it is not known whether to Palestine only or the entire Middle East, and the establishment of diplomatic relations with the Jewish Provisional Government.

The White House press secretary, Mr. Charles Ross, told correspondents today that reaction so far to the recognition had been overwhelmingly favourable. He said this step had been discussed with Mr. Marshall and Mr. Lovett before action was taken, and it had their complete support.

Mr. Ross said that the President had decided several days ago to grant American recogni-

Proclamation by Head Of Government

The creation of "Medinat Yisrael", the State of Israel, was proclaimed at midnight on Friday by Mr. David Ben-Gurion, until then Chairman of the Jewish Agency Executive and now head of the State's Provisional Council of Government.

The first act of the Council of Government, as announced by its head, was to abolish all legislation of the 1939 White Paper of the late Mandatory Power, particularly the Ordinances and Orders relating to immigration and land transfer.

In the declaration of independence, Mr. Ben Gurion called on the Arabs of Palestine to restore peace, assuring them full civic rights and full representation in all governmental organs of the State.

Mr. Ben Gurion prefaced the declaration with a review of the historic connection of the Jewish people with the Land of Israel and of their efforts to return, which never ceased throughout the generations of their dispersal, until the Nazi holocaust proved anew the urgency of the need for a Jewish State.

The Balfour Declaration of 1917, confirmed by the League of Nations, had given explicit international recognition to the

David Ben Gurion, Prime Minister

Special Assembly Adjourns

FLUSHING MEADOWS, Saturday. — The Special U.N. Assembly, called four weeks ago to discuss the U.S. propo-

---

A banner headline announces the birth of the new State. Although the State of Israel was proclaimed on Friday afternoon, May 14, 1948, the paper is dated Sunday, May 16, because no papers in Israel are printed on the Jewish Sabbath.

Chaim Weizmann being inaugurated as first President of the State of Israel.

Two days later, a mass rally was held at Madison Square Garden in New York to celebrate the birth of Israel. Ill in his room at a hotel, Chaim Weizmann heard a radio report that he had been chosen president of the State. He did not believe it until Abba Eban, Israeli representative in the United Nations, came from the rally to confirm the report. Weizmann later learned how David Ben-Gurion, the Prime Minister and actual leader of Israel, had urged that Weizmann be given the honor of being president. Ben-Gurion said: "I doubt whether the presidency is necessary to Dr. Weizmann, but the presidency of Dr. Weizmann is a moral necessity for the State of Israel."

A Head of State

The aged man's first official act as president of the State of Israel was to accept the invitation of the President of the United States to be his guest in Washington. Weizmann traveled from New York to Washington by special train, arriving to find Pennsylvania

United States recognition was followed by that of the Soviet Union and most other nations of the world.

More Than Any Other Man

The next day, a telegram arrived for the aging, almost blind scientist-statesman Chaim Weizmann, then in New York, signed by David Ben-Gurion and the other leaders of the Provisional government of the new State: "On the occasion of the establishment of the Jewish State we send our greetings to you, who have done more than any other living man toward its creation. Your stand and help have strengthened all of us. We look forward to the day when we shall see you at the head of the State established in peace."

Chief Rabbi Herzog greets President Weizmann on the first Independence Day as Foreign Minister Sharett looks on.

The grave of Chaim Weizmann.

Yad Weizmann.

Avenue decorated with flags of the United States and Israel. At the White House, President Weizmann thanked a smiling President Truman for his recognition of the new State, and presented him with a scroll of the Torah.

The following day, Chaim Weizmann set sail for Europe. Sadly leaving England out of his journey, he made his weary way homeward to the land of Israel, now engaged in a desperate and heroic war for its survival. The miracle came to pass. The tiny, poorly armed Israeli army beat back the combined forces of the invaders.

The last four years of his life saw the old warrior, who had fought with all his mind and all his heart for his people, revered as

Hechal Shlomo—the home of the Chief Rabbinate of Israel in Jerusalem.

its first president. He lived to see a troubled peace come to the land. He saw the fulfilment of the greatest promise the Yishuv had made, the ingathering of exiles. All who wished might now come freely to the land of promise. Any Jew who so desired it could gain citizenship as soon as he stepped on the shore of Israel. In the first three years of the State, 650,000 immigrants were welcomed by the 650,000 Jews who already lived in the land. The door was to remain open for as many more as wished to come.

The Institute at Rehovot continued to be a source of pride to the aged scientist, a symbol of the love of learning that had marked his life. There, when he could be excused from official duties, he made his home. There also was he buried in a simple tomb in the gardens of his home, when he died in 1952.

The whole complex of schools, laboratories, and research centers, where scientists work to make nature a better servant of human life, stands as a memorial to him, under the name *Yad Weizmann*.

Indeed, the whole living, growing land of Israel stands as a memorial to Chaim Weizmann and his many dedicated co-workers, who devoted their lives and talents to the cause of Zion rebuilt.

SOME STATEMENTS BY ZIONIST LEADERS

Zionism was the Sabbath of my life.

I believe that my influence as a leader is based on the fact that while as man and writer I had so many faults, and committed so many blunders and mistakes, as a leader in Zionism I have remained pure of heart and quite selfless.

* * *

The greatest honor I can give my children is love for our people, loyalty to self.

* * *

If a people cannot help itself, it cannot be helped at all.

* * *

I believe that a wondrous generation of Jews will spring into existence. The Maccabees will rise again.

* * *

The Jews wish to have a state, and they shall have one. We shall live at last as free men on our own soil, and die peacefully in our own home. The world will be freed by our liberty, enriched by our wealth, magnified by our greatness. And whatever we attempt there to accomplish for our own welfare will react with beneficent force for the good of humanity.

THEODOR HERZL

Zionism cannot put an end to the material Jewish problem, because not all the Jews can migrate to Palestine. Therefore the object of the movement is to create for our people a national center, the influence of which on the diaspora will be spiritual only.

The national center will not be a "secure home of refuge" for our people, but it will be a home of healing for its spirit.

* * *

Learning—learning—learning: that is the secret of Jewish survival.

AHAD HA-AM

The practical heroism of founding and planting, building and perfecting will be accompanied by the awakening of the love of God and the knowledge of His ways. New songs will be created, breathing the love of God and echoing His mighty word. New and bright realms of culture will be discovered. The old will be renewed and the new will be sanctified. This will happen when the congregation of Israel is united with the land of Israel.

* * *

Only in the Holy Land can the spirit of our people develop and become a light for the world.

ABRAHAM ISAAC KUK

Independence is never given to a people; it has to be earned; and having been earned, it has to be defended.

* * *

A time will come when there shall be neither enemies nor frontiers, when war shall be no more, and men will be secure in the dignity of man.

* * *

It is our people who once gave the world a spiritual message fundamental to civilization. The world is watching us now to see the way we choose in ordering our lives, how we fashion our State. The world is waiting to hear whether a new message will go forth from Zion, and what that message will be.
Let us be mindful that the eyes of the entire Jewish people are lifted up toward us and the longings and prayers of past generations attend our steps. May it be given to all of us to be equal to the hour and to our heavy charge.

CHAIM WEIZMANN

There is a vast storehouse filled with treasures. The key, the Hebrew language, is in our guardianship. Have we a right to throw the key into the ocean of oblivion? More than that: when we have ceased to be efficient guardians of our treasures, of what use are we in the world? I fear that in the case of such dereliction of duty the twentieth century will have in store for us not a Ghetto, but a grave.

* * *

If you succeed in conveying to the Jewish women of America the need of a sanctuary for the Jew, the need of a center from which Jewish culture and inspiration will flow, you will have accomplished a result that will bring immediate blessing to those now in distress and in terror of life, and a blessing for all future times redounding to the benefit not only of those who will make use of their sanctuary rights in Palestine, but also those who like ourselves, remaining in a happy, prosperous country, will be free to draw spiritual nourishment from a center dominated wholly by Jewish traditions and the Jewish ideals of universal peace and universal brotherhood.

HENRIETTA SZOLD

It is not a commonwealth of Jews that should be established, but a truly Jewish commonwealth. A truly Jewish commonwealth can be none other than one in which the appeals of the prophets for social justice are translated into reality.

MARTIN BUBER

185

UNIT V

BUILDERS OF
AMERICAN JUDAISM

In September of the year 1654, a small sailing ship, the St. Charles, docked at the Dutch colony of New Amsterdam on the coast of North America. Among its passengers were twenty-three Jews.

Penniless, having been robbed of their few possessions by pirates, they had come from the former Dutch colony of Recife in Brazil. The Portuguese had conquered that area and introduced the Inquisition, the dread authority of the Church which sought out and gave over for punishment those who were unfaithful to its teachings. The refugees were continuing a long history of wanderings. Their families had been driven from Spain in 1492, had lived as secret Jews (Marranos) in various countries, and had found a measure of freedom only in Holland and then in its American colonies.

Three of the newcomers were put into jail for debt. The group was told by Governor Peter Stuyvesant that they must leave. Yet in the next three years, largely through the efforts of their most outspoken member, Asser Levy, they won the right to stay, to trade and travel, to serve in the guard, and finally to be counted as citizens.

This small group of Sephardi Jews in the town that became known, after British conquest, as New York, was the beginning of the American Jewish community. It was to grow

Aaron Lopez

to become the largest and most influential Jewish community ever to exist outside the land of Israel.

Jews in the Revolution

In the century before the American Revolution small numbers of Jews settled in other cities such as Philadelphia, Charleston, and Savannah. Newport, Rhode Island—where religious freedom was guaranteed by Roger Williams, the founder of the state—had a flourishing community. The Newport synagogue building, erected in 1760, still stands as a national shrine.

When English forces took over Newport during the Revolution, many Jews, such as the wealthy trader Aaron Lopez, and the acting rabbi, Isaac Touro, faithful to the cause of independence, fled the city.

The American Revolution was aided in far greater measure than could be expected by the small number of Jews, three thousand,

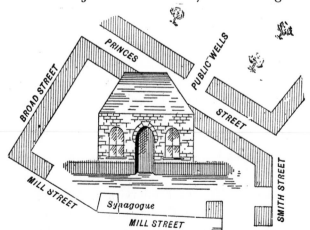

Sketch and site of the Old Mill Street Synagogue, New York.

A medal in honor of Gershom Mendez Seixas.

then in the country. Francis Salvador of South Carolina died in one of the first skirmishes in 1776. Other Jews became soldiers and officers, many giving their lives.

Gershom Mendez Seixas (1745-1816), rabbi of Shearith Israel, the first congregation of the American colonies, was so well known as a patriot that he had to leave New York when the British attacked. He returned in 1783 to continue his long ministry. He was one of the thirteen ministers to take part in George Washington's inauguration, and was appointed a trustee of Columbia College.

An outstanding name during the Revolution was that of Haym Salomon (1740-1785), a broker whose faith in the cause of liberty led him to lend money and arrange credit for the struggling American forces. An im-

Tablet in Shearith Israel Synagogue, New York.

migrant from Poland, he was one of the Ashkenazi Jews who came to America in the early days.

Jews as Citizens

The Jews of Newport, like many other groups, sent greetings to George Washington upon his election as first president of the new republic. In answer, the President wrote his famous "Letter to the Jews of Newport," in which he said: "May the children of the stock of Abraham who dwell in this land

"Letter to the Jews of Newport."

continue to merit and enjoy the good will of the other inhabitants. The citizens of the United States of America have a right to applaud themselves for having given to mankind examples of an enlarged and liberal policy—a policy worthy of imitation. All possess alike liberty of conscience and immunities of citizenship."

Many of the colonies had laws, copied after old European models, restricting the rights of Jews. For example, some required "good Christian faith" for holders of public office. The United States Constitution had no religious qualifications for citizenship. Even-

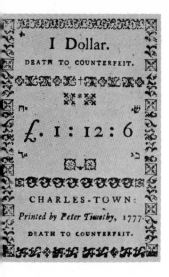

Paper money with Hebrew characters—issued by South Carolina.

tually all states removed religious restrictions from their lawbooks. The United States was the first country founded on a declaration of human rights, and providing absolute equality for Jews and Christians.

Before the Civil War

Thousands of Jewish immigrants, together with hundreds of thousands of other Europeans, entered the United States during the first part of the nineteenth century. A time of movement and change, including the revolutions in Central Europe in 1848, sent large numbers from Germany and neighboring countries to the free shores of America.

Jews who arrived in that time of pioneering and westward expansion became active in many fields. Some joined in explorations, or pioneered in trade, bringing the goods of civilization to new areas. Jews settled in all of the cities. Many took part in the first rush to California in 1849, so that within the first five years there were a dozen synagogues in the new territory.

There are many Jews who were outstanding because of their devotion to Judaism and their good work in the general community. Judah Touro (1775-1854), the son of Isaac

Touro of Newport, grew wealthy in New Orleans, and gave away his entire fortune to worthy causes. He gave $10,000, the largest single contribution, for the building of the Bunker Hill Monument. His will provided large gifts for synagogues and Hebrew schools in eighteen different cities, as well as donations to numerous hospitals, schools, benevolent societies and orphan homes. His gift to build homes for the poor in Jerusalem was administered by Sir Moses Montefiore. He left no family. On his tombstone stand the words: "The last of his name, he inscribed it in the Book of Philanthropy, to be remembered forever."

In the free atmosphere of the new country, men of vigor and enterprise were able to pursue unusual goals. An outstanding figure was Mordecai Manuel Noah (1785-1851). Active in politics, he was a publisher of newspapers and a writer of plays. He was appointed to several public offices, such as those of sheriff, surveyor and judge, in New York. As United States consul to Tunis in 1813, he helped to end pirate activity in the Mediterranean.

Mordecai Manuel Noah.

A portrait of Uriah Phillips Levy.

Most memorable of Noah's actions was the dedication of Ararat, the name he gave to Grand Island in the Niagara River near Buffalo. He hoped that it would be a "city of refuge" for Jews of Europe, a hope that was never realized. In his later years, Noah wrote that Palestine was the only place for a Jewish state.

Uriah Phillips Levy (1792-1862), another man of ambition, fought as a naval officer in the War of 1812 and rose to the rank of flag officer, the highest post at that time. In all navies of the world, sailors were flogged for discipline. Uriah Levy fought all his life to stop corporal punishment in the United States Navy, and finally was happy to see the practice ended.

In the years of controversy before the Civil War, many Jews took part in the anti-slavery cause. Three Jews, August Bondi (1833-1907), Jacob Benjamin and Theodore Weiner, took part in John Brown's attempt to win freedom for the slaves by direct action.

Isidor Bush in Missouri and Moritz Pinner in Kansas supported the often unpopular cause of abolition in their newspapers.

Rabbi Sabato Morais (1832-1897) was threatened by pro-slavery Philadelphians, and Rabbi David Einhorn (1809-1879) was forced to flee Baltimore for his life, as a result of their preaching sermons in favor of abolition.

Like other Americans when war broke out, Jews for the most part remained loyal to the part of the country in which they lived. Lending much leadership and sacrifice to the Union cause, Jewish citizens were also well represented in the armies of the South. Judah P. Benjamin (1811-1884), a United States senator from Louisiana, became Secretary of State for the Confederacy.

There are records of Abraham Lincoln's quick action when wrongs committed against Jews in the armed forces, like injustice anywhere, were brought to his attention. Four

August Bondi.

Rebecca Gratz, a painting by Scully.

A teacher and author of well-known poems and hymns was Penina Moise (1797-1880), who, even though blind during the last twenty-five years of her life, supervised the Jewish Sunday School of Charleston, conducted a girls' school, and continued her writing.

An outstanding poet was Emma Lazarus (1849-1887), whose poems were praised by such leading literary men as Ralph Waldo Emerson. She wrote odes on beauty, nature, and mythology, until the events of 1881 and the great influx of Jewish immigrants to New York, where she lived, brought her back to an awareness of her people. *Songs of a Semite* and *By the Waters of Babylon* are collections of her poems which tell of pride in her faith, sorrow for her people's sufferings, and hope for their future. As an adult, she learned Hebrew and studied Jewish history to understand her heritage better. She urged the up-

A poster commemorating the seventy fifth anniversary of the founding of The Hebrew Sunday School Society.

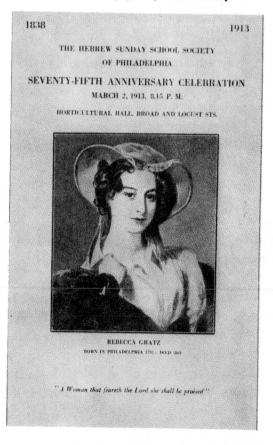

1838   1913

THE HEBREW SUNDAY SCHOOL SOCIETY
OF PHILADELPHIA

SEVENTY-FIFTH ANNIVERSARY CELEBRATION
MARCH 2, 1913. 8.15 P. M.

HORTICULTURAL HALL, BROAD AND LOCUST STS.

REBECCA GRATZ
BORN IN PHILADELPHIA 1781; DIED 1869

"A Woman that feareth the Lord she shall be praised"

Jewish chaplains were appointed to serve in Union hospitals during the Civil War.

Women of Distinction

Jewish women of the United States early showed that they were continuing the tradition of charity, compassion, and love of learning which had marked their mothers and grandmothers in all the countries of the diaspora.

Rebecca Gratz (1781-1869), attractive member of the distinguished Gratz family of Philadelphia, used her talents and influence to found the first Jewish Sunday School in America, and to establish orphan and foster homes. It has been widely believed that she was the inspiration for the heroine named Rebecca in *Ivanhoe*, for her friend, American author Washington Irving, admired her greatly and described her virtues to Sir Walter Scott, author of *Ivanhoe*.

Emma Lazarus.

building of Palestine. Her poem, *The New Colossus,* calling America "Mother of Exiles," is inscribed on a plaque on the base of the Statue of Liberty in New York harbor.

Judaism in Early America

From the beginning of its settlement, immigrants came to America from many countries. They came to seek a better life, freedom of religion and freedom of opportunity. Often they came because conditions in their home country were hard; or because they had new ideas which did not fit in well in their former society. America offered an equal chance to everyone to express himself and to make a good life.

Jews, like the others, came from many countries. The earliest, such as the first Jewish settlers in New York, were of Sephardi stock. The first synagogues that were formed in New York, in Philadelphia, in Newport, in Charleston, and in Savannah, followed the Sephardi *minhag,* or "Spanish-Portuguese"

ritual. The pronunciation of the Hebrew prayers and the tunes to which they were sung harked back to the time their ancestors had lived in Spain.

From colonial times on, there were Jews who came from Central and Eastern Europe as well. These Ashkenazi Jews would usually join the Sephardi synagogues until, early in the nineteenth century, groups from different areas grew large enough to found synagogues following their own minhag.

There were no ordained rabbis in America until a few came in the 1840's. Scholars and spiritual leaders did not seek the adventure of settling a new land. There were few Hebrew schools of any kind. Occasionally an immigrant brought with him from Europe the training needed to fulfil religious functions such as that of *shohet.* Laymen, with some Jewish education acquired in their young days in Europe, would lead services.

Isaac Leeser

The most remarkable of these acting rabbis was Isaac Leeser (1806-1868), who served as *Hazzan* and preacher for congregations Mikveh Israel and Beth El Emeth in Philadelphia. Educated in Prussia, he arrived at his uncle's home in Richmond, Virginia, at the age of seventeen. He continued his studies, taught religion to children, and began a literary career by writing letters on Jewish subjects to the public press.

Leeser saw that there were no textbooks or Bible translations, and few Jewish publications of any kind for the growing Jewish community of America. He set about to write, translate, edit and publish. Among the many works he produced was a complete English Bible translation; prayerbooks in both the "Portuguese" and the "German" tradition with translations and notes; books of instruction in Hebrew, Jewish religion and the Bible; and sermons and discourses.

The most important publication edited by Leeser was *The Occident,* a monthly magazine which appeared from 1843 to 1869. Events of interest to Jews, and problems in religious life in the New World, were discussed in its pages by leading Jews of the time.

Through *The Occident* Leeser fostered plans for improving Jewish life and education in the United States. His efforts brought about the first Hebrew day-school, the first Hebrew college, the first Jewish publication society in America. Most did not succeed, but they laid the groundwork for the time when the Jewish community would be large enough to support all these undertakings.

An Early Attempt at Reform

The same year Leeser arrived in America, there occurred the first attempt at Reform on these shores. Isaac Harby (1788-1828), an editor, author and schoolmaster, led a group calling itself the Reformed Society of Israelites, which broke away from Congregation Beth Elohim of Charleston in 1824. Some of the requests of the group were for a shorter service, translation of some prayers to English, and an English sermon to give instruction based on the Torah reading every week.

Founding its own congregation, the Reformed Society issued its own prayerbook,

Isaac Leeser (1806-1868).

and conducted services under a volunteer Reader, worshipping with uncovered heads and with the aid of instrumental music. Its aim was like that of German Reform of the same period: to "discontinue ceremonies that owe their origin to Rabbinical institutions," and to emphasize the "moral laws of Moses."

The Society ended its activity in 1833. Soon thereafter Beth Elohim adopted some Reform practices.

Reform Judaism Unites

With the arrival in the 1840's of many Central European Jews of Reform leanings, including rabbis such as Max Lilienthal (1815-1882) and Isaac Mayer Wise (1819-1900), the Reform movement was able to establish its own institutions.

Isaac Mayer Wise made Congregation Bene Yeshurun in Cincinnati a leading Reform temple. With the hope of uniting all existing congregations to follow a "Minhag America,"

Old Jewish cemetery, Chatham Square, New York.

he published a prayerbook under that name. He traveled and spoke widely, edited a weekly newspaper, *The Israelite,* and called for national conferences. He took part in many debates, some with Isaac Leeser, who opposed his reforms, and others with David Einhorn, who wished to see much more radical reforms.

Rabbi Wise founded the Union of American Hebrew Congregations in 1873, the Hebrew Union College for higher Jewish education and the ordaining of rabbis the next year, and the Central Conference of American Rabbis in 1889.

The Great Immigration

A quarter of a million Jews lived in the United States in 1870. During the next fifty years, ten times as many entered the country. The pogroms and persecution of 1881 and 1882 made life so hard for the Jews of Eastern Europe that vast numbers of them sought a new home. Two and a half million arrived in America before immigration from their part of the world was limited by United States law in 1924.

Jews and other immigrants coming in the first half of the nineteenth century were able to go where they wished, to enter many fields, and to move westward with the expansion of the country. Many Jews became peddlers, traveling to far outposts and helping to bring necessities and luxuries to farms and small villages. Eventually many of these tradesmen opened small retail stores in towns throughout the country.

The Jews who came in the great immigration following 1880 settled in large numbers in New York and other cities. They did not yet speak the language nor know the ways of the new country. Many became factory workers in the new industry of mass manufacture of clothing, which was growing up in the cities. Poor conditions, low wages, even child labor, were abuses at this time. Jews played a large part in the growth of unions, which did much to persuade employers that improving the standards of workers would benefit everyone.

Free loan societies, charity groups, and organizations for fellowship and mutual help were set up by immigrants from every town in Eastern Europe. The old tradition of charity and good deeds, *tzedakah* and *gemilut hasadim,* was carried on in the New World. Wealthier American Jews who had done well in this country helped to set up schools, orphans' homes and settlement houses for the help and education of the newcomers.

Poor as most of them were, the Eastern European Jews brought with them a sense of responsibility and a love of learning. They built small *schuls,* synagogues like those in the towns they had left. Out of their tiny salaries they took the few dollars to pay the *melamed* who taught their children Hebrew and prayers. Yiddish newspapers and magazines, theatres and lecture halls flourished.

The parents, after a hard day of work, often went to night school to learn English and citizenship. They sacrificed to try to send their children to high school and even college, so that the second generation were able to find better jobs and in some cases to become teachers and doctors.

The Second Generation

The culture and religion of the parents, the Yiddish language and the customs of the old country, were not easy to pass on to English-speaking sons and daughters. Keeping Shabbat was difficult when every penny of income was needed. The conflicting ideas and the general free atmosphere of the new country made it easy for many to leave the ways of their fathers.

The second generation wanted above all to become like other Americans. They did not realize that being better Jews would make them better citizens of America. Many of them felt that the religion of their parents was old-fashioned and belonged only in Europe.

Very few of the Eastern European Jews or their children were able to feel at home in the Reform temples between 1885 and 1920. Reform of that time, as set forth by Reform rabbis meeting in Pittsburgh in 1885, had changed most temples greatly. Services were almost completely in English, and many congregations held their main service on Sunday. Jews who were Zionists or felt close to their people in other lands found these feelings lacking in the Reform groups.

A great many of the children of immigrants were growing up with little knowledge and little respect for Judaism, and with no connection to any Jewish institution.

The Jewish Theological Seminary

Some leading American rabbis established, in 1886 in New York, a seminary for the training of English-speaking, traditional rabbis. The students had to be college graduates, familiar with American ways as well as with Jewish teachings. Rabbi Sabato Morais (1832-1897), first president of the Jewish Theological Seminary of America, as well as Rabbi H. Pereira Mendes (1852-1937) and other founders, hoped that the rabbis ordained there would be able to influence young Jews "against the inroads of indifference and irreligiousness."

In 1902, Solomon Schechter (1850-1915), Reader in Rabbinics at Cambridge University, became head of the Seminary. Under his leadership it became a first-rank institution, and the fountainhead of Conservative Judaism. He founded the United Synagogue, the organization of all Conservative congregations.

The Conservative movement had its beginnings in the "Historical" school of Judaism, of which Zechariah Frankel was a leader. The Conservative belief is that Judaism has developed through the ages, and can be studied like other historical institutions. Conservative Jews, believing that changes have taken place in the past and continue to do so today, wish to preserve and enhance Jewish tradition.

Orthodox Jewry Organizes

Orthodox Jews, faithful to all the laws in the Shulhan Arukh, and believing both Bible and Talmud to be of divine inspiration, had set up synagogues, schools and other religious institutions. Divided into numerous small communities, they did not for some time reach any type of unity. Jews of New York tried in 1888 to organize their growing numbers under the leadership of a chief rabbi, Jacob Joseph (1848-1902), whom they brought over from Vilna. Even he, however, was unable to unite the people.

Devoted to Torah, Orthodox Jews supported *yeshivot* both in Europe and in the

A very early photograph of The Jewish Theological Seminary of America.

195

Facsimile of first Hebrew periodical in America.

new land. Believing that a modern school could teach American youth both Torah and general studies, leaders, including Rabbi Bernard Revel (1885-1940), established Yeshiva University. It began in 1896 as a rabbinical seminary named after the scholar Isaac Elhanan Spektor. Under Dr. Revel's presidency, beginning in 1915, the Yeshiva grew to include a high school, a teachers' institute, an undergraduate college, and a graduate school. Under his successor, Dr. Samuel Belkin, the Stern College for Women, and graduate departments, including the Albert Einstein College of Medicine, were added.

The largest national body of Orthodox synagogues is the Union of Orthodox Jewish Congregations of America, founded in 1898. Rabbis ordained at Yeshiva University, or of similar background, belong to the Rabbinical Council of America.

Jews in America Today

Judaism in America now has three branches, Orthodox, Conservative and Reform, each with its own schools and organizations. Jews belonging to all three groups unite in all types of community work: to aid education, to collect vast sums for charity, to help their fellow-Jews and oppressed peoples everywhere, and to give support to the State of Israel.

The American Jewish community of today is mostly the product of the Eastern European immigration beginning in the 1880's. In the few generations that most Jewish families have lived in the United States or Canada, they have become an integral part of the society around them.

Problems of anti-Semitism have largely disappeared as American democracy has progressed. Problems of adjustment faded away as Jews felt themselves more at home in America. Leaders in industry, government, the professions, education and culture, the Jews realize also that America wants its citizens to be faithful members of their religious groups.

The more than five million Jews of America now form the largest, wealthiest and most secure Jewish community ever to exist anywhere. As American Jews, enjoying freedom, they are able to contribute greatly to the well-being of their country.

Medal issued on the 250th anniversary of the Jewish settlement in America.

196

In the words of Justice Brandeis:

Not since the destruction of the Temple have the Jews in spirit and in ideals been so fully in harmony with the noblest aspirations of the country in which they lived. America's fundamental law seeks to make real the brotherhood of man. That brotherhood became the Jewish fundamental law more than twenty-five hundred years ago. America's insistent demand in the twentieth century is for social justice. That also has been the Jews' striving for ages. Their affliction as well as their religion has prepared the Jews for effective democracy. To be good Americans, we must be better Jews.

Isaac Mayer Wise

(1819-1900)

"On the eighth, ninth and tenth days of July 1873, in the convention held in Cincinnati, the youngest child of Israel was born; the Union of American Hebrew Congregations was organized, constituted and established. The new chapter in our history begins with peace."

The author of these happy words, which appeared in the weekly magazine, *The Israelite*, soon after the event, was himself the author of the "new chapter" he spoke of. He had brought about the first abiding union of American Jews.

Rabbi Isaac Mayer Wise, editor of *The Israelite*, rabbi of the leading temple of Cincinnati, had worked for twenty years for an organization of congregations in the United States. He had called together conventions and meetings of rabbis. In the pages of his magazine and in lectures throughout the country he had spoken of the need for unity. He had compiled a prayerbook with the name *Minhag America*, showing his hope that all Jews in the New World would come to follow the same order of worship.

Now he saw the result of his work. Though not all congregations were represented, delegates from thirty-four temples in twenty-eight cities had voted to work together to further Judaism in the United States.

With high hopes, Rabbi Wise proclaimed, "The Union of American Hebrew Congregations is 'Israel's new glory,' and is destined to bind all the Israelites of this great country into one great union, under whose auspices the greatest glory that Israel has ever achieved will be accomplished."

Hebrew Union College

The first duty the Union set for itself, under Rabbi Wise's influence, was "to establish, sustain and govern a seat of learning for Israel's religion." The Jews of America, then numbering about 250,000, were scattered throughout the land. There were no seminaries of Jewish studies. The only rabbis and scholars were those who had studied in Europe before coming to America. Rabbi Wise himself had arrived in the United States at the age of twenty-seven, already married and a father, after receiving his education in Prague and Vienna.

To further Jewish learning in America, Rabbi Wise had tried in 1855 to establish Zion College in Cincinnati. Other attempts had been made. Isaac Leeser, outstanding Jewish editor and preacher, had founded Maimonides College in Philadelphia. Neither school received enough support to enable it to survive.

In 1874, the second meeting of the Union took place in Cleveland. This time fifty-five congregations of the mid-West and South sent delegates. The convention passed a resolution to found the Hebrew Union College in Cincinnati, in which "the future advocates of

Isaac Mayor Wise.

our religion shall be educated." A preparatory class was immediately set up.

In October of the next year, the classes of the new college began. They met in the basement rooms of a synagogue. The young men who attended did not enjoy the advantages of fine buildings or modern textbooks. Two of the three instructors, Rabbi Wise being one of them, received no pay. Yet the first Jewish institute of higher learning in America had come into being.

The new Board of Governors elected Isaac Mayer Wise the first president of the school he had founded, a position he held for the rest of his life.

An article in *The Israelite* showed how important he considered the presidency. "He considers it the highest honor which could have been conferred upon him. Neither a seat in the Senate of the United States, nor the office of Chief Justice appears to him as responsible and honorable a position as the presidency of the Hebrew Union College, where the finest opportunity is offered to contribute largely to the education of the young people of our country; to lay a solid foundation to the future greatness of American Judaism."

Rabbi Wise became the professor of history on the small but dedicated faculty of the new seminary. Founder, president, director and dean, he became personal adviser to every student, welcoming every class, inviting the entire student body to his Passover Seder each year.

The General Conference

Fourteen years after the founding of the College, the graduates formed themselves into the Central Conference of American Rabbis. This was the first union of rabbinic leaders in America. They met each year thereafter, to discuss problems and to set up standards for Reform Judaism. They agreed on a common prayerbook, the Union Prayer Book of 1884, so that services in all their temples might be similar. The leader of Reform in America, Rabbi Isaac Mayer Wise, was elected president.

Background of a Liberal

A lifetime of ambition and hard work stood behind all these accomplishments. While the young Rabbi Wise had been holding his first position in the small town of Radnitz in Bohemia, the 1845 conference of German Reform rabbis took place in Frankfurt. The ideas of the leader of the conference, Abraham Geiger, were close to those of Rabbi Wise. The younger man agreed with Geiger that the Jewish religion had changed and developed, and that the laws of the Talmud, which had directed Jewish life since the destruction of the Temple, were made to meet the needs of an earlier time. Believing firmly that the Ten Commandments and the ethical teachings of the Torah had been given by God, Rabbi Wise felt that ways of keeping the ideals of the Torah could change in different eras.

Rabbi Wise hoped that in the new country of America he would be able to carry out his ideas. He began to study English. In 1846 he and his family arrived in New York after a sea voyage of sixty-three days.

Title page of one of the early issues of "The Israelite."

The Need for Rabbis

At that time there were fewer than 50,000 Jews in the United States. There were three congregations considered to be Reform, in Charleston, Baltimore and New York. The rest were Orthodox, following the Sephardi or Ashkenazi ritual. Among all the congregations, there were only three rabbis who had been ordained in Europe. In Jewish law, any ten men may form a congregation, and services may be conducted by any learned Jew. There was great need, however, for well-educated religious leaders.

The one Jewish magazine of the time, *The Occident*, edited by Isaac Leeser of Philadelphia, took notice that Isaac Mayer Wise, who "is said to possess some Hebrew learning," had arrived. In short order, the newcomer was invited to speak in several cities, and accepted the call to become rabbi of Congregation Beth El in Albany.

Albany and Cincinnati

A time of hard work followed. As Rabbi Wise later wrote of himself, "Eighteen hours out of every twenty-four, five days of the week, he was steadily at work, six hours daily in his school, and twelve hours at his desk." In addition to directing the day school, where children learned Hebrew and German as well as English and general subjects, he read and studied, perfected his English, wrote works of Jewish history and planned his *Minhag America*.

Rabbi Wise urged his congregation to shorten the services, to observe decorum and to leave out prayers for rebuilding the Temple and return to Zion. He wished to stop observing the second day of holidays, which had been added in the diaspora. He introduced Confirmation for both boys and girls in place of the Bar Mitzvah ceremony. Many of these early reforms were accepted by his members, but from the start there were those who objected to change.

After many differences of opinion, those members who were in favor of Reform left the congregation and started a new group with Rabbi Wise as their leader. The former congregation returned to all its Orthodox traditions. The new temple was the first in America to provide for families to sit together; in the synagogue, men and women were always seated in separate sections.

Rabbi Wise had become well-known for his writings in *The Occident,* where he had many articles published although his radical views were contrary to those of the editor. Wise declared that he did not believe in miracles, nor in the coming of a personal Messiah. Editor Leeser often argued with him in his columns. In books on Judaism and Jewish history, Rabbi Wise put forth his view of Israel being chosen as a "light of the nations" to teach God's message of justice and morality to the world. He felt Judaism could be a universal religion.

In 1854 Isaac Mayer Wise became the rabbi of Congregation Bene Yeshurun in Cincinnati. Though it had been Orthodox, the congregation was ready for change and followed all reforms suggested by its new rabbi. He had found a city and a temple where he could carry out his ideas to their fullest extent. He became a leading citizen of the city, known to Christians as well as Jews; at one time he was asked, though he declined, to be state senator.

Desire for Unity

Dedicating his whole life to the cause of Reform Judaism in "the spirit of the age," Isaac Mayer Wise never intended to divide the Jewish community into different groups. He was convinced that Judaism in the free atmosphere of America must develop along the lines which he favored. Wishing to in-

A very early photograph of Hebrew Union College, Cincinnati, Ohio.

clude all Jews in his early plans at union, he emphasized that he was not in favor of radical change. For a conference he called in Cleveland in 1855, he prepared a careful statement to show he did not intend to cast aside the great tradition of the Talmud. He wrote: "The Bible as delivered to us by our fathers and as now in our possession, is of immediate divine origin and the standard of our religion. The Talmud contains the traditional, legal, and logical exposition of the Biblical laws which must be expounded and practiced according to the comments of the Talmud."

Rabbi Wise hoped to include Orthodox Jews in setting up a committee to decide on changes in Jewish observance. The Orthodox did not agree to join with him. The strongest attacks against him came, however, from other Reform rabbis. Rabbi David Einhorn was leader of a group of radical Reformers in the east who did not wish to consider Talmudic law in any way binding. They saw no need to bow to old traditions. All the laws were obsolete, they said, except the "eternal truths" of Jewish ethics. Rabbi Einhorn did not share the desire of Rabbi Wise to develop a progressive Judaism which would include Jews with traditional loyalties.

Not giving up his ambition to unite all of American Jewry, Rabbi Wise continued his efforts, until he had founded the Hebrew Union College and the other organizations of Reform Judaism. Towards the end of the century and the end of his life, he realized that the Jews of the United States seemed determined to follow different roads. The East European Orthodox Jews who were arriving in such large numbers did not share his feeling that Judaism in an age of freedom should cast off old forms and take on new ones.

Nonetheless, in all his reforms, Rabbi Wise remained loyal to many Jewish traditions which were discarded by the radical reformers. He upheld the importance of the Hebrew language, saying, "Our service ought to be conducted in the Hebrew language; for it is that which our prophets spoke." In the 1880's and 1890's many Reform congregations decided to hold Sabbath services on Sunday.

An aerial view of the campus of the Hebrew Union College.

This Rabbi Wise opposed, for he felt that the Sabbath must be kept on the seventh day as bidden in the Ten Commandments. After some decades, most Reform leaders came to agree with him.

Faith in America

Rabbi Wise had great faith in American democracy, and believed it his duty, like that of every citizen, to see that the government was true to its ideals. When Switzerland said that American Jews traveling within its borders would be kept out of districts where Swiss Jews were not allowed, Rabbi Wise went to Washington and protested. He also helped influence the United States government to speak out against czarist oppression.

Rabbi Wise felt that Jewish ideals were the ideals of all modern, democratic nations. Any setting apart of the Jews to pursue their own goals seemed unnecessary to him. For this reason, he strongly opposed the Zionist movement. All Jewish hopes for freedom and fulfillment could be attained, he felt, in America.

In 1885, a group of rabbis meeting in Pittsburgh proclaimed the ideals of Reform Judaism, making it clear that a distinct Reform movement existed. The founding of the Jewish Theological Seminary soon afterwards marked the beginning of the Conservative movement. The great numbers of Jews coming from Europe during this period guaranteed that a strong Orthodox group would carry on. Thus the American Jewish community was divided into Orthodox, Conservative and Reform branches.

Isaac Mayer Wise did not realize his dream of unity. He had, however, decided the needs and forms for the organization of Jewish life in the United States.

The Father of Reform Judaism died in March, 1900, at the age of eighty-one, after preaching a last Sabbath sermon and giving a last Sabbath afternoon lecture to his beloved students at the Hebrew Union College.

For the day of his funeral, many businesses were closed, and the superintendent of schools of Cincinnati suspended classes so that children might attend. The anniversary of his death is observed as Founder's Day by the students at the Hebrew Union College each year.

Thus ended a life of ambition and conflict, of some disappointments and of many fulfillments.

The way Isaac Mayer Wise looked at his own career can be judged by a statement he made in 1875 when he was at the height of his powers: "I thank the Almighty that I am deemed worthy of cooperation in this work of Israel's resurrection."

Front view of the "House of Living Judaism," national headquarters of the Reform Judaism.

Solomon Schechter

(1850-1915)

"America must be a place of Torah, because the future of Judaism is across the seas."

These prophetic words were written by Solomon Schechter, instructor in Talmudic studies, at his desk in Cambridge University in England in the year 1893. Familiar with Rumania, Vienna and Berlin, Dr. Schechter had never visited the United States. Yet his faith in the New World was already firm. American Jewry must be educated to fulfil its destiny as the future leader of the Jewish communities of the world. Solomon Schechter was to be one of the great builders of that destiny.

From East to West

Born to a Hasidic family in Rumania, Solomon Schechter was early steeped in the study of Talmud. At the Rabbinical Seminary of Vienna, he learned how to do research, and studied history, Hebrew lan-

Solomon Schechter.

guage, and a wide range of Jewish subjects. He no longer concentrated on Talmud alone, but he never lost the passion for thoroughness that marked the scholars of Eastern Europe.

From Vienna he moved to Berlin, where, at the Academy for Jewish Science and at the University, he learned the discipline of the scientific method of study. He admired the work of Leopold Zunz, and hoped, as Zunz had, to spend his life in research into Judaism.

A wealthy young Englishman had come from London to Berlin to study Bible and other Jewish subjects. His name, Solomon Schechter soon learned, was Claude Montefiore. The young man delighted to spend hours in talk with the brilliant newcomer from Eastern Europe.

Grand-nephew of Sir Moses, Claude Montefiore was used to making quick decisions and carrying them out. He persuaded Solomon Schechter to come with him to England as his tutor in 1882.

Leading Scholar of England

Dr. Schechter quickly became known as the leading scholar of Judaism in England. He gave lectures and wrote learned studies on Talmud, other Hebrew and Aramaic writings, and history. Dr. Schechter was able to share his ideas with thoughtful men such as writer Israel Zangwill and scholars Israel Abrahams and Moses Gaster.

While studying at the British Museum, Dr. Schechter often met Matilda Roth, a well-educated schoolteacher from Breslau. He proposed marriage, telling her that with her at his side he thought he might make a contribution to Jewish life in Europe or America. If she refused, he would become a farmer in Palestine, where his twin brother Israel had gone in the same year Solomon had come to England.

Matilda Roth agreed to marry the zealous scholar, and proved to be an understanding and helpful companion.

In 1890 the position of Reader in Rabbinics at time-honored Cambridge University became open. Dr. Schechter was elected to the position. He was able to devote his days to research, and to spend hours in the company of Christian scholars, who valued his friendship highly.

The Discovery

In May of 1896, two learned sisters who had often discussed Bible history with Dr. Schechter asked him to look at some items they had brought back from a recent trip to the Near East. Mrs. Agnes Lewis and Mrs. Margaret Gibson showed him a bundle of ragged papers they had bought from an Egyptian peddler.

Looking at two of the fragments, Dr. Schechter immediately sensed what they were. One, he said, was "part of the Jerusalem

Ben Sira fragment.

Talmud, of which few copies exist. The other may be important also."

Taking the second paper to the University library, Dr. Schechter soon found a paragraph in an English volume that corresponded to the Hebrew words he was holding. In joy he wrote to Mrs. Lewis: "I think we have reason to congratulate ourselves. For the fragment I took with me represents a piece of the original Hebrew of Ecclesiasticus. It is the first time that such a thing was discovered." With a scholar's enthusiasm, he signed his name "In haste and great excitement!"

The book *Ecclesiasticus,* a collection of wise sayings, was written in Palestine by Joshua ben Sira around 200 B.C.E. Because it was written so late, it was not included in the Bible. It was made part of the Apocrypha, the later writings which were not considered holy by the Jews. In a Greek translation, it was often read in Christian churches. Now at least a part of the original Hebrew text, lost for centuries, had come to light.

A Bible fragment from the Cairo Genizah. Upper writing is in Hebrew, 11th century. Lower writing is Greek translation.

The Geniza

For some time, travelers in Egypt had been bringing back fragments of old writings. It was known that in Cairo there was a storehouse of crumbling manuscripts, guarded by attendants who now and then removed some items for sale to tourists. This was the Cairo *Geniza*, and this Dr. Schechter now became determined to find.

Geniza, from the Hebrew root *ganoz*, "to hide or bury," means a burial place for old books and documents. Revering books, Jews would inter damaged Hebrew writings in a special room in a synagogue or cemetery, so that they would not be burnt or treated with disrespect. For over a thousand years, worn-out manuscripts of the Jewish community had been deposited in the Cairo Geniza.

In the fall of 1896, Cambridge University sent Dr. Schechter on a mission at first kept secret. He was to rescue as much as possible of the disintegrating treasure of the Cairo Geniza and bring it back to the Cambridge library.

With the help of the chief rabbi of Cairo, Dr. Schechter was allowed to crawl through a hole in the wall of the synagogue building, and to enter the dark unventilated Geniza, where old manuscripts crumbled to dust beneath his feet.

"For weeks and weeks," wrote Schechter, "I had to swallow the dust of centuries, which nearly suffocated and blinded me. I am now under medical treatment." In the six weeks of work, he seemed to become years older.

Finding it impossible to examine the thousands of partial manuscripts, the discoverer made it a policy to take all he could. Thirty bags were filled and paid for, to be sent back to England.

Before returning, Dr. Schechter went to Palestine. He visited his brother in the village of Zikhron Yaakov, happy to see him sharing in the work of building the Jewish homeland. Zion was always dear to Solomon Schechter. He wrote towards the end of his life, "Zionism was, and still is, the most cherished dream I was worthy of having." His responsibilities toward his people were, however, to be fulfilled in the diaspora.

Returning to Cambridge, Dr. Schechter set to work on the manuscripts. Among masses of material were many rare documents, including whole pages in the handwriting of Moses Maimonides, for the great sage had lived and worked seven centuries before in Fostat, old Cairo. As he had hoped, many more fragments of Ben Sira also came to light.

Two thousand Jewish manuscripts were given to the Cambridge library, and thousands more to other collections. Knowing he could do only a tiny portion of the work himself, Schechter gave of the riches he had found to many scholars. Even small portions of manuscripts could give a scholar information about long periods which had been called "dark" because of lack of records.

"Looking over the mass of fragments in the sifting of which I am occupied," Schechter wrote, "I cannot overcome a sad feeling that I shall hardly be worthy to see all the results which the Geniza will add to our knowledge of Jews and Judaism."

The finding of the Geniza made Dr. Schechter's name known not only to students but also to the mass of people. Articles about him appeared in newspapers of many countries.

The Call to America

For some time, leading Jews of America had been trying to persuade Dr. Schechter to come to New York. Rabbi Sabato Morais, chancellor, had invited him as early as 1890 to join the teaching staff of the Jewish Theological Seminary of America.

Sabato Morais (1823-1897) one of the founders of the Conservative movement.

Leading laymen of Philadelphia were able to arrange for Schechter to give six lectures in their city in 1895. This visit strengthened both Dr. Schechter and the American hosts in their belief that his place was with them. "A great people!" he exclaimed about the Americans upon his return to England.

After the death of Sabato Morais in 1897, great efforts were begun to bring Schechter to take his place. Dr. Cyrus Adler and Judge Mayer Sulzberger wrote many letters, and enlisted the aid of philanthropists such as Jacob Schiff and Louis Marshall, to make sure that the Seminary could continue to grow.

Finally, with some sadness, Solomon Schechter left his life of study at Cambridge in 1902, to accept the challenge of building up a "school of Torah" in America. One of his aims was to raise his children among Jews. He would come, he said, "for the sake of my family, and perhaps also for the sake of American Judaism, with which the future rests."

Work at the Seminary

Dr. Schechter was indeed the man to build up a "school of Torah." He organized a great library, which became the finest collection of Jewish books and manuscripts ever to be gathered in one place. Many of his **Geniza** finds were included.

The teachers that he appointed included world authorities such as Professor Louis Ginzberg in Talmud, Professor Alexander Marx in history, and Professor Israel Friedlaender in Bible.

One of Dr. Schechter's most important acts was founding the Teachers Institute at the Seminary, where men and women college students could gain a thorough education in Jewish subjects and methods of teaching. Teaching in American Hebrew schools became a recognized profession.

The United Synagogue

The real "work of heaven," in Dr. Schechter's own words, which he dedicated

Cyrus Adler.

himself to, was the founding of the United Synagogue of America in 1913. Twenty-two delegates from Conservative congregations gathered at the Seminary. The session was opened by Rabbi Joseph H. Hertz, graduate of the Seminary in its earliest days, who had just become Chief Rabbi of the British Empire.

The United Synagogue was to be a "union for promoting traditional Judaism" in America. The purpose of the United Synagogue was "advancing the cause of Judaism in America and maintaining Jewish tradition in its historical continuity." This meant, as stated by the delegates, "to establish loyalty to the Torah and its historical exposition; to further the observance of the Sabbath and the Dietary Laws; to preserve in the service the reference to Israel's past and the hopes for Israel's restoration; to maintain the traditional character of the liturgy, with Hebrew as the language of prayer."

With the aim of raising American Jews who would know and carry on their heritage, the longest statement was one on education. The Conservative union was "to encourage the establishment of Jewish religious schools, in the curricula of which the study of the Hebrew language and literature shall be given a prominent place, both as the key to true understanding of Judaism, and as a bond for holding together the scattered communities of Israel throughout the world."

The Conservative movement in America thus had its program and its goal, its organization and its seminary. Rabbis and teachers were to go forth, educated in America, and well prepared to lead American Jewry. All this was in large measure the work of Dr. Schechter.

The Highest Standards

Dr. Schechter was a man of zeal, impatient with anything less than excellence. He wished his Seminary to give the most thorough possible training to its students, so that the high standards of learning of the Eastern European community would be carried over into America. At the same time, he wished the Seminary and its schools for teachers and laymen to be organized on strict modern lines. The Seminary structure in New York came to be called "An American building with a Jewish heart."

In his last address in 1915, Dr. Schechter lamented the fact that war was raging in the world. World War I had begun. He expressed, however, his faith that mankind would return to religious ethics and love of peace. In this return, he hoped Judaism would play its part. He died later that year on November 20, the eve of the Sabbath, active to the end as teacher, guide and scholar.

His work, as he had hoped it would, had become "a source of blessing to future generations."

The Jewish Theological Seminary.

Bernard Revel
(1885-1940)

Rabbi Dr. Bernard Revel (1885-1940), first president of the Rabbi Isaac Elchanan Theological Seminary since 1915 and founder of Yeshiva College (in 1928). Dr. Revel served as President until his death in 1940.

"I see no conflict, no inconsistency between Americanism and Judaism." So spoke a learned young man of thirty, honored above many older scholars by being elected President of the new Rabbinical College in New York in the year 1915.

Dr. Bernard Revel was well chosen to head the new school, formed by the joining together of Yeshivat Etz Chaim and the Rabbi Isaac Elchanan Theological Seminary. His brilliance and his training had prepared him for the great purpose that lay before him—of combining Jewish and general studies in one university. Under his leadership was to grow the great Orthodox-sponsored institution of higher learning, Yeshiva University.

As one rabbi said in recommending him to the position, "Dr. Revel is one of the Torah giants of our generation, one who possesses general knowledge and rabbinic learning."

The Ilui

The Jewish learning of the new president was indeed remarkable. At the age of six, Dov Revel was able to recite whole pages of the Talmud by heart. He was called the *Ilui* of Pren, the Lithuanian town of his birth. Among others who hailed him as an ilui, a child genius, was the leader of the nearby city of Kovno's learned Jewish community, Rabbi Isaac Elchanan Spektor.

When Dov was twelve, his father, Rabbi Nahum Shraga Revel of Pren, died. The youngster, who had brought his father much joy in his lifetime, stood up to speak his praises at the funeral. Moving to Kovno with his family, young Dov continued his studies there, and then went to the Yeshiva of Telshe.

At the age of sixteen, Dov Revel had attained such mastery of Talmudic law that he was ordained a rabbi.

Studies in America

The young rabbi came to the United States when he was twenty-one, taking the more common name of Bernard as a translation of his Hebrew name. He immediately felt at home as a student in the Rabbi Isaac Elchanan Theological Seminary on New York's lower East Side. There Orthodox scholars, most of whom had received their early training in Europe, continued their studies of Talmud and commentaries.

Many students recently arrived from Europe, like Revel, wished also to learn English and undertake general studies. Though devotion to Torah learning left them little time, they went to night school or struggled to teach themselves Western culture.

In his own studies during the first few years in America, young Bernard Revel proved that one individual could brilliantly combine Jewish learning and general culture. Rabbi E. Bernard Levinthal of Philadelphia met Rabbi Revel at the Yeshiva, and invited him to become his assistant. He encouraged the younger man to perfect his English and to study at Temple University. After one semester, Rabbi Revel took up studies at New York University.

In 1906, Bernard Revel knew no English and had never attended a general college. Three years later he received not a B.A., or regular college degree, but the higher graduate degree of Master of Arts in philosophy at New York University.

Soon after being awarded his degree, Rabbi Revel married Sarah Rabinowitz-Travis, daughter of a leading Orthodox Jewish family of the midwest. In Philadelphia, Rabbi Revel continued his education. He studied at Dropsie College, newly organized to give advanced study in Hebrew and other Jewish subjects. As the first graduate of Dropsie, he won his degree of Doctor of Philosophy in 1912.

Beginnings of the Yeshiva

There had been hopes for many years of building up a strong institution of Torah learning for the Orthodox community of America. An early yeshivah for children was Yeshivat Etz Chaim in lower Manhattan. Its purpose when it was founded in 1886 was "to give free instruction to poor Hebrew children in the Hebrew language and the Jewish religion-Talmud, Bible and Shulhan Arukh—during the whole day from nine in the morning until four in the afternoon.

"Also from four in the afternoon, two hours shall be devoted to teach the native language, English, and one hour to teach Hebrew and Yiddish."

Although the study of religious subjects took up most of the day, some of the students were able to learn enough in the general field to pass the admission test to the College of the City of New York.

The Rabbi Isaac Elchanan Theological Seminary began in 1897 as a school for more advanced students. It took its name as a memorial to the scholar Isaac Elchanan, who had died the previous year.

At first most of the students at Yeshivat Isaac Elchanan were Eastern European immigrants between the ages of eighteen and twenty-one. Soon younger students, graduates of Etz Chaim, and other American-educated boys from many parts of the country outside of New York began to enroll.

Some effort was made from the beginning to "give instruction in the language of the land." However, most of the directors felt that the students should give full time to Torah. Other subjects, they said, were not proper or necessary for Jewish scholars and rabbis.

Rabbi Revel felt, as did most of the students, that to become leaders of American Jewry, the scholars must also learn English

In 1919, the first graduation class of Talmudical Academy, now known as Yeshiva University High School for Boys, Manhattan, posed for this group portrait. In the same year, the New York State Board of Regents registered Talmudical Academy as an approved high school, the first in the nation under Jewish auspices.

and become familiar with general culture. An article in a Yiddish newspaper, the *Tageblatt*, stated: "They are entirely justified. Jewish scholars without American culture arrive daily on every ship. On the other hand, cultured students without Jewish learning are to be found in all colleges. The Yeshiva must be the common ground where Torah and culture can be blended."

Many of the leaders of Orthodox Judaism began to agree with this point of view. Rabbi Levinthal urged that the goal of the Yeshiva ought to be "to produce devout and observant rabbis who are equipped with the knowledge of the times."

Dr. Revel Becomes President

The idea of combining Yeshivat Etz Chaim and the Rabbi Isaac Elchanan Theological Seminary had been discussed for many years. Finally in 1915 the two schools became one. Students could now begin their study at the Yeshiva at high school level and continue on to study for rabbinic ordination. To head the new institution the unanimous choice of the Board of Trustees was Dr. Bernard Revel.

The next twenty-five years, under Dr. Revel's leadership, told an amazing story of progress and growth. Dr. Revel's first task was to organize the high school department to fulfill the requirements of the State of New York and to provide all studies given by public high schools. At the same time, a full program of traditional Jewish studies was emphasized. From the beginning, in spite of the long hours and double program, students at the new Talmudical Academy ranked in the top level in scholastic competitions, and admission to colleges.

A few years later, the Teachers Institute, founded by the Mizrachi Organization of America, became part of the Yeshiva. The number of students in all branches had increased by 1924 to five hundred, meeting in a crowded building on the lower East Side of Manhattan.

Yeshiva College

Dr. Revel's most ardent hope was for a College of Liberal Arts and Sciences. He proposed such a college "with the double purpose of educating both liberally and Jewishly a number of Jewish young men who have been already imbued with the spirit and sanctity of Judaism and its teachings, so that these men may not be lost to us."

He noted that at that time, in the 1920's, Jewish students at the colleges often tried to hide the fact that they were Jewish. "Some of our talented and idealistic young men will find in a College of Liberal Arts and Sciences under Jewish auspices a congenial home," he said, where they would be able to fully express their Jewish spirit.

"Jewish young men who wish to prepare themselves for the rabbinate, for Jewish social service, for teaching in religious schools, for Jewish scholarship, or communal leadership are to be trained in an institution of higher learning of recognized rank, which is in keeping with the highest educational standards in the country."

It was not easy to gain support for such a tremendous project. Many American Jews were no longer interested in Torah study. Even some who respected Jewish tradition felt that it was a lost cause. American-born students would never be interested in higher Jewish studies, they said.

Statements in favor of the new college came from leading American educators, including presidents of many universities. They felt that a college under Jewish auspices, giving many courses which were not offered elsewhere, and emphasizing the often-neglected Jewish contribution to civilization,

Plans for America's first liberal arts college under Jewish auspices moved a step closer to reality in 1927 with the laying of the cornerstone for the Main Building of Yeshiva University at 186th Street and Amsterdam Avenue, Manhattan.

would be a real gift to America.

Rabbis' groups helped to raise funds. The Union of Orthodox Jewish Congregations of America, founded in 1898, guaranteed an annual income.

In 1926, construction of the main building for the new college began at the uptown Manhattan site. The buildings were ready for use and the opening of Yeshiva College was officially celebrated in 1928. Thirty-five students entered the freshman class.

Struggle and Growth

The year 1929 marked the beginning of the Depression. The time that followed was a difficult one. Funds to support institutions and to pay teachers were hard to find. Dr. Revel for years refused to accept any salary. Not only did he keep Yeshiva and its buildings in full operation, but he also continued to expand its program.

In 1936, Yeshiva celebrated its fiftieth anniversary and the twentieth anniversary of Dr. Revel's presidency. In the next year, Yeshiva grew to include a graduate school of Jewish and Semitic studies, which later came to be known by the name of its founder.

As Dr. Revel's twenty-fifth year with Yeshiva began, the faculty made plans for an elaborate celebration. First scheduled for the end of 1940, the meeting was postponed so that Chief Rabbi Isaac Herzog of Palestine could come.

The anniversary was never celebrated. While delivering a lecture to a senior rabbinic class on November 19, 1940, Dr. Revel suffered a stroke. Two weeks later he died, at the age of fifty-five.

Among the last words he said to his students in his final lecture were these: "You know that I never sought material success. You, my students, know that this institution has cost me much toil. I have hardly enjoyed of this world. My life's work, my life is Yeshiva."

Dr. Revel had taken over the leadership of Yeshiva during World War I, a dark time in world history. He saw that immigration from Europe was ending, and agreed with the dedication speaker who said, "Since the supply of students which we could formerly expect from foreign countries has been cut off, it is our duty to interest American young men in the study of Rabbinical culture."

Main building, Yeshiva University.

He ended his service during World War II, a much darker time. Destruction of the Jewish communities of Eastern Europe was beginning. In his last written article, he found some comfort in the fact that, " . . . before the spiritual sun of Israel has set in Europe, a sanctuary of the eternal soul of Israel has been started on this continent."

It remained for the American Jewish community to take up the great task appointed for it by history, to carry on, preserve and enhance the age-old tradition of the Jewish people.

MODERN THOUGHTS ABOUT JEWISH TRADITION

Judaism is the fear of the Lord, and the love of man, in harmony with the dicta of reason.

*   *   *

The object of Reform is to lead Israelites away from obsolete and isolating forms; to abolish antiquated customs and supersede them by such new ones as correspond to the demands of the age. Reform is an effort to rescue Judaism from indifferentism, desertion and ignorance, by inspiring Israelites with a love for Judaism and by a return to essentials.

*   *   *

Our service ought to be conducted in the Hebrew language; for it is that which our prophets spoke. Because, furthermore, our brethren in all parts of the world are familiar with the Hebrew service, and no Israelite would feel himself a stranger in the house of the Lord.

*   *   *

It is not our duty to reform the orthodox, nor is it the duty of the orthodox to reclaim the reformers. Let each worship as he thinks proper, and build up Judaism.

ISAAC MAYER WISE

There is something higher than modernity and that is eternity.

*   *   *

The Jews of America cannot live without English but will not survive without Hebrew.

*   *   *

We did not invent the art of printing; we did not discover America; we were not the first to utilize the power of steam or electricity. Our great claim to the gratitude of mankind is that we gave to the world the word of God, the Bible. We stormed heaven to snatch down this heavenly gift; we threw ourselves into the breach and covered it with our bodies against every attack; we allowed ourselves to be slain by hundreds and thousands rather than become unfaithful to it; and bore witness to its truth and watched over its purity in the face of a hostile world.

*   *   *

We usually urge that in Judaism religion means life; but we forget that a life without guiding principles and thought is a life not worth living.

SOLOMON SCHECHTER

The Bible was the cornerstone upon which was reared the enduring structure of our national life, the guide and inspiration of the sturdy and steadfast settlers of the land and of their followers who made it truly free.

*   *   *

Democracy, love of freedom and justice, is the great affirmation of Judaism, its most cherished ideal. For our passion for freedom, peace and righteousness, we have been hated and persecuted by enemies and misunderstood by friends. But love of light, learning and liberty will remain our sacred burden until it becomes the heritage of all mankind.

*   *   *

The structure of the House of Israel is neither complete nor safe without Torah, without the spiritual education of the growing generation. The stream of Jewish creative life can at no time rise to a higher level than the source of Jewish spiritual life.

*   *   *

Man must return to the great affirmations of Judaism concerning the meaning of life, to the divine optimism of the seers of Israel, to the passion for humanity, peace, and justice. American democracy must reforge its spiritual and moral weapons.

BERNARD DOV REVEL

As long as Judaism continues, nobody will be able to say that the soul of man has allowed itself to be subjugated. Its existence through the centuries is by itself proof that conviction cannot be mastered by numbers. The mere fact of Judaism's existence shows that it is impossible to conquer the spirit. Because it has been a minority, Judaism has become a measuring test for the height to which morality has risen upon earth. What the Jewish community has experienced from the nations among which it lived, has always been a measure of the extent of right and justice among the nations. From Israel's lot men could judge how far they have yet to go until the days of the Messiah.

LEO BAECK

*   *   *

We Jews are a community based on memory. A common memory has kept us together and enabled us to survive. The age-old bond of memory must be revived. What the fathers no longer hand down, the sons must get as best they can—they must study it. Our language, the Scriptures, our history must become curriculum of the most crucial importance. The sons must re-establish the bond of memory that joins the community together.

MARTIN BUBER

We have succeeded in teaching large numbers of Jews to carry their communal obligations, in terms of their contribution to Israel, overseas, national and local causes, as a normal and constant item in their annual budget. We shall have reached maturity as a Jewish community when equally large numbers of Jews include in their personal budget of time and duty such responsibilities as Jewish study, the Jewish education of their young, Jewish symbols and disciplines in the home and a commitment to the advancement of Jewish learning, art and literature.

MORRIS ADLER

I see a Jewish Commonwealth where the Jewish spirit has been reborn. I see the Jewries of the world, each at ease in the land of its residence, each devoted to that land and at the same time the bearer and transmitter of a living Hebraism. Most specifically, I see an American Jewry, emancipated, secure, free to fulfill itself without hindrance.
An American Jewry alight with a religious faith hallowed by antiquity, yet sanctioned by the best in modern thought. An American Jewry standing four square by Judaism's great moral ideals, so that the name Jew is a synonym for the practice and advocacy of justice, compassion, freedom and peace. An American Jewry literate in both its heritages, the American and the Hebraic.
I see in sum a Jewry which in its inner life has made of Judaism what it is intended to be, a source of blessing.
And I see all this set in a new brave and free world which Jews together with all men of good will, have helped to set free. Will it be a little thing—will it not rather be accounted a very great thing—to have played a part in the building of the Kingdom of God on earth?

MILTON STEINBERG

THE CHAIN
IS NOT BROKEN

THE CHAIN
IS NOT BROKEN

In this book we have met Jewish heroes who helped to lead their people into the modern age. Separated for centuries from the general society of the countries in which they lived, the Jews in the past two hundred years have taken their place as free citizens of the Western world.

In every land where they have been able to gain general education and a measure of freedom, they have proved their worth as outstanding and creative citizens. Jews have been among the leading authors, musicians, artists, scientists, scholars and statesmen of Europe and America.

In America and in Israel have grown up the two largest active Jewish communities of the present day.

Jews in the free American society have overcome early problems and have taken leadership wherever their abilities and interests have drawn them. American culture—books, magazines, art, music, theatre, television—owes much to talented Jews. Colleges and professional schools which used to have "quotas" limiting the number of students belonging to minority groups have, since World War II, opened their doors to qualified candidates without regard to creed and color. Fair play has resulted in Jews being able to take their place in college teaching, engineering, and other fields which before 1945 were open only to a limited few. In political life, Jewish ability has been recognized on state and national levels as never before.

In Israel, a community of over two million has grown up. Faithful to its promise of admitting all Jews who wish to enter, Israel has faced tremendous problems of education and rebuilding lives. It has maintained itself as the only true democracy in the Near East. Israel's high standards of education and culture, its know-how in agriculture, industry, public health and government are being taught to new nations of Africa and Asia. Hoped-for peace with its Arab neighbors will bring about a greater opportunity for the development of Israel as a model democracy, an example of progress for the world to follow.

The chain of Jewish tradition continues. In our first Unit, we saw how devout Jews of Eastern Europe carried on the traditions of piety and learning. Never-ending study of Torah led to lives of joyous observance and of good deeds.

Most of the learned Eastern European community was destroyed by the Nazis. Three million Jews living in the anti-religious Soviet Union are not able to express themselves as a community, or to give a Jewish education to their children.

In many yeshivot in America and Israel, however, Torah study continues very much in the same way as it did in Eastern Europe. The tradition of Hasidism, with its emphasis on love of God and love of fellowman, has become dear to men of every faith, largely through the writings of philosopher Martin Buber.

In our second Unit, we saw how Leopold Zunz and his followers strove to make Jewish history and thought respected subjects worthy of study. Their hope has been gloriously fulfilled. Leading universities of America teach Judaism as an important part of world culture. The Hebrew University and Bar Ilan University in Israel, as well as the Hebrew Union College, the Jewish Theological Seminary, and Yeshiva University in the United States, are centers of Jewish learning in the modern world.

Although Jewish philanthropists still set an example to others, helping one's fellowman is considered the duty of the whole Jewish community. Instead of a Sir Moses Montefiore giving out coins and pleading for his people, as we saw in Unit III, we now have great nationwide and worldwide Jewish organizations working for civil rights and other worthy causes everywhere. In every city, Jews tax themselves voluntarily by contributing to combined welfare fund drives. Besides taking care of local institutions such as hospitals, centers and social service agencies, these funds support the United Jewish Appeal, which helps Jews all over the world and aids immigration into Israel.

The building of Zion, as we saw described in Unit IV, continues with all its difficulties and all its challenges. The carrying on of all functions of a modern state, including political struggles and problems of defense, is in the hands of the Israeli people and their elected officers.

Jews all over the world share in the miracle of a rebuilt Jewish State in many ways. They contribute so that immigration can continue, for no country in the world could take in and educate twice the number of its own inhabitants in a short span of years without some extra support. They invest in the development of new industry. They gain inspiration by learning Hebrew, sharing in the culture of the new State, visiting and studying in Israel, and feeling pride in the accomplishments of their fellow Jews.

American Judaism, based on the strong foundations which are described in Unit V, continues to grow and flourish. The Jewish people, at home in America, strengthens its own institutions, of which the synagogue is the most important. Jewish adults, as well as children, are giving time and interest to learning more about their heritage.

Never before has there been a Jewish community so large, so wealthy, so free and so respected. Fortified by knowledge and loyalty, the coming generations of American Jews can strive to fulfil the vision of Israel Friedlaender. He looked forward to "a community great in numbers, mighty in power, enjoying life, liberty and the pursuit of happiness; actively participating in the civic, social and economic progress of the country; deeply rooted in the soil of Judaism; one in sentiment with their brethren wherever they are; receiving and resisting, not yielding like wax to every impress from the outside, but blending the best they possess with the best they encounter; adding a new note to the richness of American life, leading a new current into the stream of American civilization; a sharply marked community, distinct and distinguished; trusted for its loyalty, respected for its dignity, esteemed for its traditions, valued for its aspirations."

The Jewish ideals of learning and good deeds, charity and social justice, freedom of thought and responsibility in action, loyalty to one's own heritage and understanding of others, add strength to the American tradition. Through study and action Jews of today perpetuate these ideals.

The chain of Jewish tradition continues unbroken in new lands and in a modern world—a world that continues to need the message of justice, liberty, peace and love of fellowman, which Judaism first proclaimed.

INDEX

H

Ha-Am, Ahad
   see Ginzberg, Asher
Ha-Kohen, Israel Meir
   (Hafetz Hayyim),   14, 42-51
Ha-Levi, Judah,   5, 129
Ha-Matmid,   158-159
Ha-Nadiv,   94
   see also Rothschild,
   Edmond de
Ha-Nasi, Judah,   5
Ha-Shiloah,   160
Habad Hasidim,   29, 30
Hadassah,   141-142, 168
Hadassah-Hebrew University
   Hospital,   171
Hadassah nurses,   173
"Hafetz Hayyim"
   (Israel Meir Kagen),   14, 42-51
Hafetz Hayyim (book),   44-45
Haganah,   142, 143
Haham Bernays
   see Bernays, Isaac
Haifa,   143
Halukkah,   130
Halutzim,   134-135, 169
Hamburg, Reform
   congregation of,   77
Hametz,   33
Harby, Isaac,   193
Harkavy, Albert,   61
Hasidism,   13, 14, 18, 19, 26-30,
   129, 220
Haskalah,   37, 44, 157-158
Hayyim of Volozhin,   14, 34-35
"He Who Desires Life,"   44-45
Hebrew language,   8, 9, 66, 70, 72,
   78, 87, 141, 162, 202, 216
Hebrew National Schools,   106
Heberw Union College,   194, 199-200,
   202, 203, 221
Hebrew University, Jerusalem,   141,
   177-178, 221
Hebron,   129, 130
Heder,   18
Heidelberg, University of,   70
Heine, Heinrich,   64, 65, 67, 69, 90
Heritage, cultural,   3, 63-64
Heroes of Jewish Thought,   1, 12
Hertz, Joseph H.,   209
Herzl, Theodor,   125, 135, 146-155,
   176, 184
Herzog, Isaac,   214
Heshbon Ha-Nefesh,   36-37
Hess, Moses,   132, 150, 176
Hibbat Zion movement,   176
Hildesheimer, Rabbi,   78
Hillel,   53
Hirsch, Maurice de,   93-94, 117, 123,
   124, 127, 131, 149, 150
Hirsch, Samson Raphael,   59, 71, 78,
   80-87
"Historical" Judaism,   60, 66, 195
History of the Jews,   61, 167
Hitler,   47, 141, 142, 170
Holdheim, Samuel,   59, 71-72

Holland,   187
Homel pogrom,   137
House of Commons, British,   120-121
House of Lords, British,   121
Hoveve Zion,   133-134, 135, 151
Hungary,   90

I

Ilui,   25, 34, 211
Imperial Lyceum, Paris,   114
"In the City of Slaughter,"   160
India, route to,   175
Inquisition,   10, 89, 187
Iraq,   145
Irving, Washington,   191
Isaac, Levi,   13, 16-23
Isaac, Meir,   18
Islam
   see Moslems
Israel, State of,   5, 138, 141, 144-145,
   154, 172-173, 181, 196, 220, 221
   see also Palestine; Zionism
The Israelite,   194, 199, 200
"Israelite Society for Religion,"   84
Italy,   90, 95, 105
Ivanhoe,   191

J

Jabotinsky, Vladimir Zev,   138,
   161, 168
Jaffa,   103, 130, 165
Jerusalem,   12, 101, 102, 103, 108,
   129, 130, 155
   see also Zionism
Jerusalem Talmud,   206
Jewish Agency,   141, 179-180
Jewish Agency Executive,   144
Jewish Board of Deputies,   105
Jewish Colonization Association,   93,
   124, 131
Jewish Encyclopedia,   165
Jewish Girls' School, Jaffa,   165
Jewish Legion,   138, 161, 168
Jewish names,   66
Jewish National Fund,   135, 140-141
Jewish Pulication Society of
   America,   61, 167
Jewish science
   see Science of Judaism
Jewish State, idea of,   149
   see also Zionism
The Jewish State,   135, 150, 176
Jewish Theological Seminary,
   Breslau,   72-73, 78-79
Jewish Theological Seminary of
   America,   167, 195, 203, 207, 221
Jewish women, in
   United States   191-192
Jews' College, London,   106
Jews' Free School, London,   106
Jordan,   145
Joseph, Jacob,   195
*Journal for the Science of
   Judaism,*   64

Judah Ha-Levi,   5, 129
Judah Ha-Nasi,   5
Judaism, in America,   186-218
Judaism, purpose of,   83-84

K

Kabbalah,   12, 25
Kaddish prayer,   173
Kaddish of Reb Levi Isaac,   22-23
Kagen, Israel Meir
   ("Hafetz Hayyim"),   14, 42-51
Kaiser (William II),   152
Kalischer, Zvi Hirsch,   133
Kaplan, Rose,   168
Katowitz, Hoveve Zion
   conference at,   134
Keren Ha-Yesod,   178
Kerr, Mr.,   175
Kfar Gileadi,   123
Kharkov,   134
Khazars,   7
Kishinev pogrom,   137, 152, 153,
   160-161
Knesset building, Jerusalem,   124
Kol Nidre prayer,   75
Kovno, Lithuania,   37, 131, 211
Kresz, Simon,   173
Krochmal, Nahman,   60, 87
Kuk, Abraham Isaac,   184

L

Labor Zionist party,   137
Ladi, rabbi of
   see Zalman, Shneur
Ladino language,   9-10
Lamed-vav tzaddikim,   35
"Lament in Nemirov,"   160
Landowners, in Poland,   11
Landy, Rachel,   168
Languages,   9-10
Lazarus, Emma,   191-192
League of Nations,   140, 178
Learning, emphasis on,   52-87
Lebanon,   145
Lebensohn, A. D.,   44
Lebensohn, Micah Joseph,   44
Leeser, Isaac,   192-193, 194, 199, 201
Lefin, Mendel,   36
Legends of the Jews,   167
Leonidas (ship),   99
"Letter to the Jews of New rt,"   188
Levi Isaac of Berditchev,   13, 16-23,
   50
Levinthal, E. Bernard,   212
Levy, Asser,   187
Levy, Uriah Phillips,   190
Lewis, Mrs. Agnes,   206
Liberalism, 19th cent.,   55-56
Lilienthal, Max,   193
Lincoln, Abraham,   190
Lipkin, Israel
   see Salanter, Israel
Lipkin, Wolf,   34
Lithuania,   6, 8, 25, 34